Modern Presidential Electioneering

Modern Presidential Electioneering

An Organizational and Comparative Approach

Jody C Baumgartner

Westport, Connecticut
London

149005

Library of Congress Cataloging-in-Publication Data

Baumgartner, Jody C., 1958–
    Modern presidential electioneering : an organizational and comparative approach /
Jody C Baumgartner.
      p. cm.
    Includes bibliographical references and index.
    ISBN 0–275–96760–3 (alk. paper)
      1. Presidents—United States—Election. 2. Presidents—France—Election.
    3. Presidents—Russia (Federation)—Election. 4. Electioneering—United States.
    5. Electioneering—France. 6. Electioneering—Russia. I. Title.
JK528.B38 2000
324.9'1821—dc21   99–055884

British Library Cataloguing in Publication Data is available.

Library of Congress Catalog Card Number: 99–055884
ISBN: 0–275–96760–3

First published in 2000

Praeger Publishers, 88 Post Road West, Westport, CT 06881
An imprint of Greenwood Publishing Group, Inc.
www.praeger.com

Printed in the United States of America

The paper used in this book complies with the
Permanent Paper Standard issued by the National
Information Standards Organization (Z39.48–1984).

10 9 8 7 6 5 4 3 2 1

Contents

Illustrations

FIGURES

TEXT BOXES

Acknowledgments

Many people were extremely helpful to me while I was researching, writing, and producing this book, and I would like to express my gratitude for that help here. First of all, I should say that I have been especially blessed with a family which has always been exceedingly supportive, encouraging, and understanding of the various choices I have made in my life. Although at times I may fall short in showing it, this has been, and continues to be, very important to me. Jeffery L. Smithling has been kind enough to keep me supplied the past few years with the home computing components necessary to ensure that my work can continue. I have also benefited greatly from his friendship.

More tangibly, this project has been helped at various times from the assistance of Dotti Pearson, Dr. Ryan Barilleaux, Maria Hernandez, Murray Leigh, and Tim Gray, all of whom are associated with Miami University.

Other people involved in this project are deserving of far more than passing mention. Dr. Herbert Waltzer instilled in me an appreciation and passion for democratic politics that I did not have before I was fortunate to study under him. Moreover, he stepped up to the plate and agreed to read the completed manuscript for me on very short notice.

Finally, Mark H. Morris and Thomas F. Crumblin were kind enough to read each chapter as it was completed, offering many useful suggestions as well as their encouragement—this in spite of the fact that the timetable for the project was less than leisurely. Their editorial comments saved me from more than one embarrassment. Of course, any mistakes that this work might contain are mine, not theirs.

To all of you, my thanks.

1

Introduction: Modern Presidential Electioneering

INTRODUCTION

In early February of 1999 George Stephanopoulos, former adviser to Bill Clinton and a well-known political consultant, offered several suggestions to presidential aspirants in what was billed as a "survival guide" for the presidential race of 2000. The first piece of advice? Hire a firm to conduct "opposition" research on yourself.[1] This may not surprise those familiar with American politics, but even they must admit that at first glance it seems somewhat counterintuitive. Stephanopoulos makes explicit what has become part and parcel of a new conventional wisdom in modern presidential electioneering: find out what your weaknesses are before your opponent does. This puts you in a better position to more effectively preempt or respond to your opponent's attacks.

Americans have been electing presidents for roughly 200 years. Those who are familiar with the history of presidential electioneering cannot help but notice that in one sense modern electioneering practices are remarkably similar to the distant as well as recent past. For example the presidency has always been the "first prize" in our political system and political parties have always devoted much of their energy toward winning it. As James Bryce pointed out as early as 1893, parties have always favored candidates who stand the greatest chance of attracting the greatest number of votes, or in other words, of winning. Both candidates and parties raise and spend ever-increasing amounts of money in pursuit of the White House, and always have. And any good history of political campaigning in America will point out that "smear campaigns" are nothing new in American presidential campaigns.

The Changing Face of Presidential Electioneering

In spite of the fact that there is a certain continuity to the history of presidential electioneering, several changes have taken place since 1960 which differentiate the modern era from times previous. Technological advances in transportation and communications (especially television) have reduced presidential candidates' reliance on party organizations for national political communication. The crafting and targeting of political messages is increasingly sophisticated because of these same technological advances as well as improvements in survey methodology and marketing techniques. Non-party groups are now directly involved in the electoral arena rather than working through political parties to influence the process. Campaign finance laws put greater amounts of money directly into the hands of the candidate, and these same candidates have a great deal of say in how party money is spent. Political parties no longer have any control over the process of candidate recruitment, screening, and selection—in short, of who will carry aloft their party standard. Finally, campaign professionals (consultants, image-makers, etc.) have come to play an ever larger role in conducting the campaign itself.[2]

Not all of these changes occurred at once, but for our purposes in this book the organization and practices that constitute modern presidential electioneering were largely in place by 1960. Since 1972 is often cited as the start of a new era in nomination politics, one could argue that it would be a better date to mark the modern era of presidential electioneering,[3] but this date would miss important innovations and developments which together have shaped presidential electioneering into what it is today. One of the central themes running throughout this book is that candidate organizations, as opposed to party organizations, have become increasingly central to the campaign effort in the modern era. In this sense, the 1960 Kennedy campaign was the first truly modern presidential campaign.

John F. Kennedy: The First Modern Presidential Candidate?

Several facts justify using the year 1960 as a line of demarcation separating "traditional" from modern presidential electioneering. First, it is the date frequently mentioned as the beginning of the television era in American presidential politics, this in reference to John Kennedy's skillful use of television during the debates of that fall.[4] Another albeit less talked about aspect of Kennedy's skillful use of technology was that he was the first presidential candidate to have an airplane at his disposal for the campaign.[5]

Candidate Kennedy's campaign organization consisted of trusted friends, family, and campaign professionals, most notably brother Robert, pollster Louis Harris, speechwriter Theodore Sorensen, and press secretary Pierre Salinger. Importantly, of the sixteen individuals in Kennedy's inner circle, only one (John Bailey, the Connecticut Democratic Party chairman) had ever worked for the Democratic Party. In addition to staffing his organization with non-party people, Kennedy's entire campaign strategy was explicitly crafted to be outside—in fact, against—the Democratic Party. The following passage from Sorensen sums up what a Kennedy candidacy faced. "The basic difficulties always boiled down to the facts that the country had never elected a Catholic, that the country had never elected a forty-three-year-old, that the country had only elected one Senator to be President in this century."[6]

In short, the traditional powers in the Democratic Party would never have accepted Kennedy as a viable presidential candidate. Lyndon Johnson had in fact received the endorsement of every Democratic senator except Kennedy. Thus, it was determined by the Kennedy team to go around the party, directly to the people, taking advantage of a few strategic primaries (most notably, as it turned out, heavily Protestant West Virginia) in order to demonstrate Kennedy's electability. In this sense Kennedy's was the first outsider candidacy and demonstrated that candidates could successfully wage a presidential campaign with little help from their political party. This by itself marked a sea of change in presidential electioneering. In the words of the historian Robert Dinkin, it meant that

winning no longer required the [party] organization's backing because the services the traditional party offered—headquarters, canvassing apparatus, and so on—were not as essential as before. The new technical skills and financial resources necessary for a modern campaign could readily be found elsewhere.[7]

This passage encapsulates the distinction between traditional and modern presidential electioneering fairly well.

The Purpose of This Book

Given the importance of understanding presidential selection and that modern electioneering practices are virtually unrecognizable compared to those of 40 years ago, one would expect that there would be a wealth of scholarship specifically devoted to the subject. This is not the case. To be sure, the above changes in presidential electioneering have not gone unnoticed, but, as a rule, scholarly work in this area falls short of systematically examining these changes together. That is exactly what this book will do. It concentrates on the presidential electioneering practices of two types of organizations, those of presidential aspirants (or candidates) and of their political parties. In both cases the examination is restricted primarily to the national level.

Although most of the developments in presidential electioneering practices occurred first in the United States, many can now be discerned in other countries. This has led to scholarly debate over whether a supposed "modernization" or "Americanization" of political campaign practices in other countries is occurring (or has occurred). This book will help to clarify this issue. Toward that end, presidential electioneering practices in two other countries, France and Russia, are also examined here. France is chosen because in many textbooks France is used as the "other" (besides the United States) example of presidential government, and because the beginning of the French Fifth Republic (1958) coincides with the time frame of the book. Russia is included in the study as an example of a newer presidential system and because of its obvious importance in world politics.

What distinguishes this book from others about presidential campaigns and elections is its strict focus on the personnel, resources, and processes of presidential electioneering. There will be no discussion about the electorate, their voting choices, or the content or effects of political messages. Put another way, voters and political communication are outside the scope of this study. To be sure, voters are important and candidates' messages are often major determinants of the path a particular presidential campaign follows. Moreover, there is a connection between the two, however difficult that relationship may be to specify and measure. But there are literally scores of excellent studies which examine these themes and the reader is referred to these if that is where his or her interest lies (more on this shortly).

This book follows a narrow organizational approach which allows us to better see and understand the effects of presidential electioneering practices on the political system, several of which are explored in more detail. Presidential electioneering practices have several major consequences on the political system. First, it affects not only who aspires to the presidency, but candidates' subsequent success in the campaign. It speaks to questions, for example, of who runs for president? Why? What kinds of traits, skills, and background are needed to wage a successful campaign? Have these changed? Second, presidential electioneering also affects the policy choices as well as the governing style and political resources of the eventual winner. These concerns speak, in short, to the question of what is possible throughout a given administration's tenure and how the president goes about making a record and a place in history. Third, subsequent policy responsibility and accountability is also affected. Who is to blame for the failure of a given policy if the president is acting outside the mainstream of his party? Fourth, and finally, an overarching concern inherent in all of these concerns is the relationship between a president and his party[8] and the role of political parties in the political system.

The next section is devoted first to a discussion of existing scholarship on presidential campaigns and elections, some of which relates, if only in an ancillary way, to modern presidential electioneering. Throughout, the singular focus of this book as it relates to that scholarship will be brought into greater relief. Second, the outline and framework of the book is introduced and explained.

EXISTING SCHOLARSHIP ON PRESIDENTIAL CAMPAIGNS, ELECTIONS, AND ELECTIONEERING

There is an implicit voter-centric bias in most political research on presidential campaigns and elections. Most studies, in the end, are focused on voters, their opinions, and finally, their votes. To be fair, there are at least two very good reasons for this. Collectively, voters make up the central component of a democracy. While many (if not most) political scientists attempt to conduct their research in as value-free a manner as possible, they are acutely aware of how their work might be used. Even if it were possible to conduct value-free research, most would not. Therefore, from a normative perspective, it is perfectly natural to place voters at or near the center of the analysis. To be blunt, focusing research on electioneering runs the risk of a Machiavellian misuse of its results.

From a methodological perspective, voting behavior (i.e., votes themselves, as well as the voting intentions of citizens) is fairly simple to measure. First, votes are relatively easy to count. Secondly, advances in survey and polling methodology make collecting data on partisanship, voting intentions, and a wealth of other attitudinal orientations possible. A battery of surveys measuring these questions have been systematically administered by the National Election Studies (now at the University of Michigan) every four years since 1952. These data are widely available to the scholarly community. Not coincidentally, at about the same time these surveys began, the methodological orientation of political scientists began to shift away from government institutions and normative concerns to the measurable political behavior of individuals.[9]

Again, citizens have been at the heart of the academic study of campaigns and elections in one way or another for many years. Scholarship in the area of electioneering is very thin, and this is certainly the case with respect to presidential electioneering. The discipline of political science has tended to abdicate this subject either to journalists or to communications scholars.

In the next few pages, five approaches to the study of presidential campaigns and elections are outlined and briefly reviewed: the journalistic approach; the political communications approach; various studies which examine elections; research on presidential campaigning; and finally electioneering studies. The approach to this review is broad rather than deep, designed to illustrate the place of this book in the existing body of literature on presidential campaigns and elections.[10] While each of these approaches has a slightly different focus than that of this book, a student of presidential campaigns and elections should at least be familiar with them. And to be fair, all have informed this book in one way or another. With the possible exception of electioneering studies, all are explicitly or implicitly concerned with how voters behave.

The Journalistic Approach

There are many journalistic accounts of presidential campaigns and elections. These works are mainly descriptive, offering detailed, insider accounts of particular campaigns. Perhaps the most well-known and complete of this type is Theodore White's *Making of the President* series covering the elections of 1960 through 1972. In his first effort, White, like others subsequent to him in this tradition, followed the campaign from the early days and was privy to many insider decisions, events, and occurrences, which he then wove into a very intricate yet readable account. It was through this account that many of the details of the makeup and decision-making process of Kennedy's inner circle became widely known.

Since White's groundbreaking work in 1960 others have followed in his footsteps and the journalistic tradition of presidential campaigns has become fairly common. The special *Newsweek* team of Peter Goldman and others seemed to take the torch from White in the 1980s in their *Quest for the Presidency* series, and Jack Germond and Jules Witcover contributed four similar accounts of the 1980 through the 1992 elections.[11] There are many other "on the trail" or "on the bus" accounts of individual presidential campaigns,[12] but what distinguishes the White and Goldman series are their comprehensiveness and continuity. Works in the journalistic tradition are detailed, highly readable, and very interesting, especially to political observers, but while the details are fascinating and may help to explain why certain things did or did not happen in a campaign, they tend to miss the forest for the trees; moreover, they are somewhat lacking in analytical rigor. In sum, their contribution to political science is limited largely to their role as general accounts and/or anecdote or data source for individual elections (for which they are excellent).

Figure 1.1
A Communications Model of a Presidential Campaign

COMMUNICATIONS FLOW ⇨							
A Sender	*Sends*	**A Message**	*Through*	**A Medium**	*To*	**Receivers** *Creating*	**Effects**
(Presidential candidate)		("Vote for me, because...")		(TV, radio, newspaper)		(Citizens)	(Citizens vote in favor of candidate?)

The Political Communications Approach

This approach could also be labeled the "campaigning" approach, since political campaigns are basically "campaigns of communication."[13] Thus, it is hardly surprising to find that there is a good deal of scholarship in the disciplinary tradition of political communications on presidential selection.[14] In practical terms a presidential campaign is an attempt to mobilize citizen support, or more specifically, to get votes. Modeled, this idea would include several components and would look something like what is depicted in Figure 1.1.

As with any model, the reality of a presidential campaign is much more complex than this model suggests. For example, a candidate's campaign may have more than a single message, many different media are used, and actual effects may include those which were not intended (in other words, an ad may create a negative image of the candidate in the eyes of the receiver). With reference to the model, the focus of this book is on the sender (or senders). Scholars of political communications, on the other hand, typically focus on the message, the medium, or the effects of the message. More specifically, most political communications literature highlights either: (1) the increased prominence of the candidate in the political message; (2) the effect the medium (usually television) has on elections and democracy in general; or (3) the effects of political messages. The latter is a very problematic area for both political scientists and communications scholars since it is difficult to isolate the effects of a political message on behavior.[15]

With respect to the message, a good many scholarly studies support the notion that political messages, especially during presidential campaigns, are increasingly candidate-centered. Because television, the primary medium of a presidential campaign, is highly suited to an individual focus, this is no surprise. Focusing the message on the image of the candidate means, in short, that modern campaign messages are increasingly devoid of issue content.[16] As concerns the medium, much of the political communications literature focuses on the displacement of political parties by the mass media, specifically television, as the primary link between candidates and citizens in political campaigning.[17] The implications for democracy of this shift are explored by many, and (implicitly or otherwise) the verdict is often less than favorable. At minimum, most agree that the role of television in presidential primaries has dramatically changed the nature of presidential campaigns.[18]

Election Studies

There is no shortage of scholarly work which examines the results of presidential elections in the United States. Included are several quadrennial volumes worthy of note, each of which covers a broad range of subject material related to presidential (as well as congressional) elections: party nominations, polling, finance, media campaigning, voting, results, and interpretations.[19] Since presidential elections are major events, the approach taken in these works is very broad out of necessity. Common themes include the growing importance of the "invisible primary,"[20] or the pre-primary phase of presidential selection, mapping public opinion throughout the selection process (as it relates to the eventual outcome), dissatisfaction with media coverage of the process (in particular, coverage of the primary season),[21] the increased costs associated with running for president, and perhaps naturally, attempts to interpret voter turnout and the results of the election(s).

Most of this work also calls, in varying degrees, for reforming the presidential selection process. Various proposals include institutional ways to encourage third party formation or to make the two-party system more responsible and accountable, different plans to alter the primary system of presidential nominations (e.g., regionally consolidating primaries), more (or less) stringent campaign finance laws, plans to make voter registration simpler and more convenient, and a host of others, some more feasible than others. Like this book, one overarching theme that is explicit or implicit in much of this literature is the decreased influence of political parties throughout the presidential selection process. Unlike this book, works in this tradition include the results of the election and how they relate to the campaign.

Research on Presidential Campaigning

Like journalistic accounts and election studies, there is also serial (i.e., published every four years) work on presidential campaigning. The main difference between this body of work and the previous is that research on presidential campaigning focuses on the processes of the campaign rather than the results.[22] Of particular note here are Stephen Wayne's *Road to the White House* series covering presidential elections for the years

1980–96, and Nelson Polsby and the late Aaron Wildavsky's *Presidential Elections*, the first of which appeared in 1964.[23]

Both are structured similarly. Each initially covers all aspects of the "electoral arena" (for Wayne, for Polsby and Wildavsky, the "strategic environment") including voters, groups, rules, and resources. Wayne also includes a historical overview of presidential elections. Then the process of presidential selection itself is examined: the nominating season, the convention, and the general election campaign. Wayne also presents an overview of issues and mandates and both offer a section on reforms. Polsby and Wildavsky offer more by way of analysis and focus a bit more on strategy and tactics while slighting individual campaigns somewhat. Wayne highlights whichever campaign is current, not without attention to the process in general. Put another way, Polsby and Wildavsky's account is geared more toward theory, while Wayne's account is more descriptive. Each of these works are outstanding overviews of the entire process, but what separates them from this book is their inclusion of voters and political communications.

Electioneering Studies

This approach might very well be subtitled "Notes from Practitioners." Until very recently the subject of electioneering was all but ignored by political scientists, but little has changed since 1970 when one analyst rightly claimed that "works which deal competently and analytically with the subject [are] rare." As he noted, most accounts are "artistic and individualistic," dealing with either particular campaigners, their tactics (especially their use of modern technologies), or their apparent ability to control outcomes.[24] One result of Theodore White's account of the 1960 Kennedy campaign was an increased interest in a new breed of campaign professionals, or "Election Men."[25] Most books in this tradition are products of these election men, insider accounts or guides by campaign professionals.

Perhaps the best well known of the earlier works of this type was written by the co-founder of both the American and the International Association of Political Consultants, Joseph Napolitan,[26] who worked for, among others, Hubert Humphrey in 1968 and French president Valéry Giscard d'Estaing in 1974. His account is most illuminating and, like others written by consultants, tinged with a self-serving and self-promoting tone. More comprehensive is the quadrennial *Managers Look at the Campaign* series (1972 through 1996), sponsored by the Kennedy School of Government at Harvard, which gives good, first-hand, and similarly self-serving insider accounts of the strategies and tactics of the main presidential aspirants and their consultants for those years.[27] There are other interesting accounts by practitioners, but most are straightforward "how to win" manuals, advising readers on how to emulate previous wins.[28] As Gerald Pomper correctly asserted, electioneering scholarship provides little (if any) theory. An exception to this is a growing body of survey research on the attitudes of political consultants. These studies, while serving to expand our knowledge base about the industry, often seem guided by normative questions (i.e., what role consultants should play in the campaign process) and also seem to place great stock in the answers given by these largely self-promoting individuals.[29]

Summary: What We Know about Presidential Campaigns, Elections, and Electioneering

The existing body of work on presidential campaigns and elections, to state it mildly, is enormous. However, none of the approaches reviewed above deal with presidential electioneering specifically from the perspective of candidate and party organizations as this book does. The journalistic and political communications approach, as well as elections, presidential campaigning and electioneering studies all either ignore this dimension or subsume it into the general research. The key distinction between all of these literatures and this book is the organizational perspective taken here, designed to illuminate the organization and operation of presidential electioneering.

As such, the book does not fit neatly into the "traditional" campaigns and elections literature. To be sure, much of that work was useful in the construction of the framework used in this study and in the collection of data. But this book will focus on how, and with what, presidential aspirants conduct their campaigns, and therefore is very similar to Paul Herrnson's study of congressional campaigns.[30] One advantage to this approach is that it will help illuminate what kind of people, with what kind of qualities and experience, are likely to be successful in a bid for the White House. It also brings to light the relationship between presidential candidates and their party, a relationship which the winning candidate obviously takes to the White House.

THE REMAINDER OF THIS BOOK

This book is organized as follows: Chapter 2 reviews the history of presidential electioneering in the United States prior to 1960, broken down like the remainder of the book according to the personnel, resources, and processes of presidential electioneering. The purpose of the chapter is to illustrate in greater detail the claim that presidential electioneering prior to the modern era was a party-centered affair. Candidates certainly played a part in the effort, but in all aspects of the process—from selecting the party candidate to organizing and funding the campaign effort to using the party network and resources as the primary means of conducting the campaign—party was key.

Chapter 3 provides an overview of presidentialism and the formal and informal aspects of presidential selection in the United States, France, and Russia. This chapter, along with the second chapter, provides the backdrop for the remainder of the book, outlining the institutional setting in which presidential electioneering takes place. Included is a discussion of political party and electoral systems, nominating procedures (if any), media environments, and campaign finance laws in each country. Presidential electioneering does not take place in a vacuum. Obviously rules, be they formal laws or informal practices, have a large impact on the process, so a good understanding of this institutional environment is critical to an understanding of the actions of presidential candidates and their parties in the electioneering effort.

Chapters 4 through 6 begin the actual examination of electioneering practices in the modern era. By electioneering we mean the organization, resources, and activities of a political campaign which is defined here as a connected series of events designed to win office for the candidate and win control of government for the party. The general question guiding the discussion throughout the book is, "who is doing what, and with what?"[31] More specifically, Chapter 4 examines the personnel involved in presidential electioneering, Chapter 5, various aspects of the resources of presidential electioneering, and Chapter 6, the processes themselves, including both campaign activity itself as well as candidate selection. A brief introduction to these three dimensions follows.

The Personnel of Presidential Electioneering

This dimension of presidential selection is centered around two aspects of the organization: its size and complexity and its orientation.[32] With respect to size and complexity, the focus includes staffing levels of the organizations, the nature of the staff, and specialization and leadership within the organization. An increase in size and professionalization within an organization is generally an indication of greater organizational strength or institutionalization.[33] In terms of the campaign, a larger organization means more hands to perform campaign tasks; greater professionalization means a greater ability to perform more varied campaign tasks. To be specific, this section of Chapter 4 looks at the numbers of staff in the organization, specialization and professionalization within the organization, and the autonomy of the organization leadership. Beyond the numbers and nature of campaign organization this chapter examines the orientation of campaign organizations, which means both cohesion and the mission of the organization. The justification for examining cohesion of campaign organizations is fairly straightforward: greater cohesiveness brings greater strength to the campaign effort.[34] Conversely, organizational factionalism generally translates into weakness. Also examined in this section is how well the organizations seem to be oriented to the mission, namely, electing the candidate.

As mentioned previously, electioneering personnel, like electioneering resources and processes, are examined according to the efforts of candidate and party organizations. In the case of electioneering personnel we will see that party staffs are larger and more professional than in years past and are increasingly capable and willing to carry out campaign activity on behalf of, in many cases at the behest of, the candidate, which is a shift in orientation for American political parties. Candidate organizations, phenomena that are new to the modern era, are also increasingly large and capable.

There is a wild card to be reckoned with here. Before concluding the discussion of this aspect of presidential electioneering we must examine the role of a growing and increasingly specialized breed of campaign professionals in presidential electioneering. These campaign professionals are like sub-contractors, technically beholden to neither party nor candidate and are playing an increasingly important role in modern political campaigns. Their role demands that we examine this phenomenon in more detail, so before leaving Chapter 4 we will look at the industry, examining from where these professionals hail, for whom they work, and what they do.

Electioneering Resources

Chapter 5 examines the variety of resources involved in modern presidential electioneering.[35] With what, and with how much, is the campaign being carried out? In whose hands are these resources and where do they come from? These are the general questions guiding this dimension of presidential electioneering, the second and third questions are equally as important as the first. Money is obviously important here since it buys advertising, office space, the service of campaign professionals, and so on. The dimensions of campaign finance we will examine are the amounts and sources of campaign funds, how they are raised, as well as campaign expenditures.

There are other, non-monetary resources involved in modern electioneering. Questions here are similar to the ones asked of campaign finance: where are they found, how are they acquired, and who controls them? What types? First are physical resources, meaning office space and equipment. The second type of electioneering resource is information, meaning lists of voters, donors, and volunteers (actual or potential) which are used in increasingly sophisticated ways (e.g., marketing techniques, database software) to mobilize specific groups. It also includes the control of information about one's self and one's opponent, critical in crafting campaign strategy. Human resources are a third and equally important type of electioneering resource, meaning the variety of independent or non-party groups which support the electioneering effort (interest groups, single issue, ideological, or citizens' groups). A fourth and final type of electioneering resource included in this discussion is, for lack of a better term, political capital, and includes presidential incumbency, endorsements, and stature.

Throughout Chapter 5 we will see that increasing amounts of all of these types of resources (monetary and non-monetary) are needed in modern presidential electioneering. In addition, we will see that while parties are increasingly well-funded and resource-rich, electioneering resources are increasingly under the control of the candidate.

The Process of Presidential Electioneering

Chapter 6 examines the activity of, or events associated with, presidential selection. It is the "what" in the "who is doing what" question, and looks first at various aspects of candidate selection, meaning candidate recruitment, screening, and the selection of the party nominee. It is in this area that we see clearly what is perhaps the most obvious and defining characteristic of modern presidential electioneering, namely, that political parties have virtually no control over their own label. Candidate recruitment centers around questions of who and what types of individuals run, why, how many candidates enter the race, and when they start. Here, there has been a trend towards lateral entry in presidential politics, meaning less (or no) time working one's way up the party ladder and/or in government service. The other noticeable development in candidate recruitment is a trend towards earlier starts.

Candidate selection in the modern era can be reduced to a discussion of direct primaries. Much has been written about this aspect of presidential selection in the United States, but its impact on presidential electioneering is quite simple. Since the majority of delegates to the national convention are chosen in the primaries, the party nominee is selected before the convention begins. Therefore it is useful to examine and understand the numbers and dynamics involved in the primary system of candidate selection as well as the nature of the pre-primary season. Certain aspects of the convention will be examined in this section as well. Various aspects of candidate selection include when candidate organizations form, when candidates announce their candidacy, the increase in the number of states holding direct primaries, and percentage of pledged delegates selected by those states and the front-loading of primaries.

The second section of Chapter 6 then turns to campaign activity (fund-raising, polling, electoral mobilization, etc.).[36] Broadly speaking, the question here is, who is doing what campaign activities? On a different level, it may be the case that the activity is being carried out by one player (for example, the party) while decision-making rests with the other (for example, the candidate). A general list of campaign activities includes but is not limited to fund-raising, polling, electoral mobilization (voter registration and turnout), research, audio-visual advertising (production and distribution), campaign literature (production and distribution), and travel. Importantly, some of these activities (e.g., fund-raising) will of necessity be discussed prior to Chapter 6.

The role of technology is important in any discussion of campaign activity on the modern era. Before the so-called candidate-centered era, a candidate, out of necessity, relied on his party to communicate his campaign message to a national audience—there was no possible way a single person could canvass the country. Advances in communication and transportation technology have had a profound effect on political campaigning in this respect.[37] Candidates increasingly craft campaign strategy assuming the national scope which these technologies provide; these technologies also increase the demand for specialists (campaign professionals).

Conclusions

In the final chapter lessons learned from the examination of modern presidential electioneering practices in the United States are discussed, as well as what may be gleaned about presidential electioneering in France and Russia. The discussion first centers around the fact that presidential electioneering in the United States is becoming more personalized, or candidate-centered, and then examines this development in France and Russia. Various technological and institutional factors which may be responsible for this trend are noted and discussed, as are several implications of this development. Simply put, who becomes president has serious consequences for American politics. Presidential electioneering practices affect more than simply who becomes president but certainly has a great impact on that. What follows describes, details, and illustrates electioneering practices in the modern era.

2

Traditional Presidential Electioneering

ELECTIONEERING IN THE "GOLDEN AGE"

Could Abraham Lincoln have captured his party's nomination and won the presidency in the modern era of presidential electioneering? By all accounts he was a good speaker and his brevity in that respect (recall that the Gettysburg Address contains only 272 words) would certainly have worked to his advantage in the modern "sound bite" era of modern presidential campaigns. One does have to wonder, however, about other aspects of a modern Lincoln candidacy. For example, Lincoln was not a widely known national figure prior to the campaign, and perhaps most damaging is the fact that he was not an exceptionally handsome man— the most flattering description one could use would probably be homely. The point is that he could hardly be considered telegenic, and while his party ties, speaking ability, and leadership skills would certainly work to his advantage, we would be hard-pressed to imagine Lincoln as a modern-day Bill Clinton, skillfully using television to his advantage.

Why this speculation? This chapter is devoted to a description of traditional presidential electioneering. Along with the following chapter which provides an overview of the institutional environment of presidentialism and presidential selection in the United States, France, and Russia, it lays a foundation for the remainder of the book. By taking a brief tour back through time and looking at electioneering practices in the United States prior to 1960, the chapter provides a better sense of what makes modern presidential electioneering distinctive. The exclusive focus of the chapter, unlike the rest of the book, is on the United States. The reason for this is simple: there was no presidential electioneering in

France (to speak of) or Russia prior to 1960. Like the rest of the book, most of the chapter is organized according to electioneering personnel, resources, and processes of political party and (where applicable) candidate organizations in the traditional era.

Throughout the chapter it will become apparent that while candidates were never completely passive in their pursuit for top office, the story of traditional presidential electioneering is one that largely revolves around political parties. Indeed, James Bryce, the Englishman whose *American Commonwealth* still stands as insightful (if now dated in many respects) commentary on American politics, includes his chapters on the "Presidential Campaign," "Issues in Presidential Elections," and "Observations on Nominations and Election" in the section of Volume II devoted to the American party system. In spite of the fact that Bryce pays particular attention to the attributes of a winning candidate, the language he uses in his description of presidential campaigns and elections is illustrative of the importance of the party's role in the campaign effort. He writes, for example, of "the victory of a *party* in a presidential election," or the fact that the party's "duty" of "*choosing* the *candidate*" overshadows all of their other programmatic concerns.[1]

It must be mentioned that Bryce was writing during what is referred to as the "Golden Age of Parties," a period of time just prior to the Civil War to shortly after the beginning of the twentieth century. It was the heyday of American political parties, the age of the so-called urban party machines and party bosses. As implied, during this time the influence of political parties in American political life was at its height and this obviously had an effect on presidential electioneering.

The influence of political parties on campaigns has not always been as pervasive as it was during the Golden Age.[2] Beginning in the early twentieth century or so, the influence of parties began to slowly but inexorably decline. There were many reasons for this. Civil service reforms of the late 1800s began to shake the grip that party leaders had on the dispensation of public offices and government contracts. Collectively, the Progressive Movement introduced a variety of reforms intended to clean up politics by reducing the power of political parties, including the introduction of the Australian ballot, direct primaries, and non-partisan elections. Socially, the reduction in immigration in the early 1900s, the establishment of the welfare state after the New Deal, and rising levels of education and changing social mores made it more difficult for party bosses to dictate election outcomes by controlling the voting behavior of citizens. Finally, technological advances, mainly in communication (e.g., the advent of radio) made the party's role as political intermediary (or communicator) less vital than before.[3]

The point is that the picture many political scientists paint of political parties prior to the middle of the twentieth century often is exaggerated.

When we talk about party dominance in political campaigning, voting behavior, government, and community life, we are referring to perhaps a sixty-year period of time in American history. While exaggerated, this view of strong parties is useful, if only to compare and contrast the past to the present. When we refer to "traditional" presidential electioneering practices we are referring to the electioneering practices prevalent during this Golden Age of American political parties. The model, again, is slightly overstated, but it will serve as a useful starting point from which we can better paint a picture of modern electioneering practices.

Before examining traditional presidential electioneering more closely, we should first examine political party machines in more detail. In order to get a general idea of traditional presidential electioneering, we will then look at an example of a single campaign from that era, the 1880 campaign effort of the Republican James Garfield.

PARTY MACHINES IN THE GOLDEN ERA

America's first party machine was the Albany Regency (the Democratic Party of New York), built by Martin Van Buren in the early 1800s.[4] The Regency (which included the then-younger Tammany machine) was a group of patronage-bound editors, politicians, and officeholders who practiced a high degree of party loyalty, organization and, importantly, discipline. The Regency provided the model for party machines to follow.

Ties between party personnel (as such) in the Regency, as in many other urban-based party machines, were often personal, family, or business related and very strong. For example, prominent Regency leader, businessman, and banker Benjamin Knower was three-term Democratic Governor of New York William Marcy's father-in-law. He not only had a political interest but also a vested personal interest in many of the Governor's policies (in particular, controversial canal and bank policies). Even if not related by family ties, others in the organization were similarly close, a hallmark of the party machine.

Although Andrew Jackson and Martin Van Buren were the fathers of the machine model, Marcy, in one sense, was the man who defined it. It was he who coined the phrase that would later become associated with the "spoils system" of patronage politics: "It may be, sir, that the politicians of the United States are not so fastidious as some gentlemen are, as to disclosing the principles on which they act. . . . They see nothing wrong in the rule that to the victor belong the spoils of the enemy."[5] Virtually everyone who held public office in the days of the party machines was associated with a political party, since public office was considered part of the "spoils." Thus, not only were the ties among and between the personnel of political parties strong, but ties between party personnel and public officials also were strong. These ties led, unsurprisingly, to a great deal of government corruption, another hallmark of the urban party machine.

For example, the Golden Era was when voting "early and often" became a not-uncommon technique to win crucial races. The New York City Tammany Hall machine would often import voters from New Jersey and Pennsylvania for these situations,[6] and no account of traditional get-out-the-vote efforts would be complete without at least a mention of the outright purchasing of votes, a not-unheard-of practice for many years, and especially so during the Golden Age.[7] Of course, corruption in the Golden Age went beyond influencing voting.

Soliciting campaign funds from public officials was a popular way to fund political campaigns in the Golden Era. Starting in the 1830s the Democrats began levying regular "dues" (tithes) from government employees in the New York Customs House, and the Republicans were not far behind in adopting the practice. The growth of the federal government throughout the century meant more government jobs to dole out to party faithful and assess for campaign contributions later. These dues were a regular source of income for both parties and eventually became a target for reformers in the late 1800s and early 1900s.

Positions in government and favorable treatment in the doling out of government contracts was the primary way in which parties maintained discipline. And while the machine model of political parties had many less than admirable aspects, after a presidential candidate had been chosen, this discipline was such that all of the constituent state and local machines could be counted on to mobilize completely and fully in the effort to secure victory for the party. Party discipline, in one sense, was the primary and most valued of all resources in the electioneering effort. With it, a candidate could be assured of funding, networks of party workers and volunteers, favorable treatments in the party press, and more. Without it, there was no campaign.

THE GARFIELD CAMPAIGN OF 1880

The presidential campaign of Republican James Garfield in 1880 is illustrative of electioneering practices in the traditional era. The campaign is known as the "front porch campaign," so named because the bulk of Garfield's personal involvement in the electioneering effort consisted of receiving visitors (thousands of them) on the front porch of his Mentor, Ohio farm. In fact, Garfield's front porch approach worked so well that others (Benjamin Harrison in 1888, William McKinley in 1896) subsequently emulated it. But while Garfield's front porch was the focal point of the campaign and the candidate was reportedly very involved in crafting campaign strategy,[8] the Republican Party was central to the electioneering effort.

Garfield started his career in elective public office in the Ohio state senate in 1858. From that base he was elected to the House of Representatives where he served nine terms (1863–1880) and amassed an impressive legislative record. He was known to be a good orator, a skilled parliamentarian, knowledgeable about public affairs, and a fairly persuasive leader. On the negative side of the ledger, he was implicated in connection with the Crédit Mobilier scandal in 1872 but in the end was not censured for his involvement.[9] He distinguished himself so well in the House of Representatives that the Ohio legislature selected him to serve in the United States Senate in 1880, a seat he was destined never to take. James Garfield was, in sum, a good legislator, but did not command a great deal of national attention.

Leading up to the elections of 1880 there was a movement within the Republican Party, organized around the Stalwart faction of the Republican Party led by New Yorker Roscoe Conkling, in favor of a third term for former president Ulysses S. Grant. But the sentiment for a third Grant presidency was not unanimous. Most of the Republican National Committee (RNC) and many other party members, mainly the Half-Breed faction of the party, were deeply opposed and supported a James Blaine candidacy. When the Republican national convention convened in the summer of 1880, a full two-thirds of the party supported either Grant or Blaine.

Garfield attended the Republican convention as a member of the Ohio delegation. Unknown to most, for over a year there had been quiet planning within the party promoting a Garfield candidacy. As early as January of 1879, Jeremiah Rusk (a member of the RNC and a representative from Wisconsin) and Thomas Nichol (a lobbyist from Chicago) had been in touch with Garfield, inquiring about his interest in and availability for the presidency.[10] Garfield was wary, noting that "few men in our history have ever obtained the presidency by planning to obtain it."[11] In spite of the principal's seeming reluctance, others also came on board to promote Garfield's candidacy. Wharton Barker, a wealthy Philadelphia banker motivated by a desire to be remembered as a kingmaker, joined the nascent Garfield team in early 1880. These three were joined at the convention by former Wisconsin lieutenant governor and congressman Thaddeus Pound.[12] Together these men acted as behind-the-scenes convention managers. To aid in the still-unofficial "draft Garfield" movement, Barker planted a contingent of Garfield supporters behind the speaker's platform at the convention prior to the opening. As Garfield entered (late, of course, to maximize the effect), these supporters burst into "spontaneous" applause.[13]

When the convention turned to the business of nominating, Grant led Blaine in the first round of voting by 304 to 284; John Sherman (of Ohio), the third candidate of any stature (there were a total of six) polled 93. Grant probably could have eventually won under the unit delegation rule (whereby state delegations can only vote as a block), but Garfield (who opposed Grant), as chair of the Rules Committee, pushed through a rule allowing delegates to vote according to their conscience.[14] Garfield did not receive any votes on the first ballot, but on the second, Barker instructed a Pennsylvania delegate (W. A. Grier) to cast his vote for Garfield.[15] This move had no immediate effect; Garfield received no more than two votes per ballot on each of the next 33 ballots. It did, however, serve as a reminder to the convention that an alternative existed to the developing Grant-Blaine deadlock.[16]

On the thirty-fourth ballot, the governor of Wisconsin stunned the convention by casting all of his delegation's 17 votes for Garfield.[17] Garfield challenged this move on a point of order, correctly noting that he had not been nominated but was ignored by the chair (the objection was almost certainly for show). The Indiana delegation went over to Garfield on the thirty-fifth ballot, which brought Garfield's total to 50.[18] At this point Garfield was trying, out of a sense of propriety, to convince the rest of the Ohio delegation that it would be inappropriate for them to vote for him. Their first allegiance, he reminded them, was to fellow Ohioan Sherman. But Sherman, in a last minute telegram, instructed his delegates to give their votes to Garfield, and on the next ballot the "dark horse" (an unexpected choice for party nominee) James Garfield secured the Republican Party presidential nomination.[19]

Garfield and his team immediately attempted to heal party wounds. To placate the Stalwarts, he offered Levi Morton (a close associate of Conkling's from New York) the vice-presidency and after Morton refused he selected Chester Arthur, then ranked second among New York Republicans.[20] Two of Garfield's managers paid Sherman's campaign expenses (totaling $1,500) and after the convention Garfield (at the urging of others) traveled to New York to personally mend the rift with Conkling.[21] The importance of these conciliatory gestures cannot be overstated. Having started the campaign with no organization, Garfield was forced to unify the party or else face a general election campaign with nothing by way of an organization with which to conduct it.[22]

The last order of business before the convention adjourned was the actual organization of the campaign, a party responsibility. To this end, a "potent" campaign staff of party personnel was built consisting of Marshall Jewell (of Connecticut) as head of the RNC, ex-Senator Stephen Dorsey (of Arkansas) serving as National Secretary, and Levi Morton (of New York) as chief financial agent of the party.[23] James Blaine became an adviser to Garfield.

Huge amounts of resources were needed to secure a victory in November. Although Garfield cultivated several important money contacts (including Jay Gould, Chauncey Depew, and John D. Rockefeller) as the campaign wore on,[24] it was the Republican Party that was instrumental in defraying campaign costs. For example, the party conducted an expensive (and extensive) canvassing effort in New York City, constructing a list of 300,000 voters organized by precinct; roughly 12 million documents were printed and distributed during the campaign; poll taxes were paid in the South; speakers were hired and their expenses paid, all by the Republican Party.[25] Perhaps the most notable aspect of the campaign effort in terms of finance was the party campaign effort in Indiana where there were reportedly 30,000 votes for sale. At a total expense of $70,000, party manager Stephen Dorsey's arsenal of two-dollar bills bought these votes.[26]

The main reason we are examining Garfield's front porch campaign is that the effort epitomizes what was then the conventional wisdom that candidates should not be active campaigners. In this respect it stands out as a paradigm of traditional presidential electioneering. The Republican Party carried the campaign effort to the country at large, hosting clambakes in New England, barbeques in the south, staging parades, and organizing rallies in the large cities. Meanwhile, in spite of the fact that Garfield was reportedly "one of the great stump speakers of the day,"[27] he stayed on his farm in Mentor receiving guests. "An endless stream of children, politicians, Union veterans, businessmen, suffragettes, and prohibitionists made the pilgrimage to Garfield's farm in Mentor, Ohio. . . . [In fact] so many people came that the local railroad offered to stop its trains [there]."[28]

The Garfield campaign is an example, but not the only example, of the traditional practice of the party shouldering the bulk of the presidential campaign's organization, funding, mobilization, and communication efforts. Perhaps this was as it should have been, since parties, as Bryce noted, were responsible for selecting their candidate at the national party convention. As the above example makes clear, the candidate played a role in the electioneering effort but that role was minimal, certainly compared with the candidate's role in modern presidential electioneering. Next we will examine the personnel, resources, and processes of traditional presidential electioneering in greater detail.

THE PERSONNEL OF CAMPAIGN ORGANIZATIONS IN THE TRADITIONAL ERA

Prior to the middle of this century it was a truism in American politics that the further up (i.e., the closer to Washington, D.C.) one looked for political parties the less likely it was they would find any evidence of these organizations. Put another way, political parties were local, with no permanent national presence.[29] National party organizations (as such) did not truly exist. They were amorphous in formation, appearing just prior to elections and disappearing immediately afterwards. For example the RNC, although founded in 1854, did not have a permanent head-quarters in Washington, D.C. until 1970; the Democratic National Committee (DNC), founded in 1848, only did so in 1985 (prior to this they rented office space).[30]

Campaign organizations, whether party or candidate, were generally formed sometime during the year of the election (often, as in Garfield's case, at the convention) and were dissolved immediately afterwards. Although there was little (if any) national party as such, a committee was usually formed at the convention which took charge of the campaign and included a delegate from each state. These campaign organizations were on the whole much smaller than those in modern times. The Whigs, for example, backing the candidacy of General William Henry Harrison in 1840, were said to have had the "most efficient candidate organization the country had yet seen," and totaled eight legislators and their staffs.[31]

The personnel of political parties were professional politicians, the so-called "party hacks" of the urban party machines.[32] These professionals, although capable, were a less specialized class of individuals than the political professionals of today. The reason for this is fairly straightfor-ward. Campaign technology was such that with the exception of orators (and perhaps newspapermen, if they could officially be counted as party men), there was less of a need for specialized campaign personnel. This is not to suggest that political parties were anything but efficient in their conduct of presidential campaigns. On the contrary, prior to each cam-paign political parties engaged in what historian Robert Dinkin refers to as an efficient and systematic "army style" mobilization of volunteers. The presidential campaign effort relied heavily on these volunteers, who were typically organized into "clubs." James Bryce described these clubs:

[They] usually bear the candidates' names [and] are formed on every imaginable basis, that of locality, of race, of trade or professions, of university affiliation. There are Irish clubs, Italian clubs, German clubs, Scandinavian clubs, Polish clubs . . . young men's clubs, lawyer's clubs, dry-goods clubs, insurance men's clubs, shoe and leather clubs. There are clubs of the graduates of various col-leges.[33]

After the candidate clubs were organized they were whipped up into a frenzy and sent marching out to battle (recall the term "campaign" and its use in military contexts).[34] In many cases, this was taken all too lit-erally. Accompanied by marching bands, campaign battalions would take to the streets marching on behalf of their candidate.[35] One account, for example, tells of a Democratic parade (which drew roughly 6,000 spectators) consisting of 1,600 mounted men and roughly the same number on foot in Anderson, South Carolina.[36] Another report indicates that better than 25,000 businessmen, organized by profession, turned out and marched parade-style in New York City for James Blaine in late October of 1884.[37] Parades and rallies and the like were staged throughout the summer and early fall, but occurred with greater frequency the closer election day came in the attempt to build emotions and influence votes. In addition to volunteers, parties employed paid workers as well, often "thousands of paid agents . . . canvassing, distributing pamphlets or leaflets, [or] lecturing on behalf of the candidate."[38]

The point to be made here is that parties were the central element—the hub of the wheel, so to speak—of the campaign effort. While campaign clubs bore the candidates' name, they were mobilized by the party; the "paid agents" referred to above were paid by the party. And parties, recall, meant the loose confederation of state and local parties which, generally speaking, could be relied upon to carry the candidate's banner high. This latter was central to the campaign effort.

From what has been said thus far about the role of parties in traditional presidential campaigns, it should come as no surprise that personal candidate "organizations" as such did not exist. Dwight Eisenhower's "Citizens for Eisenhower" in 1952 was a notable latter-day exception, created by the candidate and run with only loose ties to the Republican Party.[39] But in the main, whatever personal candidate organizations there were in the traditional era consisted of family members, friends, and a few close advisors to the candidate. Even these advisors, it must be mentioned, were usually party men who had especially close relationships with the candidate and had likely pushed for his nomination.

RESOURCES OF CAMPAIGN ORGANIZATIONS IN THE TRADITIONAL ERA

Campaign finance prior to the modern era was fairly secretive, hardly the transparent affair it is today as the result of campaign finance reform efforts in the 1970s. Presidential campaigns, in general, were financed by parties and by wealthy individuals. And while electioneering resources include more than money, it is, and always has been, the "mother's milk" of politics (a phrase coined by the late California Democrat Jesse "Big Daddy" Unruh) because of the other resources it can buy (advertising, the services of campaign professionals, air travel, etc.).[40]

Presidential campaigns have always been costly. Prior to the 1820s and the development of political parties, presidential aspirants generally underwrote the costs of their campaigns themselves. While most presidential aspirants were men of means, this proved to be cost-prohibitive in very short order. For example Thomas Jefferson, hardly a pauper, was said to be nearly bankrupt by the end of his second term in office as a result of his costly campaign efforts.[41] In fact, the need for campaign funds in the 1852 campaign of Franklin Pierce animated the creation of the DNC in 1848 by financier August Belmont (who also became the contributor of last resort that year).

The era of party machines in American history is also known as the Gilded Age, a period which saw the accumulation of huge fortunes and various attempts by the individuals holding those fortunes to influence politics. To further their various interests, these individuals, many of whose names are familiar, quite naturally often turned to the presidency. Jay Cooke, Cornelius Vanderbilt, and the Astor family, for example, contributed heavily to the Republican Party in Ulysses S. Grant's 1868 campaign. And although the Republicans were considered to be the party of business, the Democrats had wealthy friends as well, including Cyrus McCormick, Samuel Tilden (who, oddly enough, was apparently a bit reluctant to spend money on his own 1876 campaign against Rutherford B. Hayes), and as mentioned, August Belmont, who although not wealthy himself, represented France's House of Rothschild.

Most campaigns financed by wealthy contributors saw the funds going to the campaign of a specific candidate rather than to the party. This began to change toward the end of the century. As a result of the Progressive Movement, many business leaders began to try and expand their influence by contributing to the party rather than individual presidential campaigns. But this era is best known as the era of "political kingmakers."[42] The first and perhaps best-known of these kingmakers was Mark Hanna who, from the post of chairman of the RNC, directed and helped finance William McKinley's presidential candidacy in 1896. It was, in fact, during this period that the term "fat cat" was coined, a term which referred to the common practice of "frying the fat" out of the captains of industry for campaign finance.[43]

Although many efforts were made to limit the influence of big business in political campaigns throughout much of the twentieth century, the practice of fat cats, corporations, and labor unions contributing huge sums of money to presidential campaign efforts continued right up until the campaign finance reforms of the 1970s. Whether to individual candidates or to parties, the story—in the eyes of most, a corrupt and scandalous story—of campaign finance was one of huge donations coming from a very few individuals. During the 1960s, in large part due to the rapidly increasing costs of campaigning (especially the cost of television advertising) the problem was magnified, and several presidential candidates benefitted from extremely large donations. Eugene McCarthy and Robert Kennedy were each reported to have accepted at least one donation of $500,000 apiece in 1968; Nelson Rockefeller received a single donation of almost $1.5 million (from his stepmother); and Richard Nixon benefitted directly from virtually all of a $2.8 million donation which W. Clement Stone made to the Republican Party.

In sum, campaign finance prior to the 1970s revolved in large part around large donations made by wealthy individuals, corporations, and labor unions. Sometimes these contributions were to individual candidates, sometimes to political parties with the understanding that individual candidates were to benefit.

As alluded to earlier, beyond money the most valued electioneering resource in the Golden Era was the party network, meaning the array of volunteer armies, orators, newspaper editors, and so on, associated with the party machines in the states and cities. In this respect, party cohesion, while still important in the modern era, was arguably more so in the traditional era. To the extent that the party was not completely unified in support of its candidate, the campaign suffered from a lack of resources. This meant that conciliatory efforts after the convention (like Garfield's) were not optional, and often played a pivotal role in unifying the party preparation for the general election.

Finally, some mention should be made of the technological resources available to presidential campaigns prior to 1960. It is a truism of political life that political campaigns have always taken advantage of the latest in communications (and other) technologies. This is one reason why the cost of political campaigns is constantly rising and why specialists will always be in demand. Prior to the turn of the century, technology was such that political communications were fairly simple and, comparatively speaking, fairly low cost. The campaign was waged mainly via speeches and a variety of printed material. Electronic media technology changed all this and in the process dramatically changed the equation between party and candidate as well.

The first candidate to record a speech was the silver-tongued William Jennings Bryant in 1900; Bryant was also the first to appear in a campaign movie (in 1908).[44] Short candidate biography movies (generally lasting twenty to thirty minutes) appeared first in 1936 (by Alfred Landon).[45] Both parties employed radio for the first time in 1924, and on election eve, President Coolidge took to the air over 26 stations. By the 1940s presidential campaigns were devoting up to one-third of their budget (perhaps $2 million) to radio advertising;[46] soon, television was being used in presidential campaigning and this was more expensive still (1952 was the last year that radio advertising dollars equaled the amounts spent on television).

The above is more than simply a short exercise in presidential campaign trivia. As mentioned previously, the electronic age drastically altered the relationship between party and candidate. Previously, without the party network, a candidate had no means of taking his message national. Electronic communications did not change this immediately but by the television age it certainly had. At the same time the electronic age made financial resources and campaign specialists far more important.

PROCESSES: CHOOSING CANDIDATES IN THE TRADITIONAL ERA

Candidate selection refers to one of the several phases of the campaign up to and including the party's national convention which together constitute the process of determining who will be the party nominee in the general election. The first phase considered here is candidate recruitment or how candidates decide to seek or are considered for this honor. Second, candidate screening involves the narrowing of the field of aspirants by those responsible for the eventual selection of the party nominee. Finally there is selection, or the nomination, a phase which officially concludes at the party national convention. Included in the process of choosing candidates are questions of ambition, availability, timing, and a host of other considerations which together make up the gauntlet through which an aspirant must pass through in order to become an official party candidate. In this section we will see, in short, that choosing candidates in the traditional era, as in other aspects of presidential electioneering, was a party-dominated process.

The first aspect of recruitment to be considered is the candidate's background and qualifications. In this respect electioneering in the traditional era was not entirely different than in the present era. Bryce noted that qualities of a good candidate in the Golden Era were the individual's ability as a statesman, length of national service, oratorical skills, "magnetism," family ties, stature and looks, purity of private life, public record (especially integrity), what state the candidate came from (a large state with many electors or a critical state was preferable), and most especially, how many public enemies the aspirant might have.[47] Candidates were classed (informally) according to whether they were favorites (a well known national figure with many of the above qualities, capable of drawing support from most areas of the country), favorite sons (popular in a single state only), and dark horses. The latter were often gifted but "the note of the dark horse [was] respectability, verging on colourlessness" (more on these types of candidates, the first of which was the Democrat James Polk in 1844, below).[48] It almost goes without saying that aspirants without a rich history of public and party service need not have been concerned with such niceties: a party-oriented background and a record of party service were requisites to be considered as the party nominee.

Candidate recruitment, by and large, was done by way of quietly making it known, through letters or private conversation, that an individual would be available for the party nomination. Often these communications were very subtle. The tradition until the latter part of the nineteenth century was that the "office sought the man." While the presidency was a great honor, it was considered unseemly to aspire to such a high office.[49] In line with this tradition, denials by potential aspirants were often couched in language that left open the possibility of being drafted. With respect to timing, aspirants (declared or otherwise) typically began their run (such as it was) early in the election year itself. Certainly many harbored presidential ambitions long before, but active politicking (letters, etc.) did not begin until much before then. Aspirants, even favorites, were discouraged from making their intentions known too early (probably to avoid exciting opposition). For example, former President Grant, who had gone on a world tour after he left the White House in 1877 and aspired to a third term in 1880, returned home against the wishes of his advisors in September 1879. The homecoming was considered much too early and may have contributed to Garfield's victory at the 1880 Republican convention.

This brings us to candidate screening, which in the traditional era basically meant ruling out unacceptable names. Often these decisions were not based on an aspirant's leadership or political skills but rather his blandness. As noted before, it did not pay for a presidential aspirant to have too many enemies. In other words, a potential candidate needed to be perceived as non-offensive. It was this aspect of presidential selection that led James Bryce to claim (and correctly so in the Golden Age, the era during which he was writing) that great men are not chosen to be president in the United States. "What a party wants is not a good president but a good candidate. The party managers have therefore to look out for the person likely to gain most support, and at the same time excite least opposition."[50] Those individuals who were strong-willed or excited passion were deemed too risky to carry the party banner and were discouraged (directly or otherwise) from pursuing their candidacy any further. In addition to being unremarkable, a candidate had to be skilled enough to bind disparate factions of the party together for the general election.

In the traditional era, the true drama of candidate selection was played out at the national party conventions.[51] It was there that the final deals were cut and the party nomination was decided. The outcome was determined by intricate and intense maneuvering and negotiation among party factions. Often balloting was unanimous (Martin Van Buren in 1835, Henry Clay in 1844, Ulysses S. Grant in 1869 and 1872, Grover Cleveland in 1888);[52] others, while not nominated unanimously, were selected on the first ballot (Grover Cleveland and William Harrison in 1892).[53] However voting often stretched over multiple ballots. In 1852 the Democrats took 49 ballots to nominate Franklin Pierce, and the Whigs

53 to nominate General Scott; Woodrow Wilson captured the Democratic nomination in 1912 on the forty-sixth ballot.

There were several reasons why it might take multiple ballots to choose the party nominee. Many state delegations (chosen by the state party establishments with virtually no public participation) entered the convention without having made a final or firm decision about their choice for nominee. Or, a state delegation leader might find out midway through the convention that he had been betrayed in his deal with a candidate or party faction and he would switch allegiances (deals, of course, typically involved the distribution of government jobs). Or there might simply be no agreement on a candidate. According to Bryce, delegates at the convention were motivated by any one (or more) of four desires in casting their votes for party nominee. In his words,

There is a wish to carry a particular aspirant. There is a wish to defeat a particular aspirant, a wish sometimes stronger than any predilection. There is a desire to get something for one's self out of the struggle—e.g., by trading one's vote for the prospect of federal office. There is the wish to find the man who, be he good or bad, friend or foe, will give the party its best chance of victory.[54]

Dark horse candidacies (like Garfield's) added immensely to convention drama and were made possible because of the nature of conventions. One of the functions of the national convention was to bind disparate factions of the party together. To this end the dark horse played a compromise role. At a divisive convention (like the 1880 Republican convention), an innocuous third candidate (the dark horse) would be chosen whom neither faction opposed, providing a way for various factions of the party to come together. No surprise then that when a dark horse compromise was presented it was often taken up by the body at large with alacrity.

Candidates had little direct role in this phase of the selection process. Typically they were not even present at the convention unless they happened to be part of their state delegation. This did not mean, however, that candidates had no role. Although it was against etiquette for a candidate to be at the convention, his managers and party loyalists would usually have their own headquarters at the convention where they met, planning strategy, starting rumors to exaggerate their candidate's strength, planning "spontaneous" outbursts, negotiating, and so on.[55] Using the best available technology, the candidate was in constant contact with his convention managers (e.g., via private telegraph or telephone lines specifically laid for that purpose). Recall that in 1880, for example, it was the timely telegram from the Republican Sherman that released the Ohio delegation and gave Garfield the needed votes to carry the nomination.

To recap, even this cursory examination should have made it abundantly clear that candidate selection in the traditional era of presidential electioneering meant just that: they were selected by party leaders. The public had little to do with the process, and while candidates were not entirely passive in the electioneering effort, the party nomination was first and last a party decision. In this respect, the contrast with the modern, self-starting, and primary-based method of securing the party nomination could not be more stark.

PROCESSES: CAMPAIGN ACTIVITY IN THE TRADITIONAL ERA

In many respects campaign activity is the core subject of this book. We talk about personnel in order to identify who is carrying out electioneering activity. We examine resources in order to determine with what that activity is carried out. Campaign activity itself is the "what"of electioneering, and at the most basic of levels, little has changed from the traditional to the modern era. Campaigning is still the act of carrying the message to voters and potential voters, of attempting to persuade 50 percent plus one of those voters to cast their ballot for you. Now, as before, campaigns rely heavily on the latest technologies. Finally, campaigns still emulate the successful strategies of past campaigns. Although it is hardly the science that some campaign professionals might claim it is (and most do not), the strategies and techniques that work (or seem to work) in one election will likely be emulated in the next.

In another sense, of course, a great deal has changed. Technological advances in communication as well as in transportation means that candidates, simply put, no longer need the party to carry their message to a national audience. This fact alone is of supreme importance, inasmuch as campaigning was, it could be argued, the original *raison d'être* for American political parties. In all areas of campaign activity discussed here we will see how pervasive and important political parties were in traditional presidential electioneering. To state it simply, in the traditional era, campaigns were nothing without political parties. It will also become apparent that the campaign effort itself was much less specialized in years past. One note: at the risk of being redundant, many of the aspects of personnel and resources discussed previously will be alluded to in this section. This is unavoidable, since many aspects of the machine model of political parties were so closely intertwined.

Campaign management, while not exclusively so, was very much the domain of individuals affiliated, officially or otherwise, with political parties. This is no surprise. In the traditional era it was virtually inconceivable that one would have been involved in or knowledgeable about politics without being associated with a political party. Of course the candidate himself was not without a say in the management of his own election effort, and candidates also depended on the advice of close friends, family, and so on. But because the leading political figures of the day were the party bosses and public officials (often both), presidential candidates typically lent enormous credence to their advice. This advice mainly centered around strategic issues of when (or if) to make it known one was "available" to be nominated, what issues to avoid speaking about (publicly or otherwise), and what other party figures might need to be cultivated (read, promised public office after the election or assurances that certain positions would or would not be taken on key issues) in order to secure the nomination.

The other aspect that stands out with respect to campaign management in the traditional era was that it was far less specialized. Thus, there was little need for specialists—party notables oversaw virtually all aspects of the campaign. Part of the reason that party men were so active in campaign management was the plain fact that the battle to secure the party nomination was waged at the party convention. It is in accounts of party nominating conventions that one finds explicit reference to convention managers whose job was to influence state delegations to cast their ballots for his candidate. A good convention manager had a sense of what the electorate was looking for, but more importantly, what the party was looking for and who the party could rally behind in November. Secrecy, persuasion, conviction, coercion, and an ability to understand and adroitly use convention rules were among the needed skills of a good convention manager. But above all, one had to have a good sense of where the party as a whole stood since the election effort, as noted previously, in large part depended on the full support of state and local bosses.

Campaign communication in the traditional era in comparison to the modern era, was fairly simplistic. Printed campaign material was the primary form of communicating the candidate's and party's message in the traditional era and included pamphlets (containing, for example, the party platform, short treatises by or letters from the candidate on particular issues), biographies of the candidate,[56] banners, and a variety of paraphernalia (buttons, hats, flags, etc.) with the candidate's or party's name and/or campaign slogan or theme.

At least as important as the party platform was the candidate's "letter of acceptance." Formally the document was a letter indicating a willingness to carry the party standard into the campaign battle, but in actuality it was used as a forum to outline the candidate's positions, reprinted and circulated widely. It was also used to signal various factions of the party that their positions would be given proper consideration. Of course the candidate consulted with the party on the correct positions to take on the issues before crafting such a document. Also popular during this period were campaign textbooks, consisting of a variety of political literature (including editorials, cartoons, issue tracts) which the party would bring together around a common campaign theme.

In addition to party-sponsored printed matter, the party press could always be counted on for favorable editorial treatment as well as for "news" coverage of upcoming rallies and so forth. Here again, strong connections in the party machine were vital. One all but forgotten type of campaign communication which has a rich history in presidential campaigns is music. Campaign songs, as well as chants, poems and political cartoons, are good examples of the creative uses of available campaign technology. Garfield supporters, for example, attacked the South (and thus the Democratic party) and their treatment of blacks in a campaign song about Democratic candidate General Winfield Scott Hancock:

> Sing a song of shotguns, pocket full of knives
> Four-and-twenty black men, running for their lives;
> Northern sympathizers making speeches chaffy!
> Major-General Hancock eating rebel taffy;
> English in a quandary, how to save his dollars!
> Along comes a solid South and fits them [blacks] all with collars.[57]

The other primary form of campaign communication in the traditional era was personal in nature. Specifically, speeches were a central element in presidential campaigns in the traditional era, made either by the candidate, or more likely by his surrogates. These surrogates were employed not only for their skill as orators but out of necessity. Candidates could hardly have traversed the country themselves as they do today (Harry Truman's "whistle stop campaign" of 1948 was a latter-day exception to this rule). Personal communication also included various types of gatherings (e.g., picnics, barbeques, rallies, flag raisings, parades, candidate appearances) where party faithful and others would attempt to whip up further support for the candidate.

Interestingly, the candidate himself was often discouraged from making personal appearances, especially during the Golden Age, as it was feared he might make statements which would cripple the campaign effort.[58] It was often to the candidate's (and party's) advantage to keep the candidate quiet, especially those candidates with little speaking ability (e.g., Ulysses S. Grant).[59] Stephen Douglas was the first to break with this tradition in 1860[60] but, as a rule, only those candidates who were trailing badly actively campaigned on their own behalf. Grant summed up what was then the conventional wisdom in an 1872 correspondence to Roscoe Conkling:

My judgement is that it will be better that I should not attend any convention or political meeting during the campaign. It has been done, so far as I remember, but by two presidential candidates heretofore, and both of them were public speakers, and both were beaten. I am no speaker, and don't want to be beaten.[61]

The discussion of personal communication segues neatly into one centered around the last of the three campaign activities, namely, voter mobilization. By this we mean various efforts to get out the vote, including transporting people to the polls, paying their poll taxes, as well as vote influencing, which could take the form of any of the public gatherings mentioned above or simple door-to-door canvassing. This latter was often very systematic, well planned, and executed typically on the precinct level. All of these forms of voter mobilization were done in person by, or at the least, under the direction of local party leaders.

To re-emphasize, in all of these types of campaign activity the candidate was absolutely and completely reliant on his party. Only party people were skilled enough in politics and had the connections needed to conduct a national campaign. Only they could deliver the local party machines which the candidate needed to spread his message nationally and rally support.

SUMMARY

The picture of traditional presidential electioneering presented in the previous pages was by no means comprehensive, and again, was overstated. E. E. Schattschneider once claimed that "modern democracy is unthinkable save in terms of the parties," and this was certainly true with respect to traditional presidential electioneering.[62] By the early twentieth century many things were changing which, taken together, began to erode the dominance of party organizations in the process. The various reforms of the Progressives, in particular the introduction of the direct primary, changing campaign finance laws, and communication and transportation revolutions, all together began to slowly change presidential electioneering from what it was in the traditional era to what we know it as today. In the next chapter we will explore in greater depth presidentialism and the formal and informal aspects of presidential selection in the United States, as well as roughing out an outline of the same in France and Russia.

3

Presidentialism and Presidential Selection: The Institutional Environment

MAPPING THE COURSE

Running for president is not a simple endeavor. The race is grueling and long, lasting well over a year, run at breakneck speed, and is rife with detours, switchbacks, hurdles, and other obstacles. It is not a race which the uninitiated could ever hope to complete, much less win or place. The rules governing the process are exceptionally complex and require stupendous effort and resources to understand and follow. For example, from January to mid-October of 1996 President Clinton spent over $1.3 million to comply with the myriad of complex campaign finance rules alone.

In the previous chapter we looked at presidential electioneering practices in the traditional era in the United States. In this chapter we examine the formal and informal aspects of presidential selection in the United States, France, and Russia. The chapter is designed to finish setting the stage for a discussion of modern electioneering practices.

Presidential campaigns do not take place in a vacuum. Formal rules and informal practices together constitute a particular institutional environment in which all actors who participate operate. A proper understanding of this environment is pivotal to the electioneering success of presidential aspirants and their political parties. Our discussion of presidential electioneering practices should be equally well informed, if not by all of the details of all of the pertinent statutes (we are not, after all, compliance lawyers), then by a clear understanding of the possibilities and constraints which the environment presents to presidential aspirants and their parties.

To that end, the first section of the chapter is devoted to a brief discussion of the origins of presidentialism in the United States, France, and
Russia, as well as the formal qualifications for office (in other words,
who can be president), tenure in office, provisions for re-eligibility, and
ballot access rules. These formal rules are mainly found in the constitutions of the three countries in our study. In the second section of this
chapter we examine the formal statutory environment of presidential
selection in the United States, France, and Russia. Here the discussion
turns to campaign finance laws and the formal aspects of the media
environment, by which we mean the degree to which there is a constitutional guarantee of freedom of the press as well as any provisions which
may be made for government-sponsored campaign communication (e.g.,
free television air time). The third and final section of the chapter briefly
introduces party politics in each country. As noted above, the road to
the White House is long and complex and presidential aspirants must
anticipate this. The hope is that by the end of the chapter we will have
a fairly clear picture of the terrain which presidential aspirants and their
parties must cover in order to reach the chief executive's office.

PRESIDENTIALISM IN THE UNITED STATES, FRANCE, AND RUSSIA: ORIGINS, SELECTION, AND TENURE IN OFFICE

The Origins of Presidentialism

Article II of the American Constitution specifies that the "executive
Power shall be vested in a President of the United States." While the
framers were not terribly specific about what "executive power" was,
the constitution embodies four principles which they considered vital to
the success of a chief executive and the new republic.[1] First, the framers
wanted an executive that would be independent of the other branches
of government. This was consistent with a belief that separation of powers was vital to good government and the protection against majority
tyranny of personal liberties. To this end they granted certain powers to
the president (and only to the president) and established a special body
independent of Congress to choose the president (the electoral college).
A longer term in office (four years) than that for a member of the House
of Representatives and the potential for re-election (originally unlimited,
now two terms under the Twenty-second Amendment) was designed
with executive independence in mind as well.

Second, the framers envisioned a unitary executive; in other words,
the executive power was to be vested in a single individual as opposed
to a collective (as, for example, in parliamentary systems). The reasoning
for this, discussed by Alexander Hamilton in *The Federalist*, No.

70, was to ensure that the duties of the executive could be carried out with dispatch, secrecy, and a minimum of consultation.[2] Third, and relatedly, the framers wanted an executive who had actual power, who was more than a figurehead officer of government or chief of state. Finally, they sought in the American presidency an officer who could serve as chief of state. The salary that was originally paid to the president ($25,000) was, at the time, thought to be large enough to "reflect the symbolic importance and dignity of his office."[3]

There have been a total of 53 presidential elections since the ratification of the Constitution in 1789; 42 men have served in the office, and 13 of them were elected to more than one term.[4] In the modern era of presidential electioneering a total of eight men have served in the office; one served as president without ever having been elected (Gerald Ford, 1974–77, after the resignation of Richard Nixon). Seven of these presidents were elected (Lyndon Johnson was elected in 1964 after serving from 1963–64 after the death of John Kennedy), and three were elected to the office twice (Richard Nixon in 1968 and 1972, Ronald Reagan in 1980 and 1984, and William Clinton in 1992 and 1996).

The present French regime, the Fifth Republic, was founded in 1958 as a response to the institutional paralysis of the previous regime. There were two executives in the French Fourth Republic (1946–58), a figurehead president elected by parliament and a somewhat more powerful prime minister, but neither had much authority.[5] Called upon to lead France out of crisis, Charles de Gaulle was installed as Prime Minister in 1958 and given free reign to draft a constitution. His answer to the legislative and partisan immobilism of the Fourth Republic was the proposed constitution for the Fifth Republic. The basic institutional framework of the Fifth Republic is similar to that of its predecessor, but the balance of power between institutions is dramatically different. While both executives in the Fourth Republic were virtually powerless, in the Fifth Republic the powers of both the president and prime minister are greatly enhanced.[6] The French presidency, in short, is at least as powerful and independent as the United States presidency. This is hardly an accident, since those powers are based in the same principles that animated the creation of the American presidency.[7]

Just as it was understood that George Washington would be the first American president, so it was accepted that the father of the Fifth Republic, General de Gaulle, would in 1959 be her first president. De Gaulle was initially selected president by an electoral college, but in 1962 he submitted a referendum to the French people proposing that future presidents be popularly elected. The referendum passed, and in 1965 French voters elected de Gaulle to the presidency. There have been a total of six presidential elections from 1965 to 1995 in France, and five men have served as president (Charles de Gaulle, 1958–69; Georges Pompidou,

1969–74; Valéry Giscard d'Estaing, 1974–81; François Mitterand, elected twice, 1981–95; and Jacques Chirac, 1995-present).

Russia's present constitution, dating to December of 1993, was (also) conceived and ratified in a time of national emergency and was the subject of great controversy.[8] Russian presidential pre-history dates to June of 1991 when Boris Yeltsin was the easy winner of presidential elections held while Russia was still part of the Soviet Union. The next few years were nothing if not eventful for Russians: there was an attempted coup against Soviet leader Mikhail Gorbachev (in August 1991), the Soviet Union was disbanded (Christmas Day, 1991), and the economy entered a period of protracted free fall. Throughout 1992 and most of 1993 the president and the legislature were deadlocked in a struggle to draft a new constitution, and by summer of 1993 the state of affairs between them was one of total intransigence.

In September Yeltsin disbanded the legislature by decree, further stipulating that legislative elections and a referendum to ratify a new constitution were to be held on December 12, 1993. The decree was declared illegal by both the Russian Constitutional Court and the legislature, but the military (after some hesitation) backed Yeltsin, and after a day of armed conflict the legislature was forcibly closed.[9] A whirlwind autumn of campaigning and political maneuvering resulted in the ratification of the proposed constitution, which provided for a strong Russian presidency ("super-presidential," in the eyes of some)[10] and a dramatically weakened legislature.[11] While the next two years were not quite "politics as usual" in Russia, there were no more revolutions, coups, regime collapses or changes, and Russians went to the polls in the summer of 1996 to re-elect Boris Yeltsin to the Russian presidency.

Although variations on the theme exist, the American presidency has proven to be the model for presidential government around the world. In the United States, France, and Russia, circumstances were such that at a certain decisive point in history it was determined by the majority of the citizenry that a competent, unitary, and independent chief executive was needed. The independence of the president in each country is formally embodied in the structure of each regime by way of separation of powers. In addition, presidential independence is assured by the method of presidential selection in France and Russia by direct popular election, and in the United States by the electoral college. In either case the salient point is that the president is not beholden to the legislature (or any other institution of government) for his or her job.

Tenure in Office

The details of presidential tenure, re-eligibility, and second-in-command in the United States, France, and Russia differ. In the United

States the president is elected to a four-year term and may be re-elected to one more.[12] There is a formal second-in-command, a vice-president, who, in the event that a sitting president cannot complete his or her term (for reasons of death, incapacity, removal or resignation), assumes the duties of the president for the remainder of the term. In France the term of office is seven years. There are no formal term limits, nor is there a vice-president. If a sitting president cannot fulfill his or her duties, the president of the Senate assumes the office of the presidency in a caretaker role and new elections are held within 35 days.[13] The Russian president is elected to a four-year term for a maximum of two consecutive terms. In Russia, as in France, there is no vice-president, so in the event that a sitting president cannot complete his or her term the duties of the office are temporarily performed by the prime minister for a period not longer than three months, at which point new elections are held.

The constitutions of the United States, France, and Russia each include provisions for the removal of a sitting president from office in extraordinary circumstances (i.e., impeachment). In each of the three countries the bar is set very high for such an action. In the United States, the president must have committed "treason, bribery, or other high crimes and misdemeanors," in France, "high treason," and in Russia, "high treason or some other grave crime." In France this has never happened. In the United States, impeachment proceedings have been started against three presidents (Andrew Johnson, Richard Nixon, and William Clinton) and gone to the Senate in two of those cases (Johnson and Clinton), but no president has yet been removed from office as the result.[14] Proceedings to remove Russian President Yeltsin from office have been initiated several times (most recently in the spring of 1999), but they rarely got far, since removing a president in Russia is, if anything, more difficult than in the United States or France.

The Selection of Presidents

In all three countries the formal requirements for presidential candidacy are fairly lax. France has the lowest age requirement of all three (23 years old), the same age requirement for candidacy to the National Assembly (the lower house of the French legislature).[15] In the United States and Russia the age is 35. France, unlike the United States or Russia, has no residency requirement (in the United States a candidate must be resident for 14 years, in Russia, 10). They do, however, stipulate that a presidential candidate be a citizen for at least 10 years prior to the election. Perhaps surprisingly, in France and Russia it is not required that a presidential candidate be a natural-born citizen.

After fulfilling candidacy requirements a presidential aspirant must gain access to the ballot. To do this in France, the aspirant must gather a number of endorsements (signatures) from local government officials. Specifically, a candidate is required to be "nominated" by 500 sponsors. These sponsors must hold electoral office and must be drawn from at least 30 (of a total 96) different French departments or (four) overseas territories. No more than 50 of these sponsors may come from any single department or territory.[16] To gain ballot access in Russia, aspiring candidates are required to collect one million signatures, no more than 7 percent of which can come from any one of Russia's 89 regions.[17]

In the United States the procedure for ballot access is at once simpler and more complex. The first thing to understand is that unlike in France and Russia, the United States does not technically hold a national election for president. There are in fact 51 separate elections (the 50 states and the District of Columbia). Laws governing ballot access vary from state to state, but typically, the first step for a presidential aspirant to get on the ballot is to enter a party primary of a given state which involves filing a petition (with a certain number of voter signatures) and paying a small fee.[18] The individual's name is then placed on the ballot of either of the major parties (this is, importantly, the choice of the candidate, not the party). This leads to the second important point: the nominees of the two major parties are assured of a place on the general election ballot. The two major parties enjoy a huge institutional advantage in this regard. It is much more difficult for new parties and for independent candidates to gain access to the ballot, and here again, state laws vary. Pennsylvania is currently one of the toughest states in this respect. A potential new party must gather over 99,000 signatures on a petition in 14 weeks in order for its presidential candidate to gain access to the ballot.[19]

In France and Russia, citizens constitute the electoral body. Not so in the United States. Although citizens vote for president in the United States, the president is formally selected by the electoral college.[20] Each state is allotted a number of electors (now popularly elected) equal to the number of its representatives in the House, plus two for its senators, which translates into a total of 538 electors in the electoral college (the District of Columbia is allotted three electors). Forty-eight of the 50 states award all of their electors to the candidate who receives the most popular votes in the state (Maine and Nebraska are the exception, awarding electoral votes according to the winner in each congressional district).

The system, like any electoral system, is not neutral. It advantages some and disadvantages others, and also tends to exaggerate the margin of victory for the winner. In 1992, for example, Clinton's 43 percent of the popular vote gave him 69 percent of the electoral college vote; John Kennedy's share of the popular vote in 1960 was 49.7 percent; his electoral college percentage, 58 percent; and in 1980, Ronald Reagan won 50.7 percent of the popular vote which netted him almost 90 percent of the electoral college vote. In fact, numerically, a candidate only needs to

Figure 3.1
Hypothetical Coalitions in a Three-candidate Presidential Race

Three-way Vote Distribution				Coalition Scenario #1		Coalition Scenario #2	
Candidate	"A"	"B"	"C"	"A" & "B"	"C"	"A" & "C"	"B"
Vote Share	35%	33%	31%	69%	31%	67%	33%

win in the 10 most populous states to be a mere 10 electoral votes shy of victory. Three times in American history the electoral college system has also had the perverse effect of defeating the winner of the popular election. In 1824, 1876, and 1888, the winner of the popular vote (Andrew Jackson, Samuel Tilden, and Grover Cleveland, respectively) lost in the electoral college, and thus lost the election.

But the main losers in the American system are minor (or third) parties and independent candidates. The system of awarding all of the electors in a state to the winner of the popular vote is referred to as a winner-take-all electoral system, a system which discourages all but two entrants. Thus it was that Ross Perot, a well-funded independent candidate, did not win a single electoral vote in 1992 in spite of garnering 19 percent of the popular vote nationwide. This creates a powerful electoral incentive for a candidate to align with one of the two major parties. A hypothetical example would be helpful to illustrate this point. Figure 3.1 outlines two possible scenarios for a presidential race in which there are three roughly equally competitive candidates.

Note that in the three-way race, no candidate commands an absolute majority. In this example, Candidate "A" wins, but by a very slim margin. Assuming that Candidate "A" is the strongest candidate in all possible election scenarios, and given that other attractive political incentives exist (e.g., a position in the future administration), Candidates "B" or "C" will very likely make the strategic decision to align with "A." In either case, the coalition formed by Candidate "A" and one of the other candidates easily wins the election (Coalition Scenario #1 or Coalition Scenario #2).

It is for this reason that the contest in November has always been between the candidates of the two major parties. Although there have been several third-party candidates who enjoyed considerable popular success, notably, Theodore Roosevelt and the Bull Moose Party (a.k.a., the Progressives) in 1912, Strom Thurmond and the Dixiecrat Party (a.k.a., the States Rights Party) in 1948, and George Wallace and the American Independent Party in 1968, the United States has never elected a president from any but one of the two major parties.[21] Therefore, our focus is mainly on the two major parties and their candidates.

Voting in France (for both the presidency and the National Assembly) is a two-round affair. If no candidate receives more than 50 percent of the vote in the first round, the leading two candidates move to a second round of voting, typically held a few weeks after the first. As of yet, no candidate has prevailed in first-round voting, not even the popular General de Gaulle. Officially the election campaign begins two weeks before the election, which takes place 20–35 days before the term of the current president ends.[22] Russia also uses a two-round system of electing their president.

The constitutional provisions for the selection and tenure in office of presidents in the United States, France, and Russia are remarkably similar in that they provide for a unitary, competent, and independent chief executive. Methods of selection, especially in the United States as compared to France and Russia, differ, but even here the independence of the president is assured. All three countries, especially Russia, set impeachment standards and procedures very high, which reinforces presidential independence while at the same time allowing the legislature to check a rogue president. France has the longest term of office and has no official term limits, but it is hard to imagine a French president serving more than two terms. President François Mitterand served two terms (1981–95) and was, to put it candidly, drained by the experience (he died shortly thereafter).

With respect to selection, candidacy and ballot access requirements in France are far more lax than in the United States or Russia, which might lead us to expect more presidential candidacies in France. One aspect of selection which has not been discussed yet is the fact that presidential and legislative elections in the United States are held concurrently. This is not the case (except by accident) in France and Russia. This point is worthy of note inasmuch as many feel that holding concurrent presidential and legislative elections tends to reinforce the development of a stable party system and a tendency towards two-party domination.[23] In the United States, along with the single-round plurality method of presidential election, it also tends to drive potential presidential aspirants toward aligning with one of the two major parties. Conversely, two-round presidential elections (like those held in France and Russia) which are only occasionally concurrent with legislative elections probably encourages a multi-party system and more presidential candidacies.

Table 3.1 summarizes the constitutional provisions discussed in this section. The next section turns to the constitutional and statutory environment governing campaign finance and media coverage of presidential elections.

Table 3.1

Formal Aspects of Presidentialism and Presidential Selection in the United States, France, and Russia

	United States	*France*	*Russia*
Length of Term	4 years	7 years	4 years
Re-eligibility	2 term limit	No term limits	2 term limit
Second-in-Command	Vice-president	None	None
Contingency for Non-completion of Term	Vice-president assumes duties for remainder of term	President of Senate assumes office in caretaker role; new elections held within 35 days	Prime Minister assumes office; new elections held within 3 months
Provisions for Removal from Office	For "treason, bribery, or other high crimes and misdemeanors" (difficult)	For "high treason" (difficult)	For "high treason or some other grave crime" (very difficult)
Candidacy Requirements	35 year old citizen (natural-born) who has lived in the country for 14 years	23 year old citizen (natural or otherwise); no residency requirement	35 year old citizen (natural or otherwise) who has lived in the country for 10 years
Ballot Access	Various laws governing 50 states and the District of Columbia; major parties easy access	Candidate must be nominated by 500 elected officials in 30 (of 100) regions (limit of 50 from any 1 region)	Candidates must collect a million signatures, no more than 7% of which can come from any 1 of 89 regions
Electoral Body	Electoral college	Citizenry	Citizenry
Required Election Mandate	270 votes (of 538)	Majority in first round or plurality in second round	Majority in first round or plurality in second round
Presidential & Legislative Elections	Concurrent	Not concurrent	Not concurrent

THE CAMPAIGN FINANCE AND MEDIA ENVIRONMENT

In the previous section we looked at the constitutional provisions for presidentialism and presidential selection and tenure in the United States, France, and Russia. There we noted that while there are some differences between the constitutional foundations for presidentialism in the United States, France, and Russia, all three countries arrived at similar arrangements to ensure presidential competency and independence. In this section we look more closely at the constitutional and statutory regulation of campaign finance and the mass media. The first part of this section will be devoted to campaign finance, the second to the media. In each we will see that the differences between the three countries are far greater than in the previous section, specifically, the differences which set the United States apart from France and Russia.

Campaign Finance

Deep Throat's advice to *Washington Post* reporters Carl Bernstein and Bob Woodward in their Watergate investigation was to "follow the money."[24] Money is extremely important in political campaigns, and certainly so in the television age. For example, including both the primary and general election phases of the 1996 United States presidential election season, nearly half of the $232 million spent was spent on television advertising.[25] A large amount of money is also important in presidential electioneering efforts in other countries.[26]

There are several differences between campaign finance in the United States and in France and Russia, the main one being the almost absolute transparency in campaign finance in the United States that has prevailed since the middle of the 1970s, the second, the manner in which candidates and parties go about funding their campaigns. One of the discoveries unearthed by the Watergate investigation was that President Nixon's campaign organization (as well as a few Democratic presidential candidates) had accepted some dubious or illegal campaign contributions, some of which were quite large.[27] This led to a desire to close the many loopholes in the 1925 Federal Corrupt Practices Act governing campaign finance and "clean up" political campaigns. What followed was a series of federal statutes which along with an advisory opinion from a newly formed Federal Election Commission (FEC) and a Supreme Court ruling together constitute the campaign finance regime in the United States.[28] This regime was in place for the 1976 presidential elections, and with some modification (notably, the indexing of spending limits for inflation) still sets the ground rules for campaign finance.

Perhaps the most important feature of the new system is that presidential candidates, under certain conditions, can receive public funding for their campaign efforts. To qualify, candidates must first agree to abide by spending limits in both the primary and general election phases of the campaign.[29] Secondly, they must raise at least $5,000 in each of 20 states by soliciting and collecting private contributions not greater than $250 apiece. After these conditions are met, the FEC matches the amount of funds the candidate raises for the primary season up to a preset limit; each of the major party's presidential nominees also receives public funding for the general election season.[30] Under FEC guidelines parties also receive public funding to pay for their national conventions on the condition that they limit the amount of spending on behalf of their candidate during the general election.[31]

In addition to defraying primary and general election campaign costs of the aspirants/candidates of the two major parties, the laws provide for partial public financing of minor party or independent candidates. Those aspiring to the nomination of a minor party can also qualify for public money during the primary season, but the amounts they receive are substantially less than those received by the aspirants of the major parties.[32] For the general election phase, any candidate winning at least 5 percent of the popular vote qualifies for reimbursement in proportion to the votes they receive. For example, had Ross Perot agreed to federal spending limits in 1992 (he did not), he would have been qualified to receive $25.96 million based on his almost 20 percent share of the vote. This equaled 47 percent of the amount Bill Clinton and George Bush received. Based on that 1992 vote share, he was automatically eligible for $29 million in 1996, money which he did accept. The catch in this system is two-fold. First, minor party and independent candidates must gamble that they will receive at least 5 percent of the votes in the November election to qualify for public money, and second, they must wait to be reimbursed until after the election. In the meantime they must find other means to finance their campaign efforts.

The campaign finance laws of the 1970s have had several effects on presidential electioneering (this discussion will be expanded on in Chapter 5). The first is that they have tended, on the surface, to level the playing field between the major-party candidates. Public funding, together with the funds which candidates raise, are referred to as "hard money," and hard money spending limits are the same for the two major parties and their candidates. Second, it has tended to contribute to the personalization of presidential electioneering simply by virtue of the fact that candidates are responsible for building up their own financial "war chests" and the fact that public funding goes mainly to candidates rather than parties. Third, fund-raising efforts are now oriented towards raising large numbers of small donations (under $1000) rather than small numbers of large donations. Finally, since one of the goals was greater transparency in campaign finance (and justifiably so, given that there is public money involved), candidates are forced to spend massive amounts of time and money in complying with campaign finance laws by accounting for their contributions and expenditures by reporting these to the FEC.

One final note on campaign finance in the United States before we move on to a (briefer) look at campaign finance in France and Russia. As Paul Harvey might say, "the rest of the story" concerns loopholes which have been found to circumvent the hard money limitations placed on campaign spending. This should come as no shock to anyone. Highly professionalized, televised presidential campaigns which assume nationwide travel are costly. The money, simply, will be found somewhere. Hard money is now less than half the story of campaign finance which of late revolves around the growing importance of "soft" money.[33] Soft money is money which parties can accept in order to help build party organizations and aid in voter mobilization efforts. Dispensation of it is technically controlled by the parties themselves, but both presidential candidates in the 1996 election reportedly had a great deal to say about how, when, and where this money was spent. And while soft money cannot be used for the advocacy of specific candidates, there are increasingly sophisticated ways around this.[34]

Until 1988 France had no campaign finance laws.[35] In the pre-1988 system of campaign finance French parties were officially dependent on party dues and some public financing for their funding; neither they nor candidates were allowed to accept donations. There was some public financing of campaigns, but most of this was channeled to parties rather than candidates (the exception was that presidential candidates who received a certain minimum percentage of the vote received a flat rate reimbursement). By and large, however, the bulk of campaign finance in France was illicit: "parties and politicians raised most of their money by almost openly shaking down contractors who did business with the municipalities the parties controlled. These shakedowns ranged between 1 and 7 percent of the value of the contracts."[36] It was this widespread corruption, as well as a desire to achieve a certain parity among candidates and to control the rising costs of political campaigns that led the French to reform their campaign finance system.

Three sets of laws completely overhauled the French system of campaign finance, one in 1988 and two in 1990 (there have been subsequent revisions as well, most dealing with spending and distribution limits). The old system of campaign finance applied only to the three weeks prior to the election; the new system applies to the entire year before. There has been an increase in public funding to both parties and candidates, and in return, greater transparency is required of both. Prior to the changes, parties could not accept contributions from either individuals or businesses; they are now allowed to, but there are limits to the amount they can accept. Parties and candidates are now strictly accountable for all campaign finances: all receipts and expenditures, including those for the six months prior to the start of the campaign, must be reported within two months after the election.

Presidential candidates who receive at least 5 percent of the vote in the first round of balloting are eligible to receive public funding and parties may give unlimited amounts of funds to candidates. There are, however, limits on the amounts that presidential candidates may spend, and, as was alluded to previously, strict accountability means that these limits are enforced. One of the effects of these laws, as we will see in Chapter 5, is that candidates now have a variety of strategies they can employ to raise needed campaign funds.

In Russia, the legal limit on presidential campaign expenditures in 1996 was roughly $3 million.[37] However, the plain fact is that the law was not enforced. For example, estimates suggest that President Yeltsin's campaign collected at least $100 million (and perhaps up to $500 million) in illicit contributions from Russia's business sector, and was not reluctant to spend it.

The Media Environment: Broadcast Television

Several channels of mass communication are available to presidential candidates and their parties, but television attracts the most money and attention. Therefore, this section will be devoted to broadcast television, more specifically, the ownership and regulation of, and access to, broadcast television. It is here that the United States differs the most from France and Russia, and this has noticeable effects on electioneering practices. All three countries enjoy constitutional freedom of the press, and in all three, television has penetrated to virtually all households. There the similarities end. The United States is strictly a private ownership media system while France and Russia are mixed systems, meaning that there is some government involvement in broadcast media in these countries. The United States government does not sponsor political advertising, it does not limit paid political advertising, nor does the government sponsor presidential debates.

Broadcast media in the United States are for the most part privately owned and loosely regulated by the government.[38] The regulatory agency for broadcast media is the Federal Communications Commission (FCC), a five-member body created by the 1934 Communications Act to ensure that the media "serve the public interest, convenience, and necessity."[39] FCC control of broadcast television (and radio) takes the form of limiting station ownership and the control of stations by periodic licensing procedures which examine station goals and performance, rules which mandate public and local interest programming, and those which guarantee the fair treatment of individuals and the protection of their rights. The overall track record of the FCC has been spotty at best, and the 1996 Telecommunications Act further denuded the agency of any real power.[40]

Access to broadcast television by candidates for federal office in the United States is one of the areas where FCC rules are fairly clear. Federal law stipulates that television (and radio) stations sell air time to candidates for federal office at their lowest rates.[41] Further, if a station sells time to one candidate for a particular office, they must then make equal time available to his or her opponent(s). In practice this means that any candidate with the money can get his or her message on the air. It also, obviously, puts a premium on money and raises some questions of fairness. Another form of television access is what is often referred to as "unpaid media" which typically takes the form of news coverage. Access here, in other words, depends on being newsworthy, in the first instance being perceived as a credible candidate, or failing that (or in addition to that) as a controversial candidate (conflict and controversy sell news stories). But because media outlets are private concerns in the United States, these judgements and decisions are the domain of the networks or stations alone: news is not subject to FCC equal access guidelines.

Some mention should be made of presidential debates, if only because they are sponsored by the government in other countries. They are not sponsored by the government in the United States and technically it is not mandatory that candidates participate. The first televised debates in the United States were in 1960 when each candidate agreed to debate based on their own strategic considerations (John Kennedy to counter the impression that he was too young to be president, Vice-president Richard Nixon to clarify the image that he was President Eisenhower's obvious heir).[42] There were no presidential debates in the next three elections since the front-runners in these elections (Lyndon Johnson in 1964, Nixon in 1968 and 1972) saw no strategic advantage to participate in them. In 1976, however, Gerald Ford saw the debates as a way to gain ground on front-runner Jimmy Carter, and Carter saw them as a way of further crystallizing his own support. Debates were held that year and have been held in every election year since. In 1992 President Bush attempted to avoid debating challenger William Clinton but under heavy pressure he eventually relented, illustrating the reality that presidential debates are now a permanent if informal feature of the presidential campaign landscape.[43]

The real question now is not whether to debate, but rather how, where, when, and who is to be included in the debates.[44] Arrangements for the debates, originally made by the League of Women Voters, are now handled by the bipartisan Presidential Debate Commission, formed in 1987 by the national committees of each party in an attempt to reduce the haggling involved in scheduling the debates. This goal has achieved only marginal success.[45] One constant with respect to the arrangements is that there are typically two debates between the presidential candidates and one between their vice-presidential hopefuls.

Although French broadcast media is not completely free of government control (ownership), it is increasingly less so. The French media system can be fairly classed as a mixed system leaning toward the private-ownership model.[46] Media regulations are the same for presidential and parliamentary campaigns in France. In an effort to keep the costs of political campaigns down, there is no paid political advertising allowed on radio or television.[47] Candidates are allotted free television time roughly proportional to their party's representation in the National Assembly. Specific time slots are determined by lottery, but the fact that television time is based on representation in the legislature certainly provides some incentive for candidates to align with a major party. On the other hand, by receiving any television time at all, minor candidates gain in relatively greater measure than those candidates from the major parties (at least in terms of name recognition). The government also sponsors a televised debate between the final two candidates just prior to the second round of voting.

Russia is also a mixed system of government and private media ownership, but there is far more government involvement in the Russian media than in France. For example, during the 1996 presidential elections the government made it clear to the news media that the focus of their coverage should be on President Yeltsin and General Alexander Lebed alone. Put another way, it was clearly understood that other candidates were to get no news coverage. The news media, for reasons of their own (namely, the fear that a victory for the Communist Zyuganov would usher in a new age of darkness and suppression), generally complied. Prior to the first round of voting, all candidates received ten minutes of government-sponsored television time (time slots were determined by lottery) on one of the three state-run channels. Candidates could purchase additional time, but that paid time could not exceed 30 minutes on any of the three state-run channels; paid advertising on private networks (of which there are a few) was not restricted. Each of the two second-round candidates received a total of two hours (10 minutes per day, allocated by random drawing) on state television. There was no free time allowed for the two days prior to the election, but paid advertisements were allowed. There were no debates between the Russian presidential candidates, government-sponsored or otherwise.[48]

Table 3.2 summarizes this section, highlighting aspects of the campaign finance and media (television) environment in the United States, France, and Russia.

Each country places limitations on campaign spending (although enforcement in Russia was problematic in 1996), and the United States and France publicly finance presidential campaigns (at least partially). Each country has a constitutionally free press (which broke down in Russia in the 1996 campaign) with limited government control (very limited in the United States). All are, in other words, fairly open to candidate access, at least formally.

The differences in systems are more apparent when we consider the mode of access to broadcast television. The open competition model in the United States makes candidates somewhat more vulnerable to the way in which the political press decides it will cover the election (especially evident during the primaries). Beyond news coverage, paid advertising is the primary means of television access in the United States. In Russia paid advertising is mixed with government-sponsored air time, and France does not allow paid advertising at all. Since television accounts for such a huge amount of campaign costs, we might expect from this that campaign costs would be less in France. France also bans polling

Table 3.2
Campaign Finance and Media Regulations in the United States, France, and Russia

	United States	France	Russia
Public Campaign Finance?	Yes	Yes	Yes
Campaign Finance Spending Limits?	Yes	Yes	Yes, but not enforced in 1996
Free Press?	Yes	Yes	Yes, but not during 1996 presidential campaign
Media System (Ownership & Control)	Private	Mixed; mostly private	Mixed; less private
TV Spots	Paid advertising only	Government only	Government and paid advertising
Presidential Debates?	Yes (not government-sponsored)	Yes (government-sponsored)	No
Restrictions on TV Access?	No	Yes	On private channels, no; on public channels, yes
Other Campaign Restrictions	None	Polling banned in the 2 weeks prior to election	None

during the two weeks prior to the election which, combined with television restrictions and campaign finance laws, might theoretically make for a more level playing field.

The other notable aspect of the finance and media environment is that public finance and presidential debate rules in the United States are heavily weighted in favor of the two major parties, which probably (along with other factors) helps explain why third parties rarely emerge (or last long if they do) in the United States. The next section turns to a brief examination of political parties and the party systems of the United States, France, and Russia.

POLITICAL PARTIES AND PARTY SYSTEMS IN THE UNITED STATES, FRANCE, AND RUSSIA

Political parties remain important in presidential electioneering.[49] In the United States and France it is highly doubtful that a presidential candidate could win the presidency without the backing of one of the major political parties. Since we are examining what may be a declining (or changing) party role in presidential electioneering in each country it would be useful to have an initial understanding of the shape of party politics in each. In each of the three countries we will look at the structure and organization of political parties and the party system.[50] Recall that this chapter, including this section, is designed to set the stage for the remainder of the book. Obviously this section cannot do justice to the intricacies and complexity of party politics in all three countries.[51]

Central to an understanding of the organizational strength of political parties in the United States is the fact that they developed in response to electoral needs. As the result, they are loose confederations of state and local political party organizations, corresponding to Maurice Duverger's model of cadre-style political parties.[52] This means, among other things, that the majority of the party is found below the national level. The national party committee sits rather tenuously on top of a bottom-heavy pyramid. Ostensibly the national committee controls the party, but there is no party without the constituent units. The power of political parties in the United States begins at the local level, typically with a local party committee person. As you move up the structural hierarchy you find party committees at the ward, various intermediate (e.g., city) levels, counties, and congressional districts, culminating with a state party committee.[53] The state party committees are represented on the national committee, which, again, has little power except that which is granted it by the constituent units. Both state and national party organizations (in each party) "remain weak by most standards . . . [and] almost alone among our major social institutions, have resisted the development of large, centralized organization."[54]

In general, European, including French political party organizations, are far more sophisticated than in the United States.[55] Unlike American parties, most European parties did not develop in response to electoral needs. They are far more centralized with respect to programmatic concerns, strategy, and responsibility. They are more likely to have permanent leadership and large developed party bureaucracies, are active year-round as opposed to only at elections, and have a more developed mass-membership base. Table 3.3, drawn from Maurice Duverger's classic work on political parties, summarizes the differences between the American model of cadre-style political parties and the European mass-membership model.

Party Politics in the United States

The United States is a competitive two-party system.[56] Both of the two major parties (the Democrats and the Republicans) are well developed and mature. It is the world's oldest party system: each party has been contesting elections under the same name for well over a century (the

Table 3.3

Political Party Organization: Duverger's Typology

	Cadre Party	*Mass Membership Party*
Membership	Generally few (elites)	Many dues-paying members
Activities	Mostly electoral	Ideological, educational, and electoral
Organizational Continuity	Active mostly at elections	Continuously active
Leadership	Few full-time leaders	Full-time leadership
Staffing	Few full-time workers	Permanent bureaucracy

Source: Adapted from Paul Beck (1997:62, Table II.1).

Democrats say they celebrated their bicentennial in 1972 [1772–1972]). The fact that American political parties are organizationally decentralized should not lead one to conclude that American party organizations are empty shells. On the contrary, national, state, and local party organizations in the United States have become larger and more professionalized in terms of their infrastructure and personnel in the past two decades. Both major parties in the United States now have a fairly complex organizational base, meaning that within each organization there is a high degree of organizational specialization. Each has several permanent committees, holds a variety of regular conferences, conventions and so on, and has achieved a high degree (virtually complete) of territorial penetration. Finally, each party is an independent and autonomous entity, meaning that neither is formally beholden to any other social grouping (e.g., family, organized non-political interest, the government).

Party Politics in France

The party system in the French Fifth Republic is a competitive multiparty system. Unlike the highly fragmented and volatile party system of the French Fourth Republic, it is considered stable. As of 1997, 90 percent of the seats in the National Assembly were held by four parties who typically ally along a left-right axis in second-round voting. Most would agree that this stabilization is in large part attributable to the fact that presidential elections have provided a high-stakes focal point for political parties. On the right, heir to the Gaullist Party, is the Rally for the Republic (RPR), the party of current president Jacques Chirac. The Union of French Democrats (UDF), while rightist, is more to the center than the RPR. This is the party of former president Valéry Giscard d'Estaing, a confederation formed in 1978 of three center-right parties. These two parties, aligning (very rarely) with Jean Marie Le Pen's extreme right National Front, constitute the French right. The left consists of the So-

Table 3.4
The Structure of Major French Political Parties According to Duverger's (1965) Typology

HORIZONTAL PLANE	VERTICAL PLANE Caucus (Cadre)	Branch (Mass)
Direct (Unitary)	Rally for the Republic	French Communist Party
Indirect (Federated)	Union of French Democrats	Socialist Party

cialist Party (PS), formed in 1969 as a merger of several smaller socialist parties. This is the party of two-term president François Mitterand, and it is (sometimes uneasily) allied with the French Communist Party.

Structurally, French political parties differ from those in the United States. According to Duverger's typology, parties of the French right are generally cadre parties with a direct (centralized) hierarchy; center parties are similar to American parties, and left parties are mass parties with direct hierarchies. Table 3.4 shows the structure of French political parties according to Duverger's typology.

The major French parties, although they tend to change names more frequently than those in the United States, are well developed and mature. They are organizationally complex, have permanent committees, hold regular conventions, and enjoy a good degree of territorial penetration. What should be noted here is that with respect to organizational complexity, French parties are more likely than those in the United States to be associated with an individual leader (more on this below). Each major party, by and large, also is independent and autonomous but historically has been more inclined toward programmatic rather than electoral concerns.

French parties are extremely prone to internal factionalization based on personality; this is not a characteristic peculiar to parties in the Fifth Republic. Extremely personalized parties are probably the characteristic that most distinguishes party politics in France from those in the United States. The fact that most political parties in France are associated with their leader ("Chirac's" Rally for the Republic, "Le Pen's" National Front) points to the role of personality in French party politics. But even the strongest party leader cannot completely ignore his or her party. Party organizations remain very important to presidential hopefuls in France. As in the United States, it is doubtful that a candidate could become president in France without the support of a major political party. In order for a candidate to attain the status of *presidentiable* (in American terminology, "availability"), position in his or her party is very important, as is prior service at other levels of government, which is also very party-dependent. Moreover, parties have standing organizations which candidates must make use of (at the very least to supplement their own) during the campaign.

Party Politics in Russia

Russian political parties are too young to make many meaningful statements about party politics in Russia. According to one analyst, the Russian party system "remains fragmented" and rootless with respect to society and state, "neither a two-party nor a multiparty system, but instead a fragmented and weakly institutionalized system."[57] This is hardly a surprise: in the (non-democratic) presidential election of 1991, candidates were not allowed to list a party affiliation, and the current President Yeltsin is not a member of a party. Most major parties in Russia are programmatic and are associated with strong personalities. However, several have demonstrated increasing sophistication and a good deal of territorial penetration. Examining Russia's electoral history from 1993 to 1996, we see four main political parties. The Communist Party is organized, well-funded, and territorially penetrative. The (misnamed) Liberal Democratic Party, started as a vehicle for neo-fascist Vladimir Zhirinovsky, also is fairly well organized and has penetrated most areas of the country. Other well-developed parties include the party of government and of former prime minister Viktor Chernomyrdin, Our Home is Russia, and Yabloko, a reform-oriented democratic opposition party.

There is, in sum, a great deal of difference between the parties and party systems in the United States, France, and Russia. As we continue, the effects of these differences on presidential electioneering will become apparent. The United States is one of the world's purest two-party systems. This has an enormous impact on electioneering practices and in the way political ambition is channeled. In general, American parties are more developed but organizationally somewhat less sophisticated than their French counterparts. Another difference between each country is that while the president in each is the head of state, only in France is he the head of his party. In the United States the president is the titular head of his party, but has little control over the party (and in Russia, President Yeltsin is not a member of a political party).

One thing common to all three countries is that the public in each has an increasing tendency to keep political parties at arm's length.[58] In the United States and France this has taken the form of decreased party identification and loyalty at the ballot box; in Russia, there is an outright antipathy towards or suspicion of political parties in the aftermath of the demise of the Soviet Union and the Communist Party's seventy-year hegemonic rule.[59] In keeping with the focus of this book, no further reference will be made to these social dimensions of political parties. However, it is important to add this dimension to the mix before we move

Table 3.5
Parties and Party Systems in the United States, France, and Russia

	United States	*France*	*Russia*
Number of Parties	Two	Multiple (four major)	Multiple
System Competitiveness	High	High	N/A
Party Maturity	High	Medium-high	Low
Party Complexity	Medium	High	Medium

on, especially if we are examining the supposedly decreased importance of political parties in the electioneering process. Table 3.5 distills our discussion about parties and party systems in the United States, France, and Russia.

SUMMARY

Many strategic decisions need to be made in a race for the presidency in any country. In this chapter we have exposed the major possibilities and constraints the institutional environment presents to presidential aspirants and their parties in the United States, France, and Russia. In the next chapter we turn to an examination of the personnel of campaign organizations, where the focus shifts to the "who" of modern presidential electioneering.

4

Electioneers: The Personnel of Modern Presidential Electioneering

THE USUAL SUSPECTS?

What do the following names have in common: Time Future Inc., Campaign America, Leadership '98, Campaign for a New American Century, America First PAC, and Americans for Hope, Growth & Opportunity? All were formed and registered with the FEC by early spring of 1999 for the presidential election of 2000, and all are names of what are variously known as leadership, or multi-candidate PACs, organizations ostensibly formed for the purpose of promoting a slate of candidates at various levels of government.[1] In actuality they are used as a way for presidential aspirants to begin their fund-raising and campaign efforts long before the primaries begin, a reflection of the reality that modern presidential electioneering is increasingly an effort carried out by candidate organizations—organizations which candidates themselves must build effectively and early.

Our tale of modern presidential electioneering begins by asking who is conducting the many activities associated with modern presidential electioneering. Who raises the money, recruits and directs the volunteers, develops campaign strategy, writes copy for political advertisements, and so on? A possible list of suspects would include the aspirants or candidates themselves (and their organizations), their political parties (if any), and a growing body of what we refer to generically in this book as campaign professionals.

Recall that in the traditional era of presidential electioneering the answer to this question was fairly simple. By and large election men were found in political parties. The current reality is far more complex. Polit-

ical party organizations are still very involved in presidential electioneering and in the past 20 years have been organizationally transformed,
becoming a permanent feature of the Washington landscape. But party
personnel are most emphatically not the sole, nor even the primary individuals responsible for waging presidential campaigns. To find the
people responsible for presidential electioneering in the modern era we
must look not only at parties but at the various organizations which are
created and maintained by presidential candidates themselves. In addition, campaign professionals, a new class of officially unaffiliated individuals, are playing an increasingly important role in modern
presidential electioneering.

This chapter is organized as follows: First we will explore various aspects of the personnel of political party organizations and then do the
same for candidate organizations. How many people work for them? Are
they paid or volunteer staff? How much specialization is there within
these organizations? As important, how cohesive are these organizations,
what is their mission, and how well are they oriented toward it? Then
we will examine campaign professionals, tracing the growth and specialization of the industry, examining who they work for, what their
backgrounds are, and what their role in modern presidential campaigns
is. Concluding each section we will look at the personnel of campaign
organizations in France and Russia to see how they compare to those in
the United States.

Before beginning it would be appropriate to introduce the lead players
in our cast. Table 4.1 lists the two major party presidential candidates
for the United States and second-round candidates for France and Russia
with their parties for each presidential election since the beginning of
the modern era (1960).

THE STAFF OF PARTY AND CANDIDATE ORGANIZATIONS

American Political Parties

An increase in size and professionalization within an organization is
generally an indication of greater organizational strength.[2] With respect
to parties and political campaigns, a larger organization means more
hands to perform campaign tasks; greater specialization means a greater
ability to perform more varied campaign tasks. In this section we examine the staff of party and candidate organizations, including the number of staff employed by the organization, the nature of the staff (e.g.,
are they professionals or volunteers?), the internal specialization of the
organization, staff and leadership autonomy, and mass membership (of
political party organizations). What becomes clear is that party and can-

Table 4.1
Presidential Elections, 1960–96: Major Candidates and Their Parties in the
United States, France, and Russia*

Year	Winning Candidate (Party)	Losing Candidate (Party)
United States		
1960	John Kennedy (D)	Richard Nixon (R)
1964	Lyndon Johnson (D)	Barry Goldwater (R)
1968	Richard Nixon (R)	Hubert Humphrey (D)
1972	Richard Nixon (R)	George McGovern (D)
1976	Jimmy Carter (D)	Gerald Ford (R)
1980	Ronald Reagan (R)	Jimmy Carter (D)
1984	Ronald Reagan (R)	Walter Mondale (D)
1988	George Bush (R)	Michael Dukakis (D)
1992	William Clinton (D)	George Bush (R)
1996	William Clinton (D)	Robert Dole (R)
France		
1965	Charles de Gaulle (UNR)	François Mitterand (FGDS)
1969	Georges Pompidou (UDR)	Alain Poher (Democratic Center)
1974	Valéry Giscard d'Estaing (UDF)	François Mitterand (PSU)
1981	François Mitterand (PS)	Valéry Giscard d'Estaing (UDF)
1988	François Mitterand (PS)	Jacques Chirac (RPR)
1995	Jacques Chirac (RPR)	Lionel Jospin (PS)
Russia		
1996	Boris Yeltsin (No Party)	Gennadi Zyuganov (Communist)

* Detailed listings of all candidates can be found in Appendices A-C.

didate organizations are larger, more specialized, and more professionalized than in the traditional era.

In spite of the fact that both major parties in the United States are a
far cry from well-organized powerful entities, by virtually all of the
above measures they are stronger than 40 years ago. Although American
political parties are structurally decentralized, they now enjoy a significant national presence, a presence which was fully established by the
mid-1980s. Growth and professionalization developed for each party at
different times; Republicans led the way. After Barry Goldwater was
resoundingly defeated by Lyndon Johnson in the presidential election of
1964, the Republicans appointed Ray Bliss, state party chairman from
Ohio, to head the RNC. In his efforts to revitalize the party, Bliss paid
special attention to strengthening and professionalizing state party organizations (as he had in Ohio). But the greatest contribution he made
was that he was the first national chairman of either party to attempt to
make the national committee an effective part of the party structure.
Bliss' efforts were short-lived, however, because in 1968 President Nixon,
fearful of any source of autonomous power, replaced Bliss.

The RNC languished during Nixon's presidency, but in 1976 William

Table 4.2
Staffing of National Party Committees, 1972-96

	1972	1976	1980	1984	1988	1992	1996
Democratic National Committee	30	30	40	130	160	270	264
Republican National Committee	30	200	350	600	425	300	271

Source: Paul Beck (1997:98); 1996 data from Paul Herrnson (1998a:61).

Brock was selected as chair and he immediately began to develop a direct mail program to build a regular base of small contributors. Although some party leaders questioned it, the idea was a stunning success. In the first four years, after the expenses of administering the program, the party netted over $59 million and had built a base of over two million active contributors. With this money Brock began the production of several regular party publications, ran advertisements, set up several advisory councils to develop policy (the work of which became the basis for the 1980 Republican platform), began to revive state and local party organizations, and initiated candidate recruitment operations in preparation for the congressional reapportionment of 1980. His efforts, in short, transformed the party. With the national headquarters they established in 1970, the Republican Party, in short, was a true national organization by 1980.[3]

By the time the Democrats built their national headquarters in 1985 they had recognized their relative disadvantage in professionalizing their national organizational structure. Given their longstanding electoral advantage in Congress, organizational institutionalization was perhaps less of a priority for them, but when that advantage began to narrow in the early 1980s the party took action. The man responsible for the organizational vitalization of the Democratic Party was Charles Manatt, named chairman of the DNC in 1981. Manatt basically copied the strategies that had worked for the Republicans, and in addition began looking at and implementing strategies aimed at increasing voter registration (the biggest pool of winnable votes in any given election is typically comprised of those who are likely to stay at home on election day).

Party building efforts brought several changes to each party. For example, levels of year-round staff have increased roughly tenfold in each of the major national party organizations since 1972 (of course, temporary staffing increases dramatically during election years). Table 4.2 illustrates this.

Although the focus in this book is on national party organizations, local and state party organizations have increased their staffing levels as well. The percentage of local party organizations with full-time paid staff increased roughly six-fold in each party from 1979-1992. In 1960-64, state party organizations employed average staffs of 3–4 people during non-election years; by 1979–80 that number had doubled.[4] Florida parties are a good example of the professionalizing trend in state party organizations. In 1995, the Florida Republicans had a full-time staff of 25, the Democrats, 16, and each had several part-time employees as well.[5] The point is that regardless of the level in question, the number of paid staff has increased in both parties. In this respect, party organizations in the United States are far more capable organizations than twenty or thirty years ago.

What kind of people are these paid staffers? By all accounts they are highly competent, professional individuals who often come from political backgrounds (working for an interest group, individual campaigns, or a political consultancy firm).[6] What do they do? In the words of one expert,

The staffs oversee the committee's daily operations, are influential in formulating party strategies, and play a major role in the implementation of those strategies. The campaign committee staffs are divided among functional lines; different divisions are responsible for administration, fund-raising, research, communication, and campaign activities.[7]

The national committee (and the several executive committees which comprise the national committee structure) of each party meets a few times a year, but because member concerns are localized, they are functionally all but irrelevant with respect to the daily business of running the national party organization. That job is left to the national committee chairperson, and, as might be expected, national committee chairpersons are increasingly capable.[8] Put another way, the job is not a political plum. National committee chairs are technically appointed and removed by the committee, but tradition dictates that sitting presidents and the out-party's presidential candidate name their choice for the post (in the case of the latter, for the duration of the election campaign); national committees ratify these choices without question.

Who are these committee chairpersons? They come from many walks of life but all have previous experience in politics, most in campaign politics. If the chairperson is selected by the president, he or she will almost certainly be someone whom the president trusts, who is loyal to the president, and who holds ideological views very similar to the president. The out-party chairperson is usually someone trusted by all factions of the party, which means he or she is ideologically neutral. In addition, he or she is probably not overtly associated with any of the likely aspirants for the party's nomination in the next election cycle. Table 4.3 lists each party's national committee chairpersons from 1961 through 1999 along with their previous political position.

Table 4.3
National Party Committee Chairpersons, 1961–99

Name	Tenure	Previous Political Position
Republican		
William E. Miller	1961-64	U.S. representative from New York
Dean Birch	1964-65	Campaign activist for Barry Goldwater
Ray C. Bliss	1965-69	Ohio party chairman
Rogers C. Morton	1969-71	U.S. representative from Maryland
Robert J. Dole	1971-73	U.S. senator from Kansas
George H. Bush	1973-74	U.S. ambassador to the United Nations
Mary Louise Smith	1974-77	Co-chair of the RNC
William E. Brock	1977-81	Former U.S. senator from Tennessee
Richard Richards	1981-83	Regional coordinator of Ronald Reagan's campaign (1980)
Frank J. Fahrenkopf	1983-89	Nevada party chairman
Harvey Leroy Atwater	1989-91	Campaign manager for George Bush (1988)
Clayton Yeutter	1991-92	Secretary of agriculture
Rich Bond	1992-93	Former deputy chief of staff for Vice-President George Bush
Haley Barbour	1993-96	RNC member
James Nicholson	1997-99	Colorado party committeeman
Democrat		
John M. Brown	1961-68	Connecticut party chairman
Lawrence F. O'Brien	1968-69	U.S. Postmaster General
Fred R. Harris	1969-70	U.S. senator from Oklahoma
Lawrence F. O'Brien	1970-72	Former national party chairman
Jean Westwood	1972	Campaign activist for George McGovern
Robert S. Strauss	1972-77	National party treasurer
Kenneth M. Curtis	1977	Former Governor of Maine
John C. White	1977-81	Deputy secretary of agriculture
Charles T. Manatt	1981-85	Finance chair of the DNC
Paul G. Kirk, Jr.	1985-89	National party treasurer
Ronald H. Brown	1989-93	Convention manager for Jesse Jackson (1988)
David Wilhelm	1993-95	Campaign manager for Bill Clinton (1992)
Don Fowler	1995-97	Member of the DNC Executive Committee
Roy Romer	1997-99	Former Governor of Colorado

Source: From Paul Beck (1997:91, Table 4–2).

The committee chairperson (and his or her staff) is for the most part in charge of the operation of the national party organization. Of course the chairperson is not completely autonomous—recall that he or she answers in the first instance to the national committee who technically appoints and can also remove them. Beyond this, the level of autonomy of a given committee chairman is dependent on whether the party controls the White House. If so, it is generally understood that the president determines what the role of the chairperson (and by extension the committee) is to be. The president's control over the committee has increased since Franklin Roosevelt's tenure in the Oval Office, and by the 1960s was virtually complete.[9] Some presidents have completely subordinated the national committee to their designs. Lyndon Johnson drastically cut

Text Box 4.1
Internal Organization: Departments of the Democratic National Committee

Offices of the Executive Director and DNC Chairs Assist in the administrative support for the offices of the DNC's Executive Director and National and General Chairs **Office of the Secretary** Assist in the work of managing the DNC's meetings and records **Party Affairs and Delegate Selection** Assist in the work of managing the institutional affairs of the National Democratic Party, including Party rules and delegate selection **Campaign Department** Assist in the work of the Campaign Division, including working with the DNC's Regional Political Desks, Base Vote Desks, Intergovernmental Affairs, and Training division **Office of Finance Council** Assist the Finance division in coordinating the Party's fundraising activities **Communications Department** Assist in the work of disseminating the Democratic message effectively to the Press **Compliance Division** Assist in the administrative support in ensuring compliance with DNC policies and procedures governing the solicitation and processing of contributions **Marketing Division** Assist in the support work of the DNC fundraising efforts through direct mail, telemarketing, and other media efforts **Other Divisions** Include Research, Information Services, Administrative Services, and the College Democrats of America

Source: <http://democrats.org>.

back staffing in the DNC after his 1964 victory; Richard Nixon totally circumvented the RNC in his 1972 re-election effort, virtually ignoring party chairs Robert Dole and Rogers Morton. On the other hand, some presidents, notably John Kennedy, Ronald Reagan, and George Bush, have expended considerable energy to help committee chairpersons build up the national party organization.

What do the national committees do? We can get a good sense of what they do, and how specialized modern electioneering is, by looking at the internal organization of the Democratic National Committee (see Text Box 4.1).

A final aspect of party personnel involves party membership. As mentioned in Chapter 3, cadre-style American political parties generally have few dues-paying members. There are, however, a not-insignificant number of party activists in the United States. These activists, on the whole, are well educated, come from the upper socio-economic strata, and typically come from politically active families. Since the 1960s parties have been increasingly attracting "amateur" rather than "professional" activists, a distinction which revolves around the motivation for the individual becoming involved in party politics.[10] Amateurs, according to the typology, are more "apt to be committed to a certain cause or to the whole liberal or conservative philosophy . . . [or] attracted by a particular

candidate or the positions he or she represented."[11] Amateurs are supposedly less concerned with electoral success, which is the primary motivation for professionals. Much has been made about how amateur
activists have changed party politics in the United States, but several
studies show that with respect to electioneering, amateurs are just as
likely as professionals to be effective campaigners.

French Political Parties

Political parties in France, as was discussed in the previous chapter,
are generally more centralized and structured than parties in the United
States. The major parties, in an effort to become and remain electorally
viable, have been structurally and organizationally transformed during
the Fifth Republic. All have undergone a process of "consolidation and
reorganization"[12] and now maintain "a continuous national presence."[13]
While there are few data compiled concerning the staffing of French
parties, as mentioned previously, they are sophisticated organizations,
well-staffed (the Rally for the Republic employed over 120 full-time staffers throughout the 1980s)[14] and internally differentiated.[15]

The top decision-maker in French parties is usually the president or
the party's main presidential aspirant. In the case of the Rally for the
Republic (RPR), for example, Jacques Chirac (France's current president)
easily won 70,000 of the 71,000 votes cast for the party's leadership position in 1987.[16] It was widely understood that within the RPR there was
"a system of double leadership in the party: the official one, with the
secretary-general at the top, and the unofficial one in which the RPR is
just one element of Jacques Chirac's own presidential strategy."[17] Party
Secretary Jacques Toubon often found his goals "overshadowed by the
presidential goals of Jacques Chirac" during his tenure (1979 to 1988).[18]
To take another example, one scholar noted that "more than any previous president, Mitterand . . . entered office as a *de facto* party leader" of
the Socialist Party.[19] In other words, just as in the United States, the
autonomy of the party chair is nominal. He or she is officially or unofficially subordinate to the president or the main presidential aspirant.

Membership in French parties, while not common, is relatively more
so than in the United States, but all indications are that party membership in France has seen a slight decline since an upsurge in the late 1970s
through the mid-1980s.[20] But even given that slight decline in party membership (a phenomenon common to parties in all Western democracies),
French political parties are, by and large, strong organizations, very capable of performing the tasks associated with modern presidential electioneering.

Russian Political Parties

While still in their infancy, some development, continuity, and consolidation can be seen in parties and the party system in Russia. Forty-
three parties contested the 1995 election to the State Duma. Of these,
eight had competed in the 1993 elections, and of these eight, seven won
seats in the 1995 Duma. Three of these seven ran a candidate in the 1996
presidential elections. It should be noted that the development of party
politics in Russia faces numerous obstacles, not the least of which is the
antipathy and outright hostility many Russians feel toward political parties. In addition, their president, Boris Yeltsin, is not a member of a
political party and has resisted any efforts to be associated with one,
having long held the sentiment which he expressed in April 1996: "I
cannot be a member of any political party as long as political struggle
is splitting society."[21]

Some effort has been made to build up political party organizations
in Russia. According to one analyst, the major political parties in Russia
have "undergone some organizational maturation and programmatic dif-
ferentiation" since the early 1990s.[22] Prior to the 1993 elections, many
political leaders (Yegor Gaidar, Sergei Shakhray, Sergei Stankevich, Ivan
Rybkin, Grigori Yavlinsky) engaged in party building activity. Former
prime minister Viktor Chernomyrdin has been very active in building
the one-time party of government, Our Home is Russia. At least partly
because of the involvement of these leaders, several of the main parties
have developed "more coherent leadership structures and more clearly
defined lines of authority."[23]

Easily the largest and most organized political party in Russia is the
Communist Party of the Russian Federation, which has claimed as many
as 500,000 official members.[24] Their predecessor, the Communist Party
of the Soviet Union, was banned by President Yeltsin after having been
implicated in the attempted coup of 1991 and virtually disintegrated.[25]
However, several of the surviving factions convened in February 1993
to reconstitute the party as the modern Russian Communist Party.[26] After
the December 1993 elections, Russian Communist Party deputies in the
Duma expended considerable energy on party-building activities, avail-
ing themselves of all the resources of their offices in that effort.[27] Structurally, the new incarnation of the party is less rigid and its lines of
authority are not as clear as in the old,[28] but taking the place of the old
Politburo is a Central Executive Committee which "direct[s] the regional
and local bodies and . . . preserve[s] the party's ideology."[29]

In short, the Communists are an organized and penetrative political
party, as is their close cousin, the Agrarian Party, which typically allies
with them on important matters (e.g., a presidential election). The Agrar-

ians claim roughly 250,000 members.[30] Vladimir Zhirinovsky's Liberal Democratic Party is also fairly well developed, second only to the Communist Party in terms of its organizational base. Like the Communist Party, they boast a "vast network of grassroots political organizations" throughout the country.[31] In 1996 they set up a youth branch of the party (the Young Falcons),[32] and they too have a substantial mass membership base.[33]

Candidate Organizations in the United States

Candidate organizations, as previously noted, are a new phenomenon in presidential electioneering. John Kennedy was the first presidential candidate to build and rely on his own organization in pursuit of the White House and by the end of the decade it was standard operating procedure to do so. In 1972 President Nixon took this new orthodoxy to a higher level. His Committee to Re-elect the President "functioned virtually as a surrogate party," completely divorced from the Republican Party.[34] This strategy is no longer the exception. In modern presidential campaigns it is mandatory for a presidential aspirant to have a large and efficient organization, if only because of the number of primaries and caucuses that need to be won in order to secure the party nomination.

To put it plainly, the personnel of candidate organizations are hard to track. There are almost no studies which systematically list their personnel, in part because the activity they are engaged in is rather secretive. Moreover, they are fluid in size and formation, their record-keeping is loose, and they disappear immediately after the election (if not before).[35] There is, however, some evidence which can help illuminate this area of interest. Table 4.4 shows the staff size of the organizations of the major out-party presidential aspirants from 1976 to 1992 as of January 31 of the election year.[36] One thing is immediately clear from the table: candidate organizations in the modern era are considerably larger than campaign teams (such as they were) in the traditional era.

The next thing apparent about these data is that there are few discernable patterns, which reflect the fact that at best they can give us no better than a snapshot of the campaign at a given time. Candidate organizations must set up shop and operate in many different states, some more important than others. Moreover, when a given state's primary is over the need for an organization in that state is over until the general election season begins (typically after Labor Day). For example, 1996 Clinton-Gore field director Craig Smith reported that although the campaign opened primary offices (typically employing one paid staffer) in 35 states for about four to six weeks prior to each primary, the offices were quickly closed after the primary.[37]

Variation in the data reflect candidate finances as well. After the 1996

Table 4.4
Staff Size of Out-party Candidate Organizations (as of January 31 of the Election Year), 1976–92

1976 (Democrats)							
Carter, Jimmy	188	Jackson, Henry	83	Shriver, Sargent	36	Shapp, Milton	16
Wallace, George	112	Bentsen, Lloyd	76	Harris, Fred	28	Church, Frank	10
Bayh, Birch	99	Udall, Morris	54				
1980 (Republicans)							
Connally, John	321	Bush, George	210	Anderson, John	35	Dole, Robert	20
Reagan, Ronald	300	Baker, Howard	82	Crane, Phillip	24		
1984 (Democrats)							
Mondale, Walter	337	Jackson, Jesse	51	McGovern, George	35	Cranston, Alan	28
Glenn, John	112	Hart, Gary	46	Hollings, Ernest	28	Askew, Reubin	12
1988 (Democrats)							
Dukakis, Michael	314	Gephardt, Richard	151	Jackson, Jesse	110	Hart, Gary	7
Simon, Paul	198	Gore, Albert	142	Babbit, Bruce	45		
1992 (Democrats)							
Clinton, William	129	Kerrey, Bob	127	Tsongas, Paul	23	Brown, Edmund	18
Harkin, Tom	129						

Source: Randall Adkins (1995:36).

primaries the well-funded Clinton retained better than half of his payroll; Dole, however, was forced to cut staffing back considerably after he had secured the Republican Party nomination.[38] This difference reflects the fact that Dole had competition for his party's nomination and ran out of money toward the end of March while Clinton's re-nomination was all but assured. The point? The total number of paid staffers a candidate's organization employs may vary dramatically throughout the primary season based on the level of intra-party competition, what primaries are coming up, how important the candidate considers those primaries, how the candidate and his or her major opponents are doing at that moment, how much money is available to pay staff salaries, rent, and so on.

There is one pattern evident in the data in Table 4.4: generally speaking, the more staff a given candidate had in his employ at the beginning of the primary season, the better that candidate was likely to do in the primaries. In fact, with the exception of John Connally in 1980 and Tom Harkin in 1992, the candidate with the most staffing went on to capture the party nomination. If we are willing to look to other sources for additional data, we can go one step further with this generalization. One source reports that Richard Nixon employed 337 paid staffers in 1972,[39] another that the 1980 Carter-Mondale organization employed 354.[40] Yet a different source reported that both the Clinton and Dole campaign organizations employed "hundreds of paid staff members" throughout the 1996 campaign.[41] This means that the 1992 campaign of Bill Clinton

Text Box 4.2
The Structure of the 1996 Dole Campaign Organization

In charge of Dole's campaign were **National Campaign Chairman** Donald Rumsfeld and **Campaign Manager** Scott Reed. These two (mainly Reed) coordinated efforts with an **Advisory Group**. Reed, in turn, coordinated the efforts of the following:
- **Media Consultants** (prior to September, Don Sipple and Michael Murphy; afterwards, Greg Stephens, Alex Castellanos, and Chris Mottola)
- **Pollster** Tony Fabrizo
- **Political Director** Jill Hansen
- **Communications Director** John Buckley

Source: Adapted from Stephen Wayne (1997:210, Figure 6.1).

notwithstanding (129 staffers on January 31, per Table 4.4), we can cautiously surmise that a presidential aspirant needs an organizational staff of roughly 300 in order to capture his or her party's nomination.

It is hard to make many generalizations about the structure of candidate organizations. Most are fairly centralized, the hierarchy such that a few individuals make most of the important decisions. Examples of tightly run campaigns include the Goldwater (1964), Nixon (1972), Reagan (1984), Bush (1988) efforts as well as both of the Clinton campaigns. In both Goldwater's and Nixon's case, the campaign operation was kept close to the candidate mainly because of a fundamental distrust of the Republican Party (Goldwater because he was a candidate from outside of the "establishment," Nixon for other, perhaps less definable reasons). Clinton's 1992 and 1996 efforts were both very centralized and exceptionally well-organized. On the other hand, the Bush campaign of 1992 was reportedly "disjointed, uncoordinated, and internally competitive with three separate groups—the White House, the reelection committee, and the campaign's media operation—vying for power."[42] Text Boxes 4.2 and 4.3 show the basic structure of the Dole and Clinton campaign organizations in 1996.

Some candidates retain decision-making power during the campaign, but most defer (in most cases) to the experts whom they have hired. The 1996 Dole organization had several problems (high turnover, infighting) but their difficulties were in large part due to Dole's management style. In short, Dole reportedly has a problem with delegation based on a general lack of trust of advisers. His tendency during the campaign was to first make decisions on his own and subsequently not communicate them properly to the rest of the staff. The problem of trust was exacerbated by the fact that Dole started the campaign without a team which had been with him through his other presidential races, and so was forced to rely on many new faces.[43]

If we factor in coordination between the candidate organization and the party organization, it is safe to say that Republican campaign organ-

Text Box 4.3
The Structure of the 1996 Clinton Campaign Organization

There were two separate organizations directing the Clinton campaign. The actual **Campaign Organization** was headed by **Consultant** Richard Morris (who resigned in August) and **Campaign Manager** Peter Knight. These two coordinated matters with the **White House** team (below), and the efforts of the following:
- **Pollsters** (Mark Penn, Douglas Schoen)
- **Media Consultants** (Robert Squier, Bill Knapp)
- **Communications Director** Ann Lewis

The **White House** team was directed by **White House Deputy Chief of Staff for Political Affairs** Harold Ickes. He, in turn, coordinated the efforts of:
- **Press Secretary** Mike McCurry
- **Communications Director** Donald Baer
- **Political Director** Douglas Sosnick
- **Senior Adviser** George Stephanopoulos

Source: Adapted from Stephen Wayne (1997:213, Figure 6.2).

izations on the whole are more centralized than those of the Democrats, if only because the Republican Party is a more centralized organization. Power in the Democratic Party, more so than in the Republican Party, resides with the state organizations and various factions, and this affects the structure of the campaign. Walter Mondale's 1984 effort was hindered by the fact that the candidate had many ties within the Democratic Party and consulted with them all; the campaign, in other words, lacked direction. Both the Reagan effort of 1984 and Bush's 1988 campaign had a high degree of coordination with national and state party organizations. In each case, fund-raising and mobilization efforts were generally left to the party while the candidate organization handled all aspects of strategy (including resource allocation, scheduling, campaign content) and communication (including media relations). Both of the Clinton campaigns relied similarly on state party organizations to mobilize the electorate.

One final development should be noted with respect to candidate organizations. In the modern era, it has become increasingly common for the candidate's family to take to the hustings on behalf of the candidate. John Kennedy's family was the first, his brothers, sisters, and mother, Rose, taking to the campaign trail in 1960. Since 1976 it has become standard practice for relatives of the candidate to take to the campaign trail across the country. In their role as surrogate for the candidate, they are able to extend the candidate's reach farther than he or she would be able to do alone.[44]

Candidate Organizations in France

Ample impressionistic evidence suggests that French presidential candidate organizations, at least those of the more successful candidates,

Table 4.5
Reported Percentage of Campaign Expenditures Spent on Staffing: Selected
French Candidate Organizations, 1995

	Laguiller	Hue	Chirac	Jospin	Voynet	Cheminade
Percentage of Expenditures	—	2-3%	2-3	15	20	23

Source: Irène Hill (1997:95).

have grown larger and more complex in terms of their personnel. Recent
accounts of presidential electioneering in France suggest that the locus
of campaign activity is increasingly found in "candidate-based teams
with party support."[45] Jacques Chirac's 1995 campaign machine was
"highly organized,"[46] having attracted "an army of political personalities
and militants."[47] It is difficult to be more precise than this with respect
to actual numbers. One account of the 1988 campaign reports that Mitterand had a staff of 80, Chirac, more than that, and Raymond Barre (the
candidate of the Union of French Democrats) around 20.[48] There are
some data on candidate organizations for the latest presidential election
(1995). Table 4.5 shows the percentage of campaign expenditures that
went towards staffing for several candidates. There is obviously a great
deal of variation in these data which almost certainly reflects differences
in total budgets rather than staff size (it is hard to believe, for example,
that the eventual winner, Jacques Chirac, spent less on his staffing needs
than other candidates).

A notable aspect of Chirac's 1995 campaign was the fact that his
daughter Claude was his "main political adviser," having started working on the 1995 effort shortly after her father's 1988 loss (actually, in
September of 1989). In fact, we can see family members in prominent
positions in candidate organizations in all three countries (as well as in
the traditional era in the United States). In the United States there are
the examples of John Kennedy's brother Bobby, George W. Bush Jr.'s
involvement in his father's campaign, or Pat Buchanan relying on his
sister Bay. This increased use of family and close friends in an inner
circle of advisors is another distinguishing characteristic of modern presidential electioneering.[49] Chirac, like many French politicians, also made
use of the scholarly community in 1988, having commissioned noted
French scholar Jean Charlot to examine his 1988 defeat and advise him
on his 1995 effort.[50]

Finally, there is much more of a tendency in France than in the United
States for candidates who occupy positions of government to use their
positions for campaign purposes. In 1988, for example, Mitterand had
his own staff in place at party headquarters (headed by Lionel Jospin)
as well as a team working out of the Elysée (the offices of the president);

Chirac was able to use the resources of the offices of Prime Minister, Mayor of Paris (he was both at the time), as well as RPR headquarters.[51]

Candidate Organizations in Russia

The Russian presidential election of 1996 highlights the differences between traditional and modern presidential electioneering. The Communist Party candidate Gennadi Zyuganov ran a traditional party campaign in every sense. After a certain amount of intra-party positioning, he secured an official nomination from his party and proceeded to, for the most part, rely on the party for the direction and conduct of his campaign. Yeltsin, for his part, was the epitome of the candidate-centered model. He had no party to rely on. His campaign was conducted by his own organization(s), allies, and a team of campaign professionals. Of course this simplifies the reality of the campaign, but the point is that one candidate was the candidate *of* his party, and the other stood as a candidate *without* party, as the candidate of the nation.

There were several groups working to re-elect President Yeltsin in 1996. One, headed initially by Kremlin insider Oleg Soskovets and subsequently by Yeltsin confidant and head of presidential security Aleksander Korzhakov, was the "official" team.[52] The second, formed in late January to convince Yeltsin that he was receiving bad advice from the "official" team, was founded by Anatoli Chubais with the backing of powerful business and media elite (more on this below). These two organizations would compete with each other throughout the campaign, but in turn would come to answer to Yeltsin's daughter Tatiana Dyachenko, who took over as campaign coordinator after Soskovets was replaced.[53]

Although President Yeltsin's campaign effort was not officially connected to a political party, many groups worked to aid in his re-election. In fact, the totality of the re-election effort was exceptionally confusing. For example, 15 separate groups collected the signatures required for Yeltsin to be placed on the ballot.[54] Other efforts to re-elect the president included those of various political parties, notably, Reform's New Course and Our Home is Russia (each of which also claimed to be the "official" Yeltsin campaign organization).

Eventually all of these groups were brought together by Sergei Filatov to form the All-Russian Movement for Support for the President which served as an umbrella organization for over 250 political parties and 21 organizations (unions, civic groups, and social organizations). This gave the Yeltsin campaign a pre-existing (if very disparate) organizational base.[55] The organization employed roughly 100 people and displayed some signs of professional organization throughout the campaign (for example, it had a "Center for Work With Political Parties and Political

Movements" division which issued campaign manuals to branch organizations).[56]

Thus, Yeltsin's "campaign organization" was in fact at least three distinct organizations: the Chubais and Korzhakov (formerly Soskovets) teams as well as the All-Russian Movement. Finally, it should be mentioned at least in passing that government machinery was equally important to Yeltsin's campaign effort, helping, for example, to mobilize roughly 100,000 people to get out the vote for second-round balloting.[57] In addition, many members of government (including Prime Minister Viktor Chernomyrdin and several deputy prime ministers) actively worked for the president's re-election.[58]

Most of the other major presidential candidates relied on their own organizations as well; many went out of their way, in fact, to disassociate themselves from the parties they belonged to. For example, retired General Aleksander Lebed did not run as a representative of the Congress of Russian Communities, the party under whose label he had only months before been elected to the Duma. Instead, he formed his own "political group" (Trust and Conscience) consisting mostly of retired military officers to contest the election.[59] For the most part Yabloko party leader Grigori Yavlinski ran his own campaign as well, ignoring the party altogether.[60]

THE ORIENTATION OF PARTY AND CANDIDATE ORGANIZATIONS

In this section of the chapter we examine the orientation of campaign organizations, or to be more specific, their cohesion and mission. To what extent do all members of the organization (in this case, party and candidate organizations) share a similar goal or mission, and how well do they subsume other interests (e.g., personal ambition) to the pursuit of it? Theoretically, a greater degree of cohesiveness and the existence of a narrowly specified and defined goal within an organization translates into greater organizational strength.[61] With respect to electioneering, greater organizational cohesiveness and an electorally oriented organization brings greater strength during the campaign effort. First, an examination of how unified party and candidate organizations are during the election effort.

Party Cohesion

This section centers around one general question: how unified is the party? Is the party split by factional infighting? Have they healed the wounds (if any) incurred by the nomination? Are candidate organizations rife with personal infighting over who is in control, or is there a clear structure of command?

The opposite of party unity is party factionalism, and it is instructive to remember that factionalism, whether rooted in personality, ideology, or issues, inheres in party politics. In fact both of the major parties in the United States were born of factional dispute. The modern Democratic Party was born in 1832 from the more populist, Andrew Jackson wing of the Democratic-Republicans; the Republicans grew out of the anti-slavery wing of the Whigs. It was noted in Chapter 2 that unified parties were crucial to the electioneering effort during the traditional era of presidential electioneering in the United States; little has changed in this respect.

There is no completely satisfactory or direct way to measure party cohesion, but some impressionistic evidence points to increased cohesiveness in American political parties. In a fairly ambitious effort, Denise Baer and David Bositis reviewed the state of American political parties in 1992, concluding that American party organizations are generally more cohesive entities than 40 years ago.[62] And while related only peripherally to the campaign effort, legislative parties are appreciably more unified in the United States since 1960.[63]

Of course American political parties are not without internal division. One manifestation of internal differences in each party are the existence of various extra-party organizations. For example, the Democratic Leadership Council (DLC) was formed in 1985 by moderate and conservative Democrats and see their mission as rescuing the party from its (real or perceived) captivity by liberal special interests. The DLC is a force within the party with which to be reckoned. Their membership includes such party notables as Senator Joe Lieberman (the current chair), Senator Sam Nunn, and Missouri Representative Richard Gephardt. Importantly, Bill Clinton once served as chair of the organization and current DNC chair Roy Romer is also vice-chair of the DLC. Other examples of extra-party organizations include Jesse Jackson's Rainbow Coalition, or Republican Senator Jesse Helms' conservative Congressional Club.[64]

An indirect measure of party cohesion are the proceedings and mood of the party national convention. Divisive and split conventions indicate a divided party, and this spells trouble for the party and its candidate in November. One analyst explicitly suggests that national conventions are

tests of political moods and electoral fortunes. At least since 1964, it has been easy to spot the likely November winner based simply on the tone of the proceedings. Upbeat, confident conventions mean victory: Democrats in 1964, 1976, and 1992, and Republicans in 1968, 1972, 1980, and 1984. Fractious, quarrelsome conventions signal defeat: Democrats in 1968, 1972, 1980, and 1984, and Republicans in 1964, 1976, and 1992.[65]

In 1964, for example, the Republican Party was divided over the direction it should take. This division manifested itself prominently in the nomination struggle between the conservative Barry Goldwater and the more moderate, "establishment" candidate Nelson Rockefeller. Though Goldwater won the nomination, the rift that was created by the struggle was too deep to be easily mended. Goldwater lost badly to Lyndon Johnson and an exceptionally unified and energized Democratic Party that year. Four years later the violence surrounding the Democratic national convention in Chicago, as well as the perception that Hubert Humphrey had "stolen" the party nomination, gave the impression that the Democrats were deeply divided. This virtually assured Republican Richard Nixon of his November victory. As the result of being the major beneficiary of party reforms, George McGovern secured the Democratic Party nomination in 1972. However, those reforms and his nomination alienated party regulars and McGovern's subsequent campaign was, according to one account, "an exercise in futility."[66]

While the main goal of the modern party convention is to present as unified a face to the public (and the other party) as possible, convention planners have to balance this goal with the need to placate the bruised egos of losing candidates, recognizing that they often represent a substantial segment of the party. This is often very difficult. Sometimes it means allowing losing aspirants to address the convention, but this can be detrimental to the goal of presenting a unified party to the national audience: allowing major differences to publicly surface at the convention is often fatal to the campaign. So for example, Ronald Reagan's lukewarm embrace of the 1976 Ford candidacy at the convention detracted from Ford's campaign. The prominence given to Jesse Jackson's speech in the 1988 Democratic convention is widely believed to have been detrimental to Michael Dukakis' campaign effort; similarly, Pat Buchanan's "culture wars" speech at the 1992 Republican national convention probably hampered George Bush's campaign (it was for this reason that Buchanan was not allowed to address the convention in 1996).[67]

Mission

With respect to the mission of the party organization, it should first be remembered that American political parties developed in response to electoral needs (primarily congressional), especially after the expansion of suffrage in the 1830s. From the original congressional caucuses and Andrew Jackson's Democratic populist appeals, political parties have always had winning control of the presidency and Congress as their main goal. How well are modern political parties oriented to this goal? Concurrent with the growth and professionalization of party organizations has been a shift in their orientation toward candidate service (especially at the congressional level, particularly the House of Representatives).[68] In fact the organizational renewal efforts of both parties (the Democrats following the lead of the Republicans) discussed earlier were in large part an attempt by party organizations to re-establish their role in a changing electoral (i.e., increasingly technology-driven, candidate-centered) environment. In practice this has meant providing legal and strategic advice, public relations assistance, political information acquired by the organization's research departments, and some (limited amounts of) direct financial aid. In addition, national parties distribute money to state party organizations for the party-building activities and voter mobilization efforts of the latter.

A recent addition to the arsenal of party service to candidates is "issue" advertising. As the result of a 1996 Supreme Court ruling, parties can engage in unlimited issue advocacy advertising, providing that the ads do not explicitly call for the election or defeat of a particular candidate.[69] The "creative" use of issue advertising has allowed parties to become far more involved in the presidential election effort of late. For example, the Democratic Party began running issue advocacy advertisements portraying the Republicans (mainly Newt Gingrich) in a negative light as early as October of 1995 (for the 1996 election). During the course of the campaign they spent well over $40 million on issue ads designed to help President Clinton's ratings and set the terms for the election campaign. The Republican Party intervened in the Dole campaign effort in late March of 1996 (after Dole had exhausted his funding) to run ads designed to boost Dole's image.[70] In short, American political parties are increasingly oriented toward candidate service, if only to insure their continued survival and relevance.

French Political Parties: The Role of Personality

It was noted in Chapter 3 that French parties are more personalized than those in the United States. Therefore it should come as no surprise to find that French party politics are almost defined by their factionalism. Factionalism has always been prevalent in French political parties, but in the words of one expert, "all [French parties] suffer increasing internal divisions."[71] Party factionalism reflects the tendency of French parties to be either the creation of, or personal vehicles for, individuals. For example,

- The modern Socialist Party was the creation of François Mitterand;
- The Union of French Democrats was formed to provide parliamentary support for Valéry Giscard d'Estaing;

- The Union for the New Republic (forerunner to the Rally for the Republic) was a vehicle for Charles de Gaulle;
- The modern Rally for the Republic was remade in 1976 in Jacques Chirac's image;
- Until very recently, Jean Marie Le Pen and his National Front were almost indistinguishable from each other.

Often it is difficult to discern if intra-party differences in France are ideological or personal. There were, for example, several ideological groupings in the French Socialist Party in the 1980s, but most were associated with individuals (mainly François Mitterand and Michel Rocard).[72]

Presidential politics are at least partially responsible for this. One observer noted that "by the late 1970s, rivalries between potential [Socialist Party] presidential candidates had emerged as the most powerful source of intra-party conflict."[73] In 1987 the French Communists saw their first intra-party dispute—traditionally rare in very disciplined Communist parties—over the presidential aspirations of Pierre Juquin and André Lajoinie.[74] Illustrating the importance of personality in French party politics, it is not unusual for French presidential aspirants to switch parties to suit their electoral designs.[75] Most recently, the Rally for the Republic's Edouard Balladur ran under the UDF label after losing the RPR nomination to Jacques Chirac.[76]

Just as in the United States, after the party nomination has been captured by a particular candidate in France the goal is to unify the party in preparation for the election. Electoral considerations are almost as important to French political parties as they are to American parties, and in this respect the differences between parties in the two countries has begun to blur somewhat. "Major parties orient their strategy and adjust their tactics on the basis of" presidential elections in France.[77] In spite of the aforementioned factionalism of the French left, most accounts credit them with being very unified during Mitterand's 1981 and 1988 campaigns.[78] For example, although Michel Rocard had presidential intentions in 1981, he gave Mitterand his full support after Mitterand announced his candidacy; the left united shortly afterwards.[79] Conversely, his opponent, the incumbent Valéry Giscard d'Estaing saw his UDF fall apart.[80] Again in 1988, the right (both the RPR and the UDF) was considered "fractured" while the "factionalized" left was unified enough to re-elect Mitterand.[81] In 1995 the right healed their first-round differences quickly and well; the Socialist Lionel Jospin could not, on the other hand, unify the forces of the left.[82]

In France, as in the United States, sound electoral strategy means candidates must distance themselves from ideological or programmatic extremes. Similar to, for example, Robert Dole's implicit refutation of the Republican Party's stance on abortion in 1996, Lionel Jospin distanced himself from the Socialist Party's record during the 1995 campaign. This is important inasmuch as this type of refutation hardly sits well with party regulars, and may in turn affect their commitment to the campaign. There is, of course, an institutional reason for French presidential candidates to position themselves apart from party, namely, the necessity of building a coalition for the second round of balloting.[83] This coalition is typically forged by the candidate (e.g., as when the Socialist François Mitterand successfully courted the French Communists in 1980).[84]

Overall, personalities dominate French party organizations which are, to simplify, merely "vehicles to win election to the presidency."[85] Party labels, by and large, are mere conveniences for French presidential aspirants.[86]

Russian Political Parties

Although the major Russian political parties have achieved some amount of legislative cohesion,[87] their youth and the prominence of personalities within most makes it unwise to pass judgement on their overall cohesion. Factions still dominate. A good example of intra-party fighting during the 1996 presidential election was the struggle between the leaders of Russia's Democratic Choice over which candidate to endorse in the election. Party leaders Yegor Gaidar and Anatoli Chubais supported Yeltsin; Sergei Kovalev favored Grigori Yavlinksi.[88] Another example of party disunity is the fact that some regional branches of Yavlinski's Yabloko (e.g., the Yaroslavl branch) decided to back President Yeltsin rather than their own Yavlinski.[89]

The campaign effort of the Communist Party also suffered from factionalism, mainly ideological rather than personal. This is hardly surprising. As mentioned earlier, many factions were formed after the Communist Party of the Soviet Union disintegrated,[90] so the modern Party "contains a variety of ideological tendencies, some more orthodox communist than others."[91] While the modern incarnation of the party is less inclined to "ideological absolutes" than its predecessor, there was a good deal of ideological infighting as the 1996 campaign wore on, reflecting a division between hard-line ideologues and those more pragmatically (electorally) inclined.

The Orientation of Candidate Organizations

While it might be easy to assume that since everyone in the candidate organization is working only to elect the candidate, most presidential campaigns suffer from some infighting within the organization, especially among top-level staffers; typically these people are the hired consultants. In all fairness, given the high stakes and egos involved, infighting within candidate organizations is probably to be expected. Usually infighting is kept fairly quiet, made known either after the campaign or when someone on the team is replaced. This, when it happens, is usually to revitalize (the perception or the reality of) a faltering campaign. In late February of 1996, after Dole placed second in the Delaware primary, he fired two of his senior strategists, campaign deputy chairman William Lacy and chief pollster William McInturff. McInturff was being held responsible for polling blunders in both Delaware and earlier in New Hampshire (where he failed to predict Pat Buchanan's victory); Lacy was fired because McInturff was his "lieutenant."[92]

The presidential campaign of Russian president Boris Yeltsin in 1996 was rife with infighting. In many ways the Yeltsin team reflected the internecine court politics familiar to observers of insider Kremlin politics. David Remnick's account of the Yeltsin campaign's intra-organizational struggle is illuminating, highlighting the struggles between the groups of Anatoli Chubais and Aleksander Korzhakov.[93] The arrest of two members of the Chubais team (Sergei Lisovski and Arkadii Yefstafev), authorized by Korzhakov and motivated largely by a desire to solidify his post-election position, was a perfect illustration.[94] Yeltsin's campaign effort was, in short, almost fatally divided. Factional struggles within and between organizations campaigning for the incumbent president made a unified effort all but impossible. In fact, one can speculate that if the president had not had the weight and support of so many organizations behind his effort (including the state administrative apparatus), his re-election bid would have been unsuccessful as the result of this confusion.

CAMPAIGN PROFESSIONALS: THE NEW "ELECTION MEN"

Along with technological advances, one of the defining characteristics of modern presidential electioneering has been the growth, specialization, and use of campaign professionals in the campaign effort. They are the new experts, the professional electioneers. Electioneering formerly was the sole domain of party functionaries and personnel, but technology and the proliferation and specialization of political consultants, campaign managers, pollsters, fund-raisers, and so on, has changed that. As early as 1976, Robert Agranoff observed,

The party professional has given way to a different type of professional—the advertising and public relations man, the management specialist, the media specialist, the pollster—who performs services for the candidates based on skills he has acquired in nonpolitical fields.[95]

Campaign professionals are increasingly responsible for "calling the shots" in modern presidential campaigns. In fact many consultants have become a secondary center of attention during the campaign, often becoming media personalities as well. Witness, for example, James Carville's appearances on "The Late Show with David Letterman" or the sitcom "Mad About You." Campaign professionals play such a prominent role in presidential campaigns that they are often offered and accept presidential appointments after the election.[96] George Stephanopoulos, for example, parlayed his role in the 1992 Clinton campaign into a White House appointment (and subsequently a position working for a major television network).

What types of people are these campaign professionals? They are generally white males, younger (about two-thirds under 50), and highly educated (almost all have a college degree, almost half a graduate degree). Their demographic profile, in short, matches that of many professional classes. Nearly two-thirds have experience working for a political party, better than half in the office of an elected public official or government, and about a third have worked in the news media. About one-quarter are motivated in their career choice by the money, another quarter by their political beliefs, and about a third by the "thrill of competition."[97]

Growth of the Industry in the United States

Although political consultancy has a long history in political campaigning in the United States, it was not until this century that it became a business. Californians Clem Whitaker (a political reporter) and Leone Baxter (a public relations worker for the Redding, California Chamber of Commerce) teamed up successfully on a local referendum campaign in 1933. They married shortly thereafter and formed the first political consultant firm in 1934.[98] In 1936 Alfred Landon became the first presidential candidate to retain the services of an ad agency, and for the next 20 years others (mainly Republicans) followed suit, drawing on the expertise of various agencies in producing television spots. In 1960 the Kennedy campaign assembled an entire team of consultants who provided the candidate with a variety of services, including media advice, polling, and political strategy.

In 1969 Joe Napolitan, who had worked on Hubert Humphrey's 1968 presidential campaign, founded the American Association of Political Consultants (AAPC). The AAPC's original membership numbered 25, and in the past 30 years the profession has grown almost exponentially to number roughly 4,000[99] (another measure suggests that if one includes part-timers, there are as many as 35,000).[100] In just one small segment of

Text Box 4.4
The "1998–99 Political Pages" Listing from *Campaigns and Elections*

■ Attorneys — Elections & Compliance	■ Print Advertising Graphics & Design
■ Campaign Management	■ Political Publications & Newsletters
■ Database/File Management	■ Political Web Sites on the Internet
■ Direct Mail — Printing and Processing	■ Press Relations & Events
■ Direct Mail — Strategy & Creative	■ Research — Opposition
■ Educational & Training Programs	■ Research — Issues, Voters, & Legislative
■ Fax Services	■ Research & Information Online
■ Field Operations & Organization	■ Satellite Services
■ Fundraising Consultants	■ Software & Computer Services
■ Fundraising Software & Computer Services	■ Speech Writing/Ad Copy Writing
■ General Consultants & Strategists	■ Speakers, Analysts & Press Sources
■ Initiative & Referendum Consultants	■ Targeting
■ Internet / Web Site Consultants	■ Telephone Contact Services
■ Mailing & Telephone Lists	■ Video Duplication
■ Media Buying	■ Video, TV & Radio Production
■ Media Consultants	■ Governmental Relations & Lobbying
■ Media & Speech Training	■ Grassroots Lobbying: Strategy & Planning
■ Online Information Services	■ Grassroots Lobbying: Products & Services
■ Petitions & Signature Gathering	■ Public Affairs — Issues Management
■ Polling — Survey Research & Analysis	■ Public Affairs — Public Relations & Events
■ Polling — Focus Groups	■ Public Affairs — Research & Polling
■ Polling — Interview Services	■ Public Affairs — Advertising & Media
■ Printing & Promotional Materials	Production

Source: Campaigns and Elections (1998, front cover).

the industry, opposition research, the number of firms in operation has grown more than 200 percent in the 1990s alone.[101]

Specialization of the Industry in the United States

As the industry of campaign professionals has grown, so too has it become more specialized. Virtually every form of campaign activity (fund-raising, polling, electoral mobilization, accounting and compliance, research, the production and distribution of audio-visual advertising, direct mail and literature, internet services, and so on) can be found represented in *Campaigns & Elections*, the trade magazine founded in 1980 for campaign professionals. Text Box 4.4 is taken from *Campaigns & Elections* "1998–99 Political Pages," the annual issue which lists industry firms and the products and services they offer, and illustrates the wide array of specialties within the industry.

Newer technologies contribute significantly to greater specialization within the industry. International Business Machines has the distinction of producing the first political campaign software, "Campaign Manager," in 1983.[102] Since then technological advances have exploded. Among the newer technologies and techniques being used in electioneering are:

- Telebanks with computer-aided dialing for canvassing of specially selected target categories of voters;
- On-line computer organizational links;
- Toll-free numbers for instant feedback, fund-raising, and attracting volunteers;
- New polling techniques (moment-to-moment, push polls);
- Use of the Internet (Email, the World Wide Web);
- Satellite teleconferencing;
- Targeted infomercials and campaign literature;
- Computerized opposition research.[103]

The point here is rather simple. The above are all fairly recent and complex technologies, and newer and specialized technologies and techniques require trained specialists to employ them. As an industry, campaign professionals have continued to adapt to that reality.

Television and image-making are especially important in the specializing trend of campaign professionals. Modern presidential campaigns assume major media presence, and have, to say the least, come a long way since Richard Nixon refused a major advertising firm's proposal to organize his campaign around the latest media techniques in 1960.[104] As early as 1976 Senator Henry Jackson of Washington hired speech instructors to help him speed his oral delivery and improve his pronunciation, lost twenty pounds, had plastic surgery to correct sagging eyelids, let his hair grow, and got a new wardrobe better suited for television.[105] Ronald Reagan took this aspect of electioneering to a new level and, according to one analyst, after him "melodrama was part of the job specification."[106] This lesson was not lost on Bill Clinton, who saved his faltering campaign in 1992 by a dramatic and effective appearance with his wife on "60 Minutes." Al Gore, in preparation for the announcement of his 2000 candidacy, consulted Michael Sheehan, a former actor, on body language, intonation, and wardrobe.[107]

Professionalization of the Industry in the United States

Political consultancy in its many forms is also increasingly professionalized. As mentioned, the field has its own professional association and, to keep practitioners abreast of new developments, the AAPC and *Campaigns & Elections* (among others) conduct seminars for managers, consultants, and other campaign workers. There are also seven schools in the United States, some in operation since the mid-1980s, which teach the craft of campaigning.[108] One caveat to the professionalizing trend should be noted here. A code of ethics is a vital component of any profession, and here the AAPC falls short in the eyes of some. The Pew Research Group found that although most consultants were aware of the

AAPC's code of ethics and believe that the association should be able to enforce it (by censuring its members), the vast majority (81 percent) doubted the code's effectiveness, and over half (54 percent) said it had little effect on their own behavior.[109]

Most consultants do not consider party an important part of a winning campaign equation; Joe Napolitan, founder of the AAPC, states this explicitly.[110] However most do hold a favorable, if more complex view of the role of parties in the electoral process, as well as the relationship between consultants and parties.[111] At minimum, most consider parties important enough to work only for candidates of one party or the other. Put another way, only rarely do they "play both sides of the fence." But in their view, it is mainly they, not parties, who help candidates win.

The services campaign professionals offer go overwhelmingly to candidates. And, they seem to profit greatly from this: Dick Morris was reported to have earned roughly $1.5 million from the Clinton campaign in 1996, Squier Knapp Ochs (a media firm), $2.5 million, and Mark Penn and Doug Schoen (pollsters), $1 million.[112] Table 4.6 details some of Clinton's expenditures on campaign professionals in 1996.

Campaign Professionals in France

Campaign professionals are also finding France's political soil fertile. For some time in French presidential campaigns, "traditional party elites [have been] losing their importance as they become ousted in favour of the new breed of technocrats," as candidates increasingly turn to campaign professionals for major decisions in presidential campaigns.[113] The industry of campaign professionals in France is both growing and specializing. There was some imitation of American campaign politics involved in this development, at least in the beginning. Theodore White's account of the Kennedy campaign was translated into French in 1961; the co-founders of the International Association of Political Consultants (IAPP) in 1969 were the American Joe Napolitan and the French consultant Michel Bongrand.[114]

In his 1965 bid for the presidency, Jean Lecanuet was the first French presidential candidate to employ a political consultant (Michel Bongrand). Joe Napolitan worked for Valéry Giscard d'Estaing in his successful 1974 presidential bid. Importantly, campaign professionals began to be associated with winning candidates, and since much of what informs the strategy and tactics of a political campaign is what worked (or what seemed to work) in the previous one, it has become virtually unthinkable to run for the French presidency without a team of campaign experts. Giscard d'Estaing, for example, relying on campaign professionals, bypassed his own UDF entirely in the 1981 elections. François Mitterand's campaign in 1981 was reportedly handled far better than his

Table 4.6
Clinton Payments to Consultants, April 1995 through July 1996 (in Thousands of Dollars)

Firm	Service Provided	Paid
Squier Knapp Ochs & November 5 Group Broadcast	Advertising	$8,741
Malchow, Adams & Hussey Direct	Mail Fund-raising	1,636
Penn & Schoen Associates	Polling	995
Dick Morris	General Strategy	231
Larry Hayes	Accounting	217
Share Systems	Telemarketing	122
The Smith Co.	Telemarketing	119
Greenberg Research	General Consulting	113
Cranford, Johnson, Robinson Associates	Media Consultants	96
Morris & Carrick	General Consulting	90

* A total of $12.9 million was paid to a total of 35 firms; the above list represents the 10 which received the most money.

Source: From the Campaign Study Group, as reported by Ruth Marcus and Ira Chinoy (1996).

previous one in 1974, the credit for which belongs to campaign manager Jacques Ségéula (who also played a "dominant role" for Mitterand in 1988).[115] Ségéula, in fact, now works for candidates in other countries (e.g., the Austrian SPÖ), further illustrating the growth of the French campaign professional industry.[116]

French presidential elections were born into the age of television, and as in the United States, television plays a major role in presidential campaigns in France. This of course affects how candidates present themselves (personal appearance, speech patterns, etc.) and increases the importance of image and media-handling techniques. No surprise then that there has been an increased reliance on campaign and media specialists. Virtually all presidential candidates since de Gaulle have taken "professional public relations advice on television appearances."[117] Chirac, for example, averse as he was to being "managed" for television, underwent a complete make over for the 1988 campaign,[118] presenting a revamped, "new-style Chirac" to the country;[119] image specialists, not his party, were responsible for this. The importance of television is seen in candidate budgets: in 1995, seven of the nine first-round candidates allocated greater than 30 percent of their total expenditures on advertising; three spent more than 50 percent.[120] A good deal of this spending went toward television production costs.

Campaign Professionals in Russia

Although his campaign organization was fragmented, certain aspects of the Yeltsin campaign were entirely professional. Collecting the signatures necessary for candidate registration was "largely a commercial operation, with hired professionals deployed to circulate the nominating petitions."[121] Yeltsin's use of a team of American consultants was widely reported by the Western press (most prominently in *Time* magazine). The following group of American consultants were in Moscow for most of the campaign:

- Steven Moore, a public relations specialist;
- George Gorton, a "longtime strategist for California Governor Pete Wilson";
- Joe Shumate, a pollster;
- Richard Dresner, who worked with Dick Morris in the late 1970s and early 1980s on Bill Clinton's gubernatorial campaigns;
- Dick Morris, then a top Clinton campaign advisor.[122]

Although it remains unclear exactly how important these American campaign professionals were to Yeltsin's re-election effort,[123] they were routinely utilized by the Yeltsin campaign. For example, the campaign relied heavily on their survey research for image and message refinement. In fact, hiring a team of campaign professionals was the price Yeltsin paid for the financial support of media magnate and businessman Boris Berezovski.[124]

Russia now has its own crop of home-grown campaign professionals. Video International, the firm that had been successful in the president's campaign for support in a crucial 1993 referendum,[125] was responsible for packaging and selling Russians a "new" Yeltsin.[126] Throughout the Yeltsin campaign effort large amounts of money (raised outside of the legal bounds of campaign finance laws) went "to pollsters, media strategists, and public relations strategists," including Russian firms like Politika, the Center for Regional Research, the Intellectual Communications Agency, Imya, and Nikolo-M (named after Machiavelli).[127] Other candidates besides Yeltsin made use of campaign professionals as well. For example, Grigori Yavlinski hired a team of campaign professionals from St. Petersburg.

SUMMARY

The overall conclusion is that in terms of their personnel, campaign organizations are larger, more specialized, and more professionalized than a few decades ago. This suggests, at the least, that presidential campaign politics is no place for amateurs (if, indeed, it ever was). Running for president has become big business, still for political parties, but increasingly for the officially unaffiliated campaign professionals who work for the candidates and their increasingly sophisticated organizations. Political parties have increased in strength since 1960, and in the United States their increased presence at the national level has been documented. The paradox here is that larger, more professional and service-oriented party organizations are more capable of campaign activity at the same time that political campaigns have become less labor-intensive,[128] which is at least partially explained by the fact that presidential campaigns are now conducted on a much larger level in terms of their overall reach. In the next chapter we will look at what these organizations bring to the campaign effort by way of resources.

5

The Resources of Modern Presidential Electioneering

INTRODUCTION

Almost every journalistic or scholarly account of campaign finance makes reference to the vast sums of money required in a race for the presidency. Indeed, the totals are staggering for the average citizen to consider. For example, George W. Bush, the Republican Governor of Texas and early front-runner in campaign 2000, reported official campaign contributions of $37 million by July 15, 1999. With this amount, he announced that he would not be accepting federal matching funds for the campaign.[1] These funds were raised, recall, better than 18 months before the November 2000 election.

In Chapter 4 we looked at the personnel of modern presidential electioneering ending up with a good picture of who are the electioneers in modern presidential campaigns. In this chapter we ask another fairly simple question: with what do electioneers conduct the campaign? Rather than focus, as many accounts of campaign finance do, on the massive amounts of money spent in the campaign, this chapter takes a more holistic and nuanced look at the resources of modern presidential electioneering.

The chapter is divided into two sections and, because money is so important, the first section is devoted to campaign finance. Money can be thought of as a first-order resource, without which many other resources would be hard or even impossible to acquire. Beyond looking at amounts of money spent in the race, the chapter will look at who raises the money, how and from where, who controls the spending of it, and where it goes. Like the previous chapter, a distinction will be made between the finances of party and candidate organizations. A third dimension is added as well, at least in the case of the United States, which includes soft money and issue advocacy advertising (alluded to earlier) for which it is difficult to assign responsibility to either party or candidate.

The section on campaign finance, in particular that part of it which deals with the finances of candidate organizations, will take up much of the discussion in this chapter. But other, non-monetary resources used in presidential electioneering are deserving of attention as well. In the second section of the chapter we will discuss these other resources, specifically, physical resources (e.g., organizational headquarters, technology), information, allies of the organizations, and political capital.

CAMPAIGN FINANCE: MONEY, MONEY, AND MORE MONEY

Estimates suggest that Abraham Lincoln and Stephen Douglas together spent approximately $150,000 in the 1860 presidential race; in 1960, Richard Nixon and John Kennedy spent roughly $20 million between them. By 1996 the amount of money spent by major party candidates totaled over $233 million. Electing presidents has always cost a great deal of money, but in the modern era costs have skyrocketed, even with inflation factored in. Direct primaries where multiple candidates campaign in each state, cross-country travel, television advertising, and the services of campaign professionals have all contributed to the ever-rising price tag associated with selecting our chief executive.[2]

This section is devoted to a discussion of the money involved in modern presidential electioneering. As in the previous chapter, a distinction will be made between the campaign finance efforts of the party and candidate organizations; those efforts which are indeterminate will be covered separately. The discussion will be further divided according to the phases of the campaign, specifically, the pre-primary (or "invisible primary") period, the primary season, the party national convention, and the general election campaign itself. Perhaps obviously, there is less to talk about in some of these phases for each type of campaign organization. For example, the invisible primary period is mainly associated with candidates and their organizations; the national conventions are primarily a party affair. Finally, not all of these phases correspond directly to phases of the election seasons in France or Russia, so these countries will be covered at the end of each section. First, a look at the finances of political party organizations in the United States.

Table 5.1
National Committee Hard Money Receipts, 1976–96 (in Millions of Dollars)

	1976	1978	1980	1982	1984	1986	1988	1990	1992	1994	1996
Democrats	$13.1	11.3	15.4	16.5	46.6	17.2	52.3	14.5	65.8	41.8	103.1
Republicans	29.1	34.2	77.8	84.1	105.9	83.8	91	68.7	85.4	87.4	187.2

Source: Paul Herrnson (1998a:58).

The Finances of Political Party Organizations

Consistent with the institutionalization of party organizations (i.e., growth and professionalization) has been an institutionalization of their means of finance and a steady increase in their revenue. This has allowed them to play a larger, albeit changing role in electioneering, and has made them once more "very important players in party politics and elections."[3] One of the important aspects of party building discussed in Chapter 4 was the regularization of the means of party finance. Since the 1970s telephone solicitation and various fund-raising events have been used to seek large and small contributions from party faithful; direct mail is consistently used to solicit donations of under $100.[4] Hard money (money contributed to a political party for campaign purposes and regulated by the FEC) receipts for each party have risen almost without interruption from 1976 through 1996 (see Table 5.1).

It is important to remember that the figures in Table 5.1 include only hard money. Here individuals are limited to donations totaling $20,000 per year to the national party; PACs can contribute $15,000 in any given year. The table shows that Republicans enjoyed a considerable advantage throughout the late 1970s and most of the 1980s in raising campaign hard money, which reflects the fact that they had, by the 1980s, developed a fairly sophisticated direct mail system. The fact that Republican supporters are a more homogenous group probably makes it easier for them to solicit contributions, and the party's minority status in Congress prior to 1994 (and Clinton's control of the White House after 1992) likely lent more urgency to their fund-raising appeals.[5]

Parties play no formal role in the primaries but each of the major parties receives federal grants for their national conventions ($12.4 million in 1996) and may also solicit and accept funding from local businesses (host committees) in the cities where the convention is held.[6] Through 1984 this latter option was exercised sparingly; neither party raised even a third of the amount of the federal convention grant in this manner. However in 1988 the Democratic Host Committee contributed roughly twice the $9.2 million granted the party by the federal govern-

ment for the convention; in 1992 both parties' host committees contributed substantial amounts but neither collected amounts equal to their
federal grant.[7] It was in 1996 that host committees came into their own
with respect to convention funding. They were, in fact, where most of
the convention funding was found. In all, the Democrats collected almost
$21 million through Chicago's Committee for '96, while the Republican
San Diego Host Committee took in roughly $11 million. Both parties
accepted one donation of over $2 million and another of over $1 million,
which in the mind of some, wreaks havoc with campaign finance laws
that were designed to end the era of "fat cats."[8] Parties also receive federal funds for the general election campaign ($11.6 million in 1996). In
general, though, their official role (i.e., hard money expenditures) in the
general election is minimal.

Candidate Organization Finance: Sources

Presidential aspirants have several sources for needed campaign funding, and those who hope to have any electoral success pursue funding
early and energetically. If they agree to federal spending limits and sat-
isfy a few other requirements (see Chapter 3), presidential candidates are
eligible to receive federal matching funds where the government matches
all donations of under $250 for the primary season and funds the general
election campaign.[9] In 1996 the spending limits for the primary season
were $37.1 million (more precisely, $30.9 million for campaign activities
themselves and $6.2 million for fund-raising expenses). For the general
election the limits were set at $74.2 million for each of the two major-
party candidates ($61.8 million for campaign activities and $12.4 million
for fund-raising expenses). There are, importantly, no limits set for the
legal and accounting expenses incurred to comply with the law.[10]

How do candidates raise funds? Generally speaking there are two
fund-raising strategies, those targeted toward smaller donations (under
$250) and those designed to elicit larger ones (between $250 and $1,000).
The distinction is important. Small donations matter because only those
donations of under $250 are matched by the federal government (or, the
first $250 of larger donations). Large donations are important simply
because they add up quicker. Individual contributors can give up to
$1,000 to a candidate for the primary season.

One of the staples of campaign finance in the modern era is direct
mail, the strategy typically employed to raise smaller donations. This
strategy is usually one of the only options available to lesser-known aspirants or those who do not have an established donor network. Patrick
Buchanan, who challenged the incumbent George Bush in 1992 for the
Republican Party nomination, was exceptionally successful with direct
mail.[11] In all he raised over $4 million via direct mail by the end of May

(1992); 76 percent (about $5.5 million) of his total funding came from donations of under $200. In the end he qualified for about $5 million in matching funds. Similarly, Paul Tsongas raised roughly 43 percent of his total ($8.1 million) in donations of less than $200; public funding constituted approximately 36 percent of his fund-raising effort.[12]

While direct mail is an effective fund-raising tool, fund-raising events work better.[13] It is the preferred way to solicit large donations and also serves to demonstrate that the practice of going after fat cats is not over. For example, in 1996 Phil Gramm kicked off his presidential bid with a barbeque that raised $4.1 million; Lamar Alexander announced his candidacy at a party which brought in $2.2 million. The eventual Republican nominee Robert Dole added $1.5 million to his coffers with a gala in New York, and President Clinton raised almost $6 million in a week of dinners and similar events.[14] Clinton, in fact, raised approximately 42 percent ($10.5 million) of his funding from donors who contributed $750 or more.[15]

The large donor strategy works especially well for candidates with extensive political or other ties. Here, the value of donor networks becomes evident. In both 1988 and 1992 George Bush relied on a network of donors known for large gifts and on past contacts for help in soliciting more of the same. As the result he raised $16.5 million in 1988 and $18 million in 1992 in donations of $1,000—well over half of his primary season fund-raising in each year. If we factor in individuals who gave $750 or more, large donations accounted for 82 percent of his total contributions. This is in stark contrast to his direct-mail efforts: less than 10 percent of his campaign funding came in the form of donations of less than $100. In 1988 Michael Dukakis employed a similar strategy, forming a finance committee of people who pledged to raise at least $10,000; by May of 1988, 900 people had been successful in doing so. In addition, 230 individuals raised a minimum of $25,000 and another 130 raised $100,000 or better.[16] In the spring of 1999 George W. Bush, Jr., relying on his father's (as well as his own) contacts, formed the Pioneers, a group of individuals who were each committed to raising at least $100,000 for the campaign. By late June (1999) his sister, Doro Bush Koch, had been successful in raising $120,000.[17]

Candidate Organization Finance: The Invisible Primary

As should be apparent by now, it is increasingly important for serious presidential aspirants to begin raising funds early. Most analysts agree that a presidential aspirant needs from $20–30 million in the bank by the end of January of the election year if he or she is to have any chance at winning their party's nomination.[18] Obviously, more would be even better. The reason why is fairly straightforward: an increasingly front-loaded primary season. The term "invisible primary" refers to the fact that winning the nomination increasingly depends on a candidate's ability to raise the early money necessary to make a serious bid in the front-loaded primary season. Those who cannot are winnowed out quickly.

Simply put, early money—a great deal of it—is critical to get out of the gate and ahead of the field early. Since 1980, with the exception of John Connally that year, the candidate who started the primary season with the most money went on to become the party nominee (Connally raised slightly more money than Republican rival and eventual nominee, Ronald Reagan). As early as January and throughout the spring of 1999 there were press stories circulating regarding the early fund-raising efforts of several presidential aspirants (notably, George W. Bush and Vice-President Al Gore) for election 2000,[19] this a full year before the first primary (in fact, some other Republican aspirants were already complaining that Bush was drying up the donor pool).[20]

How much money is needed? Table 5.2 shows the total and average amounts of money raised by the top five fund-raisers in each of the six campaigns from 1976 to 1996 in the year prior to the year of the election. A decline is evident in 1992, a year when all candidates started campaigning late, but the upward trend continued in 1996. Candidates are continuing to raise and spend greater amounts of money prior to the beginning of the primary season.

In order to raise these massive amounts of money presidential aspirants creatively work around campaign finance laws, laws intended to regulate funds raised for and spent on the advocacy of a particular candidate. One way to raise money early is to form candidate exploratory committees or tax-exempt foundations which technically do not advocate the election of a particular individual, and therefore are not subject to FEC guidelines. So, for example, Jack Kemp formed Empower America, a conservative think tank and advocacy organization, in early 1993; similarly, Bob Dole founded the Better America Foundation soon after that, at least partially in response.[21] Lamar Alexander's nonprofit Republican Exchange Satellite Network was a vehicle for him to discuss policy and thus widen his base of appeal. Since it was not subject to FEC guidelines, he was able to fund the network with a few large donations (13 of $100,000; 200 of $10,000 or more). And, once his campaign officially began in 1995 he was able to (and did) return to these same donors for more funding.[22]

The more commonly employed strategy is to form leadership (or multi-candidate) PACs, "political action committees headed by . . . federal politicians, but independent of their campaign committees. . . . [and] registered with the Federal Election Commission as non-connected, multi-candidate political committees."[23] These allow presidential aspirants to engage in almost unlimited fund-raising prior to the beginning

Table 5.2
Money Raised by the Top Five Fund-raising Candidates Through December of the Year Preceding Presidential Elections, 1975–95 (in Millions of Dollars)

Year	Candidate	Receipts		
1975	George Wallace (D)	$6.0	*Total of all Candidates:*	$15.04
	Henry Jackson (D)	3.4	*Average of Top Five Candidates:*	$3.01
	Lloyd Bentsen (D)	2.1		
	Ronald Reagan (R)	1.9		
	Gerald Ford (R)	1.7		
1979	John Connally (R)	$9.2	*Total of all Candidates:*	$30.46
	Ronald Reagan (R)	7.2	*Average of Top Five Candidates:*	$6.09
	Jimmy Carter (D)	5.8		
	George Bush (R)	4.5		
	Edward Kennedy (D)	3.9		
1983	Walter Mondale (D)	$11.5	*Total of all Candidates:*	$28.03
	John Glenn (D)	6.4	*Average of Top Five Candidates:*	$5.61
	Alan Cranston (D)	4.7		
	Ronald Reagan (R)	3.6		
	Gary Hart (D)	1.9		
1987	George Bush (R)	$19.1	*Total of all Candidates:*	$70.76
	Pat Robertson (R)	16.4	*Average of Top Five Candidates:*	$14.15
	Robert Dole (R)	14.3		
	Michael Dukakis (D)	10.8		
	Jack Kemp (R)	10.2		
1991	George Bush (R)	$10.1	*Total of all Candidates:*	$18.84
	Bill Clinton (D)	3.3	*Average of Top Five Candidates:*	$3.77
	Tom Harkin (D)	2.2		
	Bob Kerrey (D)	2.0		
	Paul Tsongas (D)	1.31		
1995	Bill Clinton (D)	$25.6	*Total of all Candidates:*	$102.5
	Bob Dole (R)	24.5	*Average of Top Five Candidates:*	$20.5
	Phil Gramm (R)	20.9		
	Steve Forbes (R)	20.0		
	Lamar Alexander (R)	11.5		

Source: Emmett Buell (1996:13–15, Tables 1.3 and 1.4); data for Ronald Reagan's 1983 campaign courtesy of Bob Biersack (FEC); 1995 data from Anthony Corrado (1997:143, Table 4.2).

of the primary season. Ostensibly independent, leadership PACs consist of five or more candidates for federal office and are supposed to help party-building by supporting a slate of candidates. However, it is widely understood (and accepted) that they raise and spend money primarily on behalf of their presidential candidate.

Ronald Reagan was the first presidential candidate to create a leadership PAC. In 1977 he transferred money left over from his 1976 candidacy to his newly formed Citizens for the Republic in preparation for the 1980 campaign; over the next two and a half years the PAC raised $6.7 million. Although approximately 10 percent of this money was used to help other candidates for other offices, most was used for Reagan's benefit "to hire a staff, establish fund-raising networks, build direct-mail lists, develop a political operation, recruit volunteers, and subsidize Reagan's travel."[24] By 1988 leadership PACs were a standard tactic for raising early money: 10 of the 13 major-party candidates in 1988 formed and used leadership PACs, spending $25.2 million between them.

There are several advantages to forming a presidential leadership PAC. First, while individuals can only contribute $1,000 to candidate organizations themselves, they can give $5,000 to a PAC. Second, by circumventing federal spending limits they allow the candidate to begin their campaign effort early by building and operating shadow campaign organizations. Although these organizations cannot spend money directly on the candidate's election campaign, they can, for example, spend money on overhead (e.g., staffing needs) and general political costs (e.g., polling, consulting, travel) that indirectly benefit the candidate. Third, leadership PACs allow candidates to develop a network of political support; using leadership PAC money judiciously to contribute to the campaigns of others (up to $5,000 per candidate) is a way for a presidential hopeful to curry favor. Bob Dole, for example, received endorsements from many of the Republican officials to whom his leadership PAC had contributed in 1996.[25]

Finally, leadership PACs give a candidate a head start on building a direct mail program and a donor network. After a few years of fund-raising a leadership PAC will have developed a list of proven contributors. These lists are expensive. When the official campaign begins, the candidate's official organization can buy or rent the leadership PAC's donor list for a fraction of its fair-market cost. Reagan, for example, used his leadership PAC's list of 300,000 donors in 1980; in 1984, Walter Mondale got a list of 25,000 from his, saving approximately $1 million; similarly, Bob Dole and Jack Kemp each saved about $2 million in 1988.[26] In 1996 Dole began his official campaign with a list of some 500,000 donors from his Campaign America.[27] Finally, there is a new twist in the use of leadership PACs. State-based leadership PACs seem to be increasingly popular. Lamar Alexander, for example, formed several state leadership PACs in 1999 (Virginia and Tennessee prominent among them). State leadership PACs provide all of the benefits of federal PACs but are even further removed from the regulatory regime of the FEC since states have their own campaign finance rules.[28]

One last note with respect to candidate fund-raising. As of the spring of 1999, most of the major presidential candidates are making use of their own World Wide Web sites to solicit campaign funds. Some of these sites are more sophisticated than others[29]; some (Elizabeth Dole, John McCain) even automatically email campaign updates to subscribers. Based on evidence from the 1998 Congressional elections it is unclear

Table 5.3
Prenomination Expenditures by In- and Out-party, 1960–96 (in Millions of Dollars)

Year	Out-party	In-party	Total
1960	$2.1 (Democrat)	$.5 (Republican)	$2.6
1964	10.0 (Republican)	1.0 (Democrat)	11.0
1968	20.0 (Republican)	25.0 (Democrat)	45.0
1972	23.7 (Democrat)	5.7 (Republican)	38.4
1976	40.7 (Democrat)	26.2 (Republican)	66.9
1980	71.5 (Republican)	35.7 (Democrat)	107.2
1984	79.6 (Democrat)	27.1 (Republican)	106.7
1988	89.7 (Democrat)	112.7 (Republican)	202.4
1992	65.3 (Democrat)	79.9 (Republican)	145.2
1996	184.6 (Republican)	44.6 (Democrat)	229.2

Source: James Davis (1997:108).

how successful they will prove to be, and there are compliance problems associated with online giving.[30] However, candidate web sites (at all levels of government) are now considered "mandatory," and we should expect to see this fund-raising strategy become standard practice.[31]

Candidate Organization Finance: Primary and General Election Spending

Raising large amounts of money before January ensures that a candidate will be able to be at least minimally competitive in the primaries. Candidates use this money for advertising, staff salaries, office space and equipment, the service of campaign professionals, and so on. Equally as important as starting the primary season with a large amount of money is being able to continue to raise it consistently throughout the primary season.[32] Unsurprisingly, there has been an increase in the amounts of money raised and spent by candidates during the primary season. Table 5.3 shows primary season (prenomination) expenditures from 1960 to 1996. Since expenditures for each party's candidate vary depending on whether the party has control of the White House, the table is organized according to the expenses of the in- and out-party of the given year.

Money is especially important if primary battles are highly contested, crowded into a short period of time and across several regions at the same time. In 1996, as the result of serious early challenges from Pat Buchanan and the well-financed Steve Forbes, Bob Dole ran out of money shortly after he secured the party nomination (in fact, by the end of January Dole had spent nearly $28 of the allowed $37 million).[33] This put him at a distinct disadvantage to President Clinton, whose renomination was uncontested. From then until the Republican national convention Dole engaged in some very creative (and necessary) financial management. For example, he sold computer equipment and other office supplies from the Dole nomination campaign to the Dole election committee for $1.4 million. This amount may seem like a pittance, but it helped to keep his organization alive, paying staff salaries, travel expenses, and so on.[34]

In spite of the fact that party national conventions are increasingly used as an advertising springboard for the general campaign, presidential candidates have no role in financing them. Candidates receive public funds for the general election, an amount, like primary funding (and convention funds for the parties), which is indexed for inflation ($67 million apiece in the upcoming 2000 election). If candidates accept federal funding for the general election, their fund-raising stops after the nomination has been won (with the exception of funds raised for accounting and compliance purposes).

This leads to an aspect of candidate finance which is becoming increasingly important and should be discussed here. In order to help candidates comply with the myriad of rules and regulations, the FEC allows candidates to raise unlimited amounts of money for legal and accounting expenses.[35] These funds, kept in a separate account, are raised (subject to a $1,000 per contribution limit) to the tune of several million dollars. In 1996 Clinton-Gore raised $7.8 million in compliance funds; by May of 1999 Al Gore had solicited money from better than 900 individuals for his compliance fund, individuals who had also contributed to his campaign fund in the first quarter of 1999. The twist here is that compliance funds can, with some creativity, be used to campaign. After Dole ran short on funds in the spring of 1996, he used compliance funds for staff salaries, events, and travel, all on the pretense that they were legitimate costs of fund-raising for the compliance fund, and he also borrowed $1.2 million from the fund to keep his campaign afloat.[36]

Before we turn our attention to soft money and other gray areas of campaign finance, let us take a brief look at how campaign hard money finances are spent. Table 5.4 outlines the prenomination expenses of President Clinton and Robert Dole in 1996. Although Clinton spent much more money proportionately than Dole in overhead and advertising (about 10 percent more) and Dole outspent the president on fund-raising and campaign events, the table reveals remarkable similarities in how each candidate allocated their funds.

The Rest of the Story: Soft Money

It is fairly easy to organize a discussion of FEC-regulated hard money around either parties or candidates. Of late, however, a major chapter in the story of campaign finance revolves around the growing importance

Table 5.4

Prenomination Expenses of President Clinton and Robert Dole in 1996 (in Dollars and Percentage of Total)

Expenses	Robert Dole		William Clinton	
Overhead				
Travel	$3,056,131	8.9%	$2,807,709	9.2%
Salaries	3,034,964	8.8	3,386,424	11.1
Taxes	1,387,439	4.0	1,936,312	6.4
Computing / Office Equipment	1,293,316	3.8	1,416,836	4.7
Telephone	1,118,858	3.2	1,337,986	4.4
Lawyers / Accountants	936,969	2.7	1,556,967	5.1
Office Furniture / Supplies	590,785	1.7	839,101	2.8
Rent / Utilities	566,664	1.6	733,699	2.4
Bank / Investment Fees	92,234	0.3	9,072	—
Food / Meetings	19,944	0.1	26,236	0.1
Total	$12,097,302	35.1%	$14,050,342	46.2%
Fund Raising				
Direct Mail	$7,420,198	21.5%	$2,030,118	6.7%
Events	2,343,440	6.8	2,148,325	7.1
Telemarketing	320,590	0.9	413,668	1.4
Total	$10,084,228	29.3%	$4,592,111	15.1%
Advertising				
Electronic Media	$6,306,732	18.3%	$8,741,437	28.8%
Other Media	174,842	0.5	96,736	0.3
Total	$6,481,574	18.8%	$8,838,173	29.1%
Other Campaign Activity				
Campaign Events / Other Nonmedia Campaigning	$4,037,933	11.7%	$1,592,211	5.2%
Persuasion Mail / Brochures	967,693	2.8	206,380	0.7
Staff / Volunteers	13,413	—	20,606	0.1
Total	$5,019,039	14.6%	$1,819,197	6.0%
Donations				
Political Parties	$6,555	—	—	—
Ideological Groups	6,364	—	—	—
Civic Organizations	2,475	—	—	—
Total	$15,394	—	$64,303	0.2%
Other				
Polling	$743,213	2.2%	$1,012,286	3.3%
Nonitemized Expenses	10,325	—	11,571	—
Total	$753,538	2.2%	$1,023,857	3.3%
Total	$34,451,076	100%	$30,387,983	100%

Source: Stephen Wayne (1997:55, Table 2.6); originally reported by the *Washington Post* (April 18 1996, p. A3, and August 24, 1996, p. A11).

of unregulated "soft" money, money which is donated to political parties and is intended to help party building.[37] In 1996 the solicitation and spending of soft money virtually exploded. One analyst reports that in the 1995–96 cycle, the DNC spent $95 million and the RNC, $111 million. These figures represent better than a 200 percent increase from 1992.[38] Soft money represents a re-emergence of fat-cat corporate giving. In 1996 Phillip Morris distributed better than $2.6 million between the two parties (mostly to Republicans), Seagram, $1.8 million (most of theirs to Democrats), RJR Nabisco, close to $1 million; several others exceeded $500,000.[39]

Presidential candidates have some control over how these funds are spent because, in spite of the fact that soft money cannot be used for advocacy of specific candidates, there are increasingly sophisticated ways around this. And, candidates labor hard to raise these funds for the party. From the 103 infamous White House coffee klatches held from January 1995 to August 1996 the DNC collected $27 million.[40] In 1996 Clinton aide Harold Ickes' "job [was] to ensure that the DNC raised the unregulated soft-money to pay for TV ads," ads which (indirectly) promoted the Clinton re-election effort.[41]

Soft money is used in a variety of ways which benefit presidential campaigns, "to operate telephone banks, to print and distribute campaign literature, and to recruit field organizers and other political operatives."[42] In 1992 and 1996 both parties' presidential candidates used soft money channeled to state party organizations to help defray the costs of operating their organizations in the states. This, in turn, freed up more money for media advertising and reduced their need for national staffing. Much of the soft money that parties collect goes to state and local party organizations, as it was intended. It helps pay for federal and non-federal activities that are shared with states (fund-raising, voter mobilization, administration) and that benefit both federal and non-federal candidates, organizational expenses (e.g., buildings, equipment), and is sometimes earmarked for specific state and local candidates.[43]

But the primary way soft money was spent in 1996 was both parties' use of what are known as "issue" ads. The DNC made heavy use of these ads in the fall of 1995 in order to frame the upcoming election and throughout the spring and summer of 1996 (while Dole was out of money). The RNC stepped in to assist the Dole campaign by running issue ads between the end of the primary season and the convention. Produced by each candidate's media consultants and firms, these issue ads were "indistinguishable from the commercials the Dole and Clinton campaigns produced for themselves."[44] It was noted in Chapter 1 that the content of political ads is outside the scope of this book, but examples here will be instructive in order to illustrate how closely "issue" ads resemble candidate campaign ads; see Text Box 5.1.

Table 5.5 gives some idea of the magnitude of issue advocacy spending by showing the amounts of money spent in selected states on issue ads in the prenomination period of 1996.

Campaign Finance in France

Campaign finance in France was, until recently, a much less transparent affair than in the United States. As mentioned in Chapter 3, much

Text Box 5.1
Political Party "Issue" Ads: Two Examples from 1996

Democratic National Committee Ad, "Finish"	Republican National Committee Ad, "More"*
Announcer:	**Announcer:**
"Head start. Student loans. Extra police. Anti-drug programs. Dole-Gingrich wanted them cut. Now they're safe. Protected in the '96 budget because the President stood firm. Dole-Gingrich? Deadlock. Gridlock. Shutdowns. The President's plan? Finish the job. Balance the budget. Reform welfare. Cut taxes. Protect Medicare. President Clinton says, get it done. Meet our challenges. Protect our values."	"Did you know there are over five million illegal immigrants in the U.S.? And that you spend five and a half billion dollars a year to support them with welfare, food stamps, and other services? Under President Clinton, spending on illegals has gone up. While wages for the typical worker have gone down. And when efforts were made to stop giving benefits to illegal immigrants, Bill Clinton opposed them. Tell President Clinton to stop giving benefits to illegals, and end wasteful Washington spending."

* "Finish" was released on May 6, 1996; "More," on June 20, 1996.
Source: Brooks Jackson (1997:237).

campaign finance in France prior to 1988 was illicit—there were campaign finance scandals literally every few months.[45] It was not until 1988 that any official accounting of party and candidate fund raising and spending was done. Certainly modern-style presidential electioneering in France, as in the United States, costs more money. Estimates suggest, for example, that Jean Lecanuet's 1965 "modern-style campaign" cost four to five times as much as François Mitterand's more traditional-style campaign.[46] So, although "the information we have before 1988 is hypothetical . . . all the estimations go in the same direction." Put simply, presidential campaigns in France have become "infinitely more expensive."[47]

French political parties have several sources of revenue. First, they levy elected public officials for regular dues. For example, in 1986 Socialist Party members of parliament were levied $1,256 per month, which amounted to $4.4 million for the party that year.[48] Members of political parties in France (as in most political parties in Europe) pay annual dues; for instance, membership dues for the Rally for the Republic (RPR) were around $31 in 1990–91.[49] Between 1990 and 1992 dues from elected officials and members accounted for roughly 15 percent of total (reported) party revenues for the RPR. Overall revenues for the party have increased of late, in part due to the party's direct mail program (inspired by American parties) which raised better than $30 million from 1984 to 1990, based on a donor base of 250,000 (a "hard core" of 80,000).[50] It is safe to assume that the finances of the RPR are at least passingly similar to those of the other major French parties. In all, budgets for political parties in France have risen dramatically in the past 20 to 30 years. Unofficial estimates suggest that party spending by the Socialists and the RPR doubled, and perhaps tripled, in the 1980s.[51]

Table 5.5
Political Party Issue Advocacy Spending in the Prenomination Period, 1996

Democrats	Expenditures	Republicans	Expenditures
California	$4,156,092	California	$4,018,821
Pennsylvania	3,809,470	Pennsylvania	1,735,443
Florida	3,578,159	Illinois	1,553,663
Ohio	2,984,535	Ohio	1,295,910
Michigan	2,647,529	Tennessee	946,688
Washington	1,910,807	Georgia	839,699
Illinois	1,857,482	Washington	684,000
Wisconsin	1,470,784	Missouri	661,980
Minnesota	1,401,058	Colorado	496,485
Colorado	1,258,217	Iowa	420,720
Oregon	1,115,941	Michigan	346,260
Missouri	1,113,584	New Mexico	332,393

Source: Common Cause, Letter to the Honorable Janet Reno, October 9, 1996, from Anthony
Corrado (1997:148, Table 4.3).

As in the United States, France provides public funds for elections and much of this money goes to political parties. The formula for public funding is two-part: 50 percent of total public funding is distributed based on the number of votes a party receives in the election and the other 50 percent is distributed according to the number of seats a party receives in (both houses of) parliament. Table 5.6 shows the distribution of public funding to parties in 1995.

Since a good proportion of public money in France is channeled to parties, it might seem that campaign finance laws would drive candidates to their parties for money.[52] Not so. The overall "paucity of organizational and financial resources available" to parties provides little incentive for candidates to look to them for financing,[53] and parties are only one possible source of funding for presidential aspirants. Of the slightly better than $15 million spent by Jacques Chirac and François Mitterand in 1988,[54] for example, only about $6 million came from their parties.[55] French presidential candidates also receive public funding based on a three-tiered plan. In 1995 any candidate who appeared on the first ballot but received less than 5 percent of the vote was entitled to $1.1 million; if they received greater than 5 percent on the first ballot the figure jumped to $5.1 million. The two candidates who made it to the second ballot could claim up to $6.8 million in state funds.[56]

Candidates can accept donations from individuals and, like in the United States, there is a cap set on the amount a person can contribute to a presidential candidate. In 1995 that limit was set at $4,710 (for the sake of accounting, contributions of over $157 are required to be made by check). A new twist to campaign finance laws in France allows pres-

Table 5.6
Public Funding to French Political Parties in 1995 (in Millions of Dollars)

	Public Funding Based on (Thousands of Votes)	Public Funding Based on (Members of Parliament)	Total
Rally for the Republic	$9.2 (5203)	$16.2 (345)	$25.4
Union of French Democrats	8.6 (4830)	15.9 (337)	24.5
Socialist Party	8.3 (4704)	6.1 (129)	14.4
French Communists	4.0 (2253)	1.7 (36)	5.7
National Front	5.6 (3153)	0 (0)	5.6
Other Parties	3.5 (1972)	1.1 (23)	4.6

Source: Irène Hill (1997:91).

idential candidates, who are not allowed to buy television time to campaign, to advertise for contributions in the press. In 1995 many did so in the major newspapers, including Prime Minister Edouard Balladur and Lionel Jospin. Candidates can also raise money by way of loans and the sales of campaign paraphernalia at public rallies. Finally, most analysts agree that illegal donations (from individuals, businesses, and unions) have not ceased entirely.[57]

Some patterns can be seen in French presidential candidate finance in 1995. Candidates generally approached the raising of needed campaign funds in one of three ways, relying mainly on either the state, their party, or the contributions of individuals. Table 5.7 shows this by listing the percentage of total funds a candidate received from a given source; interestingly, the eventual winner, Jacques Chirac, received only 1 percent of his finances from his party.

Unlike in the United States, spending limits were *lowered* for the 1995 presidential election. In 1988 the spending limits were $18.8 million for first-round candidates, $25.1 million for second-round candidates;[58] officially reported expenditures were roughly $15.2 million each for François Mitterand and Jacques Chirac (actual figures were almost certainly much higher).[59] In 1995 spending limits were lowered to $14.1 million for first-round candidates and $18.8 million for second-round candidates. As it happened, few reached the spending limits. Chirac (a second-round candidate) and Balladur (a first-round candidate) came close to their limits, spending 97 percent and 93 percent, respectively. The other second-round candidate, Jospin, spent 73 percent of the limit, a reflection of the fact that his was only a three and a half month campaign. One other candidate spent slightly over half of the limit (Hue, at 54 percent), and the remainder spent less than half, probably a problem with resource

Table 5.7
French Presidential Candidate Fund-Raising Strategies, 1995

Mainly State-financed		Mainly Party-financed		Mainly Individual-financed
Lionel Jospin	49%	Lionel Jospin	45%	Jacques Chirac 60%
Robert Hue	66	Philippe de Villiers	51	
Jean Marie Le Pen	78			
Dominique Voynet	91			
Arlette Laguiller	95			
Jacques Cheminade	99			

Source: Irène Hill (1997:96).

gathering rather than with thrift (it should also be remembered that the official campaign period is only a few weeks long in France).

Before we close this section on campaign finance in France there are two aspects of campaign finance in France that very closely resemble the picture in the United States. First, candidates seem to be able to find and exploit loopholes in campaign finance laws in France as well. Somewhat analogous to pre-candidacy PAC activity in the United States, "great sums are spent by presidential aspirants without any accountability whatsoever prior to the official campaign."[60] This is done, undoubtedly, to get a head start on the campaign (another report backs this up, noting that presidential aspirants commission polls months in advance of the election season).[61] Second, although paid political advertising on television is banned in France, advertising consumes much of the campaign budget. In 1995 seven of the nine first-round candidates spent more on advertising (in all media) than anything else, and three of them spent more than half of their total budget on it.[62]

Campaign Finance in Russia

There are only a few relevant facts about campaign finance in the Russian presidential election of 1996. First and foremost, the laws were not enforced at all. This is not as unusual as it may seem to Western observers, since few laws in Russia are, in the Western sense, enforced. Russia is (at best) still in the embryonic stages of becoming a law-governed society. Second, Yeltsin was in almost complete control of the financial resources of the campaign. Since the major fear in Russia (as elsewhere) was that a victory by the Communist Party would spell a return to an authoritarian political system and a command economy, Yeltsin unsurprisingly attracted the support of virtually every major business in Russia, including all of the major banks. Not only did Yeltsin reap this support directly (in the form of several hundreds of millions of dollars in illicit contributions), he also prevented others from being able to raise needed campaign funds.

One exception to this was the campaign of General Aleksander Lebed whose finances benefited from his arrangement to support the president in the second round of voting. Though Lebed initially had few financial resources, his electoral pact with the president gave him access to, and support from, Yeltsin's financial backers.[63] Yeltsin also gave Lebed the opportunity to appear on network television, making Lebed's candidacy somewhat unique in that regard as well. Another exception was the campaign of Vladimir Zhirinovsky, which "appeared to be financially well endowed; only Yeltsin and Lebed outspent him on television advertisements."[64]

In sum, modern presidential electioneering costs a great deal of money, far more money than traditional presidential electioneering did. Candidates and parties are in a continual struggle to raise more money and are largely successful. The process of raising and spending these ever-increasing sums of money is now far more transparent due to campaign finance regulations, but this fact has not eliminated illicit campaign finance in France and Russia and creative ways to get around these laws in the United States.

NON-MONETARY RESOURCES

As crucial as money is, other resources—some of which can be acquired with money, some which cannot—can be equally important to the presidential electioneering effort. To illustrate, recall that in the traditional era, party discipline, which could not be purchased, was the wellspring of most, if not all, electioneering resources. We look at four types of resources in this section: physical resources, mainly campaign headquarters; information, about one's opponent, one's self, or the electorate; human resources, or allies; and finally, a rather amorphous category labeled political capital which includes presidential (or vice-presidential) incumbency, endorsements of other political leaders, and stature. The discussion in this section will be more qualitatively oriented and in some cases (e.g., in the case of stature) will be strictly impressionistic and speculative.

Physical Resources

Both major parties in the United States have a large physical plant, maintaining impressive national offices in Washington. The benefits a national headquarters brings to the electioneering effort are obvious. They provide a location for fund-raising events; meetings with candi-

102 Modern Presidential Electioneering

Table 5.8
Out-party Candidate Organizations, 1976–92: Numbers of States (as of
January 31 of the Election Year)

1976 (Democrats)							
Wallace, George	12	Bentsen, Lloyd	8	Bayh, Birch	4	Shapp, Milton	2
Jackson, Henry	9	Carter, Jimmy	8	Shriver, Sargent	4	Church, Frank	1
Udall, Morris	9	Harris, Fred	4				
1980 (Republicans)							
Reagan, Ronald	25	Connally, John	15	Crane, Phillip	8	Dole, Robert	2
Bush, George	19	Baker, Howard	10	Anderson, John	7		
1984 (Democrats)							
Mondale, Walter	18	Glenn, John	13	McGovern, George	5	Hollings, Ernest	3
Jackson, Jesse	15	Hart, Gary	8	Cranston, Alan	4	Askew, Reubin	2
1988 (Democrats)							
Jackson, Jesse	22	Gore, Albert	13	Simon, Paul	7	Hart, Gary	2
Dukakis, Michael	18	Gephardt, Richard	9	Babbit, Bruce	5		
1992 (Democrats)							
Brown, Edmund	18	Clinton, William	8	Kerrey, Bob	8	Tsongas, Paul	2
Harkin, Tom	10						

Source: Randall Adkins (1995:36).

dates, strategists, journalists, and allied groups; campaign research efforts; party records; and not least, for a permanent staff to work. They
also house what have, for each party, evolved into extremely sophisticated communications centers, including radio and television studios
and their own World Wide Web sites.[65] Both parties also boast of year-
round organizations in the states, not the case even as late as the 1960s
when state party "headquarters" was often the home or office of the state
party chair. In addition, many (if not the majority of) local party organizations now maintain permanent headquarters as well.[66]

One of several strategic decisions candidates face in preparation for
the primary season is deciding in which states to build organizations
with the limited funds they have. The commitment to set up physical
headquarters in a given state means that the candidate considers that
state important enough to expend scarce resources toward that end. We
know that in 1996 the Clinton campaign had, at various times, field offices in 35 different states (see Chapter 4). Like levels of staffing of state
candidate organizations (Table 4.4), there is a great deal of variance in
the number of states in which candidates build organizations, and similar factors explain this variance (level of intra-party competition, which
primaries are coming up and how important they are, how the candidate
and his opponents are faring at the moment, how much money is available, and more). See Table 5.8 for the number of states with out-party

Table 5.9

Out-party Candidate Organizations, 1976–92: A Summary (as of January 31 of the Election Year)

Year	Candidate	Number of Staff	State Offices
1976 (Democrats)	**Carter, Jimmy**	**188**	**8**
	Wallace, George	112	12
1980 (Republicans)	Connally, John	321	15
	Reagan, Ronald	**300**	**29**
1984 (Democrats)	**Mondale, Walter**	**337**	**18**
	Glenn, John	112	13
1988 (Democrats)	**Dukakis, Michael**	**314**	**18**
	Simon, Paul	198	7
1992 (Democrats)	**Clinton, William**	**129**	**8**
	Harkin, Tom	129	10
	Kerrey, Bob	127	8

candidate organizations as of January 31 of the election year from 1976 to 1992.

Another reason for the variability in the data in Table 5.8 is that candidates, at least better known candidates, are often able to supplement their own operations with those of the state party organizations in states where they have received endorsements from party leaders. So, for example, George Bush's 1988 effort was given a substantial boost from the backing of state party organizations in New Hampshire, South Carolina, and Illinois. Georgia Governor Zell Miller lent his party organization's support to candidate Bill Clinton in 1992, and Bob Dole benefited from party organizational efforts in New York, South Carolina, and several New England states in 1996.[67] But to make the point again, it is difficult to make many meaningful statements about these data other than to note that the more successful aspirants were more likely to have headquarters in more states. However, if we combine the data from Tables 4.4 and 5.8, we see that the eventual nominee in each election cycle had the greatest number of either staff or state offices (see Table 5.9; nominee is in bold).

One final note with respect to physical resources. Rapid advances in technology in the past few decades have made these technologies more available and affordable, facilitating rapid communication (faxes, email) between different parts of the country as well as helping campaign teams organize and manage their many tasks, data, and so forth with the use of powerful desktop computer technologies. This latter has had a profound impact on electioneering. Simply put, computers have "colonized every level of the campaign process,"[68] making it possible for candidates to do "in house" many of the tasks (e.g., management of extremely large databases) that they formerly turned over to vendors.[69]

As mentioned in Chapter 4, the major French parties have permanent headquarters from which to conduct party business and electioneering activity. Main headquarters are found in Paris, but the major parties maintain local offices as well, although these are often less well-funded.[70] In addition, like their counterparts in the United States, French presidential candidates typically have their own headquarters and offices, often more than one. In 1988, for example, both Mitterand and Chirac had staff at their government offices (president and prime minister, respectively) and at party headquarters as well; these latter were responsible for campaign coordination with branch offices. In addition to official offices, the campaigns often utilized apartments rented for the duration of the campaign.[71] In 1995 Chirac maintained multiple offices for the campaign, and Lionel Jospin, taking the lead from Mitterand (for whom he had worked as head of the campaign in 1988), maintained a campaign headquarters separate from the Socialist Party.[72] What little information we have, in other words, indicates clearly that like American presidential candidates, French presidential candidates rely heavily on their own physical plant as well as those of their parties in the quest for the presidency.

In Russia the distribution of physical resources was more equitable between the Yeltsin and Zyuganov camps than in campaign finance. Here the advantages of a large and highly organized political party were clear. The Russian Communists and the Zyuganov team had cultivated and re-invigorated the regional bases of power inherited from the Soviet era (which had not completely withered away) in preparation for the 1995 elections to the Duma.[73] The end result was a "rich network of regional offices"[74] of which they were able to make use.

When we look at Yeltsin's campaign we see incumbent advantages that make what we are accustomed to in the United States pale in comparison. Yeltsin's main campaign team(s) occupied better than four floors of the exclusive President Hotel, owned by the office of the president.[75] In addition, most of Russia's 89 regions had up to four separate Yeltsin campaign headquarters, and local government offices also served as unofficial Yeltsin satellite campaign offices. In fact, observing Yeltsin's "pork machine" campaign politics (more on this below), one analyst observed that some regional campaign headquarters "doubled as patronage machines reminiscent of Tammany Hall."[76] Finally, it was clearly to President Yeltsin's advantage that he had access to, and control of, the presidential jet, while Gennadi Zyuganov had to contend with Aeroflot for his transportation needs.[77]

Information

This section explores the control of three types of crucial campaign information: information about the electorate, about one's opponent and his or her activities, and about one's self. Information about the electorate has evolved into a large and sophisticated database industry by which voters, donors, and volunteers (real or potential) can be reached. This is increasingly important as campaigns move from "broadcasting" toward "narrowcasting," the targeting of select groups with specialized appeals as opposed to blanketing a national audience with a generic message. "Big used to be beautiful in political communication, but not anymore, now that targeting small, some would say exotic, audiences allows communicators to put exactly the right information into the right hands at the right time."[78] Information about the electorate is increasingly sophisticated and increasingly available; its increased availability makes it less expensive, but its increased sophistication increases the importance of the consultants needed to manipulate it.[79]

Information about the opposition is also important in political campaigns (to return to the military metaphor, similar to military intelligence). James Farley, manager of Franklin Roosevelt's first two campaigns, took opposition research to what at that time was a new level with a research team that processed as many as 15,000 newspaper clippings from around the country every day into usable reports for the candidate.[80] Both major parties in the United States now have large research divisions which expand considerably during election years. In addition, candidates have their own research teams, some very sophisticated. In 1992 and 1996 the Clinton campaign organization had a world-class team which processed polling data and information about his opponents, providing Clinton with reports at lightning speed. They also kept the media abreast of Clinton's positions. For example, while the major networks were still assessing the first presidential debate, the Clinton team was faxing the media "his" rebuttal to Dole's remarks.[81]

Controlling information about yourself, your message, and your activities is far more difficult in modern presidential electioneering. While candidates are in control of the content of their paid advertising, they have far less to say about how the news media treats them and their message. And there is no way to get completely around the scrutiny of the news media, which is so intense that it probably serves as a disincentive for some potential presidential aspirants to consider a candidacy (e.g., Colin Powell in 1996). Media scrutiny can damage a campaign. In 1968 Richard Nixon let early Republican front-runner George Romney take center stage; Romney, being a less well-known name, needed the exposure. Nixon took a back seat and waited, convinced that in the end the exposure would backfire on Romney, which it did. Nixon's "handlers," in short, kept the press at bay, at the same time telling them that their candidate was a "new" man. In 1972 Nixon took this strategy even further, avoiding the national news media almost entirely.[82]

Nixon had learned that the news media is an exceptionally powerful kingmaker in an era of television and primary elections and his 1972 campaign set a precedent for most campaigns to follow. From then on, candidates have limited and controlled the press' access to the candidate. This strategy works well. One analyst noted that in 1988, "the less accessible candidate (Bush) was better able to communicate his message than the more accessible one (Dukakis); the kinder and gentler rewards of victory went to the nominee who was better able to keep the pesky media at bay."[83] The Bush team understood the rules of the game better than the Dukakis campaign; they kept Bush so far away from reporters that some resorted to using binoculars and megaphones to try and see and communicate with the candidate.[84]

Candidates increasingly try to find ways to get their message out without the mediation (in their eyes, distortion) of the news media. Another popular way to circumvent the news media is using what is referred to as "new" media, or talk, variety, and entertainment shows (both television and radio). Nixon had used this strategy as early as 1968, appearing on the "Tonight Show with Johnny Carson" and "Rowan and Martin's Laugh-in"; similarly, John Anderson appeared on "Saturday Night Live" in 1980.[85] Attracted by the fact that new media conveys their message unadulterated by newscasters and analysts, candidates used this strategy heavily in 1992 (and somewhat less so in 1996). Hosts of these programs are less likely to take adversarial stances in their discussions with the candidates, thus making it a far more attractive venue. Additionally, candidates often reach audiences whom they might otherwise miss with appearances on these shows. Ross Perot, for example, announced his candidacy in both 1992 and 1996 on "Larry King Live"; Clinton appeared on the "Arsenio Hall Show" in full Blues Brothers garb playing the saxophone. Finally, the Internet has opened up a completely new medium of communication, one in which candidates can retain complete and absolute control over their message (at least on their own sites).[86]

Patterns of control over information in France follow those in the United States fairly closely. Parties, candidates, and consultants are making greater use of a growing body of increasingly sophisticated information about actual and potential voters, donors, and volunteers. The growth of the polling industry in France helps illustrate this (see Table 5.10). It is also safe to surmise that, unlike in the United States, those presidential candidates already in public office make great use of their offices to access whatever information about the electorate that the government may have compiled.[87]

Table 5.10
Formation of Polling Firms in France

Year Founded	Name	Director(s)
1938	IFOP	Jean Luc Parodi, Laurence Parisot
1963	SOFRES	Jérôme Jaffré
1970	BVA	Pierre Giacometti
1975	IPSOS	Jean Marc Lech
1977	Harris France	Philippe Mechet, Jérôme St Marie
1979	IFRES	Dominique Genée
1980	Faits et Opinions	Jean François Tchernia
1985	CSA	Roland Cayrol

Source: Irène Hill (1997).

The Russian media was favorably disposed to the incumbent president Yeltsin in their coverage of the 1996 presidential election. This was no accident since the media was pressured throughout the campaign by a Yeltsin "heavy squad . . . to give positive coverage to the president and to ignore or attack his opponents."[88] One analyst claimed that "Yeltsin's most cherished campaign resource was his monopolistic control over all three national television stations."[89] Anecdotes and examples of media bias throughout the campaign abound. The president of one of the national television networks was a member of Yeltsin's campaign team[90]; journalists were paid to cover the president favorably[91]; on the last day of the media campaign Russian Television "broadcast a lengthy interview with President Boris Yeltsin . . . [who was] helped along by friendly questioning." At the close, "the interviewer . . . wished Yeltsin 'victory, victory, and victory.' "[92] Around election day Russian Television aired a highly touted and award-winning film about Stalin's purges ("Burnt by the Sun") and another about the Bolshevik murder of the Tsar Nicholas' family; another network aired a two-part documentary about the activities of the secret police between 1917 and 1953.[93] These films were designed to evoke negative memories of Communist rule which would (it was assumed) be associated with Yeltsin's opponent Gennadi Zyuganov.

After General Lebed brokered his deal with Yeltsin to support the president in the second round, he received some media support. The European Institute for the Media concluded that "Lebed was the only candidate besides Boris Yeltsin that received more favorable than unfavorable coverage on television."[94] Zyuganov did receive some favorable media coverage, mainly from the less centrally controlled local media.[95] But Stephen White and his colleagues summed up campaign coverage of the 1996 presidential election in Russia well: "Control of state administration gave Yeltsin campaigners generous mass media coverage, the use of government telecommunications and travel facilities, and oppor-

Table 5.11
Growth in the Number of PACs, 1974–96

Year	1974	1976	1978	1980	1982	1984	1986	1988	1990	1992	1996
Number of PACs	608	1146	1653	2551	3371	4009	4157	4268	4172	4195	4079

Source: Margaret Conway and Joanne Greene (1995:157, Table 7.1); 1996 information from
   the FEC <http://www.fec.gov>.

tunities for stage-managed events."[96] The effects of media control by
Yeltsin cannot be overestimated; it would be difficult to believe that it
had no effect on the outcome of the election.

Human Resources: Supporting Groups and Allies

This section examines allies and potential allies of candidates and parties during the presidential campaign. Specifically, it deals with growth
in the number of independent groups and who they are allying with,
contributing to, and working for. In the past, groups worked almost
exclusively through political parties; now, they are just as likely to align
directly with candidates.

There has been a virtual explosion in the United States of interest
groups and their PACs in the modern era of presidential electioneering,
mainly due to campaign finance laws which regulate interest giving to
campaigns. The number of PACs has grown almost seven-fold from 1974
to 1996 (see Table 5.11). Fewer than 1–2 percent of presidential candidates' hard money contributions come from PACs,[97] but PACs contribute
heavily to parties, and this money goes to the campaign effort through
the soft money conduit referred to in the previous section. Both political
parties have institutionalized their relationships with interest groups and
PACs in recent years, helping to arrange fund-raising events and providing information to PACs to channel needed resources to critical
states.[98]

Other independent groups have entered the electoral arena as well. In
the 1980s many (mainly ideological) groups began advertising directly
on behalf of the candidate. For example, in 1984 (the high point), $16.3
million was spent by various groups on behalf of Reagan (or against
Mondale); $1.2 million was spent for Mondale (or against Reagan). In-
dependent expenditures have declined of late (a little over $4 million in
1992), but the pattern of Republican backers outspending Democratic
supporters persists.[99] It should be noted that this type of support risks
alienating the more moderate center of the electorate since it typically
comes from the more hard-core extremes of the party; as such, it is often
unwelcome.

Another development in the modern era is the increased amount of campaigning carried out by ad hoc citizen groups (e.g., Citizens for Kennedy, Volunteers for Nixon, Democrats for Eisenhower, Republicans for Johnson).[100] There were, of course, "candidate clubs" similar to these groups in the traditional era, but those groups were mobilized by the party. Now candidates mobilize these volunteer efforts themselves; examples of this abound. Eugene McCarthy and George McGovern both recruited heavily from college campuses in 1968 and 1972; Jimmy Carter's Georgian "Peanut Brigade" followed him on the campaign trail in 1976; Jesse Jackson relied heavily on volunteers recruited through churches in 1984 and 1988; Pat Buchanan received a great deal of support from committed conservative followers, especially in caucus states where these supporters could participate directly. In 1988 Pat Robertson's campaign effort rested on the assumption that the three million people who signed petitions to convince him to run would be an active source of support throughout the campaign.

Democrats can typically rely on the support of organized labor who, as a group, are increasingly active in campaign politics. For example, the 1980 Democratic National Convention had the largest single-interest group delegation in history with 302 members of the National Education Association serving as delegates.[101] The intensity of labor support during the campaign depends to some extent on the candidate: for Walter Mondale it was very strong; for the "New Democrat" Bill Clinton, less so.[102] In point of fact, the Democrat's relationship with organized labor is one that seems to be becoming a double-edged sword. The more moderate wing of the party has backed away somewhat from being too closely associated with organized labor, convinced that their involvement in politics is perceived negatively by many Americans.

In France the alliances that matter most are the party alliances made after the first round of balloting. Typically this means that the Communists support the Socialist candidate (it has never been the other way around) while the two main parties of the right support whichever candidate of theirs makes it to the second round. This arrangement, however, cannot be assumed, and it sometimes means assuring prominent members of the coalition party a place in the new administration. Mitterand, for example, brought several Communists into government after his victory in 1981 (which created a minor stir, being the first time they had been represented in government).

There is a long tradition in France of candidates enlisting the aid of independent groups (*comités de soutien,* or support committees), especially in runoffs between two candidates of the same party. Impressionistic and anecdotal evidence points to an increased importance of these alliances in campaign politics.[103] For example, although the 1981 campaign of Valéry Giscard d'Estaing was organized and run "mainly from the Elysée and from his personal headquarters . . . his local campaign was often placed in the hands of comités de soutien."[104] Mitterand's success (indeed the success of any Socialist candidate) in 1981 and 1988 depended in no small measure on the support of organized labor, which is much more institutionally tied to the party than we are accustomed to in the United States.

It is probably unfair to examine coalition formation and allies in Russia for the presidential election of 1996 because, in a sense, the election was a national referendum on the future of the Russian regime. By the time second-round voting took place, the various political forces in Russia had for the most part coalesced into reform and anti-reform camps.[105] To simplify the story, suffice it to say that the mobilized interests favoring reform outnumbered those who did not. Yeltsin supporters (pro-reform) came from almost all sectors, and perhaps most critically from the business sector. As previously noted, "every major corporation or bank in Russia backed the president" either formally or informally.[106] A major turning point in the campaign came in the spring when rival businessmen and media magnates Vladimir Gusinski and Boris Berezovski reconciled their differences in order to help re-elect the president.[107] Yabloko also backed the president, albeit indirectly (saying it could not support Zyuganov, nor could it ask its supporters to say "no to both," an option on Russian ballots that is a holdover from the Soviet era).[108]

The Communists showed their impressive organizational strength in enlisting allies. After the 1993 elections they had worked to strengthen trade organizations and unions as well as other sympathetic groups and reactivated the Komsomol (the youth wing of the old party).[109] Zyuganov could also count on the support of the Agrarian Party whose alliance with the Communists strengthened his rural support base[110] and various smaller parties and associations. With former Soviet prime minister Nikolai Ryzhkov, Zyuganov brought these forces together in a "Bloc of National and Patriotic Forces, a coalition of nationalist and communist forces" which comprised a total of 136 organizations.[111] Many trade unions gave their support to Zyuganov, though a few of the more hardline ones refused, highlighting Zyuganov's difficulties in positioning himself as a middle-of-the-road presidential candidate.

Political Capital

This rather vague category of non-monetary resources includes three different dimensions. The first, incumbency, is fairly easy to define. Presidential incumbency brings with it several advantages. An incumbent, especially in the modern age of media scrutiny, has a national platform from which to campaign. Virtually everything the president does in a given day is potential "news," and incumbent presidents make great use of this fact, employing the ceremonial powers of the office (meeting heads of state, honoring military or civilian leaders), assured that their image will be seen by millions that night. Presidents can also use the office to curry favor with particular blocs of voters by dispensing aid, grants, contracts, and so forth. They must, of course, use caution in doing this because potential exists for such moves to backfire if they are perceived as being obviously partisan. Finally, popularity for an incumbent can be an enormous help in securing other resources. For example, in 1996 Clinton spent only $4.6 million to raise $37 million (the limit) in primary season funding (Dole spent $10 million raising the same amount).[112]

Incumbency is the ultimate resource in seeking the party nomination. Although sitting presidents in the modern era are sometimes challenged for their party's nomination (Ted Kennedy challenged Jimmy Carter in 1980; Pat Buchanan challenged George Bush in 1992), every incumbent president who has sought renomination in the modern era has received it. In fact, George Bush used his vice-presidency as a resource, seeking his party's nomination based on the record of the outgoing administration. But vice-presidents are often in a bind in this respect. Many of the advantages of presidential incumbency are theirs, if to a lesser extent (e.g., the national platform), but they often have to try and distance themselves from any objectionable aspects of the previous administration. Richard Nixon faced this dilemma in 1960; more recently, Al Gore, who has enjoyed the fruits of an increasingly visible and public vice-presidency as well as being acknowledged from the beginning of the Clinton administration as the heir-apparent, will be faced with the same problem (Gore was already distancing himself from certain aspects of the Clinton presidency as early as June of 1999).

A second aspect of political capital involves the endorsements of other political leaders. As discussed briefly above, endorsements from governors and other elected officials can make a huge difference in a campaign, opening the door for other critical resources (staff, volunteer networks, office space) to flow into the campaign. Bob Dole's primary victory in South Carolina, for example, has been attributed to his endorsement by former Governor Carroll Campbell, Jr., Senator Strom Thurmond, and Governor David Beasley. Support from Beasley was especially important because of his ties to the religious right, a conservative group of voters who made up roughly a third of that state's primary voters.[113] Endorsements can also bring other, more intangible benefits to a campaign. For example, Jack Kemp's endorsement of outsider Steve Forbes in March of 1996 lent a certain credibility to the Forbes candidacy.

Endorsements for the Republican nomination of 2000 began taking shape very early. By March of 1999 nearly half of the country's 31 Republican governors had officially endorsed George W. Bush, and nearly

100 elected leaders had made the trek to Texas to see the governor at his home and express support.[114] By late June Bush had the endorsement of 115 House members and 20 Senators[115]; he also received the support of John Kasich, an early entrant in the presidential race who withdrew his candidacy in July. The full effects of these numerous early endorsements have yet to be seen,[116] but it is hard to believe that there will not be some effect on the emergence or vitality of other candidacies, and it is almost certainly the case that Bush will benefit from the organizational ties of these elected officials.

Stature, the final dimension of political capital, is the least easily defined. One recent work perhaps described it best:

So what do we mean by "stature"? We find it a bit like obscenity: We're not sure we can define it, but we know it when we see it. For lack of a better definition, stature is a combination of high-level experience in public affairs, an even temperament, and a general air of political gravitas.[117]

Stature is not altogether dissimilar to Bryce's notion of presidential "availability." In the first instance it determines, if only in a general way, how credible an individual's candidacy will be with the general public. In this sense, trying to determine an individual's stature is hardly more than a guessing game, but one that can be played with some degree of certainty, at least with the obvious choices. Bob Dole had stature in the 1996 presidential race; Colin Powell would have if he ran; Pat Buchanan (among others) was probably lacking. Looking to 2000, all of the more prominent names mentioned early have stature: Bill Bradley, Al Gore, George W. Bush, Elizabeth Dole. It is simply easier to imagine certain people occupying the office of the presidency than others, and this is the bottom line with respect to stature. Beyond public perception, stature is a great help in securing endorsements from other political leaders, who doubtless include stature in their calculus along with other, more "practical" political concerns.

As might be expected, what constitutes political capital in France and Russia varies in many ways from the United States, and from each other. The post of prime minister is especially important for those with presidential aspirations in France and Russia, giving an individual easily as much national visibility as a president; being the mayor of each country's capital city does the same.

Incumbency also brings advantages to a presidential candidacy in both countries. Yeltsin made shameless use of his office in his campaign effort, making 33 trips throughout Russia in four months of campaigning, at each stop dispensing federal aid.[118] This aid often took the form of payment of back wages to state workers; sometimes it was federal funding to the regions, an effort to sway regional governors to his side; and sometimes it took the form of a publicized personal gesture, like promising (and delivering) a car to an ordinary citizen in Vorkuta. Appealing to both Russian and Soviet nationalism and "in a bid to win the support of veterans," the president decreed on April 16 that the red Soviet-era victory flag would henceforth serve (alongside the Russian tricolor) as an "official symbol for ceremonies marking the victory over Nazi Germany."[119] A newly decreed Russian holiday (June 12), marking the date of Russia's first presidential election, was a thinly veiled ploy to hold a pre-election rally in Moscow.[120] Other examples abound.

Endorsements in each country are also important, not only from political leaders, but from the academic community as well (a different set of professional ethics within the academy as well as a political culture that places greater stock in an intellectual class accounts for the difference between the United States and France and Russia in this regard). In Russia in 1996 it mattered a great deal that General Lebed allied with Yeltsin; there, great stock is placed in military leaders. Yeltsin, in fact, received endorsements from all sectors of society, including Aleksii II, Patriarch of the Orthodox Church; the widow of Chechen leader Dzhokar Dudaev (an ethnic Russian); leaders from all the member-states of the Commonwealth of Independent States (as well as, more generally, leaders of the Western world); and other public figures (for example, Nikita Mikhailov, who starred in "Burnt by the Sun").[121]

In France, Georges Pompidou benefited greatly from the implicit (only) endorsement of outgoing President de Gaulle in 1969. Withheld endorsements can often cause a great deal of harm to a candidacy (this is true in the United States as well). In 1995, after RPR's Edouard Balladur managed to secure the nomination of the Union for French Democrats, UDF founder Giscard d'Estaing took his "revenge" on Balladur by supporting RPR's Jacques Chirac in the election.[122]

Finally, what constitutes stature is somewhat different in France and Russia. Both countries are more apt to identify with a strong leader. So it was in France that de Gaulle was seen as France's savior; similarly, Yeltsin benefited greatly from pictures (shown around the world) of him atop a tank defying the putschists in the 1991 coup attempt. (This should not be taken too far, however, as similarities can be seen between the stature of these two leaders and that of George Washington at the beginning of the American Republic.) Further illustrating cultural differences in defining stature, Mikhail Gorbachev, seen by the West as a world leader (*Time* magazine once named him Man of the Year), ran for the presidency in 1996 and while many in the West placed great stock in his candidacy, he polled only 0.5 percent of the first-round vote. Most people in Russia see him as an incompetent who destroyed Russia's greatness. This simply illustrates the point that stature, while important, is not only difficult to define, but is culture-bound as well.

SUMMARY

Resources are increasingly important in presidential electioneering. Parties are better off financially than even a few decades ago, but their official role in modern presidential electioneering in the United States is minimal. Candidates are generally reliant on their own efforts and federal funding to defray campaign costs. From the little qualitative evidence available it seems that a similar situation prevails in both France and Russia. For example, one analyst plainly states that French "candidates make greater uses of their own resources" as opposed to those of their party.[123] This was certainly the case in the Russian presidential election of 1996 where the extraordinary sums of money spent by the incumbent president Yeltsin, sums which dwarfed the spending of all other candidates combined, were raised by his campaign team.

Increasingly greater attention is being paid to the acquisition of nonmonetary resources as well. A physical plant (permanent or temporary headquarters), control of information, and the cultivation of allies are more important not only to parties, but especially to candidates. This is true in all three countries. Political capital is also important. Most analysts would agree with the commonsense but difficult-to-prove notion that a candidate's stature works as a catalyst in the process of resource acquisition; organization and visibility from a previous run for the presidency also is probably helpful.[124]

In Chapter 6 we move to the actual processes and activities of modern presidential electioneering.

6

Electioneering Processes and Activities: The Campaign

INTRODUCTION

Many metaphors and images are used in discussing presidential campaigns, each suggesting a different way to understand presidential selection. For some the process is a candidate-centered "quest" for the presidency, a "marathon" a candidate must endure and win in his "pursuit of the White House"; for others the presidency is the grand prize in an "election game" where presidents are "made" or "sold" to the public; for still others it is a more neutral "road to the White House."[1] In this chapter we look at two final dimensions of modern presidential electioneering, namely, the process of candidate selection and the activities associated with modern presidential campaigns. What becomes clear as we move through the chapter is that there is at least a grain of truth in all of these metaphors.

Because this chapter deals with processes and activities, it is organized according to the various phases of the campaign; but consistent with the rest of the book, the roles that candidates, parties, and campaign professionals play will be noted and highlighted. The first section is devoted to a discussion of candidate recruitment; the second deals with candidate screening and the process by which the field of presidential aspirants is narrowed to one candidate per party. The final section deals with presidential selection, or the general election campaign, examining campaign activity—activity that is, of course, ongoing throughout the entire process. The various activities discussed in this section include strategy (the blueprint for the campaign) and tactics (its implementation), polling, electoral mobilization, and communications.[2]

What becomes evident is that the process of choosing a candidate is structured such that political parties have almost no role other than being a supporting member of the cast. In fact the language we (political scientists) use to describe how an individual goes from citizen to president no longer accurately portrays the process. Candidates "recruit" themselves; by doing well in the primaries and staying flush with cash, they "winnow" and "screen" themselves. The process encourages and rewards organized, efficient, professional self-starters who have an extraordinary amount of money and stamina. Moreover, the art (or science?) of campaigning itself is no longer a matter of conveying a simple message from candidate to citizenry. Candidate communication is an increasingly professional and sophisticated affair, informed by market research, polling and survey data, and executed with almost laser-like precision.

CANDIDATE RECRUITMENT

Candidate Recruitment in the United States: Who Runs for President?

The personal characteristics of presidential candidates in the modern era, as a rule, are only slightly different from those in the traditional era. In the past, only white males were considered viable candidates for the office and only white males have ever secured major-party nominations. This, however, may be changing. In 1984 the Democrats nominated a woman, Geraldine Ferraro, as their vice-presidential candidate, and Elizabeth Dole was at one point considered a top prospect for the Republican presidential nomination in the election of 2000. Virtually all presidents have been Protestant Christians. Although the Democrat Al Smith was the first Catholic to receive his party's nomination (in 1928), it was not until John Kennedy was elected in 1960 that the country selected a Catholic. And it was not until 1988 that one of the major parties nominated someone of other than Northwest European ancestry (Michael Dukakis). Most party nominees also come from the larger states, a significant factor in the November election.[3]

Elected presidents are typically middle-aged: the oldest president when inaugurated was Ronald Reagan (age 69), the youngest, Theodore Roosevelt (age 42). A major concern for the Dole campaign in 1996 was the perception that he was too old (73 at the time), in spite of the fact that he was in good health. The modern system all but demands that presidential candidates of any age be in very good physical condition (and release medical reports to prove it). Indeed, Woodrow Wilson's comment that the system of presidential selection in the United States rewards wise athletes—a small class—is perhaps more apt now than when he made his observation, given the longer campaign season over greater amounts of territory in the modern era. In fact, some claim that the length and brutality of the primary season in the United States helps ensure that quality candidates are selected, since only the very strongest can survive.[4]

Elected presidents are typically married, and married only once. The only bachelor presidents have been James Buchanan and Grover Cleveland, and the only divorced (and remarried) was Ronald Reagan. Marital problems and the like used to be a virtual death knell for a presidential candidacy: Nelson Rockefeller (1964), Gary Hart and Pat Robertson (1988) were all hurt by marital problems or sexual improprieties (alleged or real) in the modern era. It remains to be seen whether Bill Clinton's troubles in this respect have changed public expectations of what level of sexual propriety is appropriate for a president, if indeed it will continue to matter at all.

Little has changed since Bryce made his well-known observation about great candidates (not great men) being chosen president of the United States. Good campaigners, however defined, are more likely to be successful in modern presidential politics. There is a far greater premium in the modern era on a candidate's independent ability to raise money, build and maintain public support, and organize a campaign well (or at least have the good sense to delegate this task to someone who can). In this respect, President Clinton may have been the quintessential presidential candidate. As far as the disposition of modern candidates, increased and constant media scrutiny demands that candidates possess both a thick skin and certain charismatic style (telegenic appearance, speaking ability). Conversely, uncharismatic candidates face an uphill climb (for example, George McGovern, Michael Dukakis, or Robert Dole).

With regard to background and experience, the type of prior governmental experience needed for a successful run for the presidency has changed in the United States. A position that holds the potential for national exposure is increasingly important, though oddly, knowledge of national government seems less so (Jimmy Carter and Bill Clinton come to mind). The United States Senate was a particularly good jumping-off point from 1960 through 1972, when all major-party nominees came from that background (as did Bob Dole in 1996). Governorships have become a good launch pad in the modern era (Ronald Reagan, Jimmy Carter, Michael Dukakis, Bill Clinton); the vice-presidency (past or present) seems to help in securing the party nomination (Richard Nixon, George Bush, Walter Mondale); and, a past run at the presidency seems to help as well (Barry Goldwater, Richard Nixon, George McGovern, Ronald Reagan, George Bush, and Bob Dole).

Table 6.1
Number of Major-Party Candidacies Per Election Cycle, 1960–2000

Year	Out-party Candidacies	In-party Candidacies	Total Per Cycle
1960	5 (Democrat)	3 (Republican)	8
1964	7 (Republican)	2 (Democrat)	9
1968	4 (Republican)	5 (Democrat)	9
1972	13 (Democrat)	3 (Republican)	16
1976	14 (Democrat)	2 (Republican)	16
1980	9 (Republican)	4 (Democrat)	13
1984	9 (Democrat)	1 (Republican)	10
1988	9 (Democrat)	6 (Republican)	15
1992	9 (Democrat)	3 (Republican)	12
1996	11 (Republican)	2 (Democrat)	13
2000	10 (Republican)	2 (Democrat)	12

Note: See Appendix A. Election 2000 data includes all candidates who were listed with the
FEC as of July 15, 1999; see <http://www.opensecrets.org>. By November 1, 1999,
the number of Republican candidacies for Election 2000 had decreased significantly
(by six), mainly due to George W. Bush's extraordinary money-raising success.

How Are Presidential Candidates in the United States Recruited?

Recall that in the traditional era one of the chief considerations in the
determination of an individual to make a run for the White House in
the United States was that individual's position in the party. One had to
have "paid his dues" or "come through the ranks" in order to be seriously considered for the job. This is referred to by some as "apprentice-
style" recruitment, for fairly obvious reasons, and by and large it no
longer prevails.[5] The mode of candidate recruitment that currently prevails is known by some as "entrepreneurial-style."[6] Entry into presidential politics is lateral, meaning less (or no) time working one's way up
the party ladder and/or in government service, dependent only on the
candidate's own efforts and resources. In other words, presidential aspirants are self-appointed; parties now have virtually no role in candidate recruitment.

This has had several effects. First, in spite of the fact that running for
president entails great risk to career, reputation, family, and so on, there
has been a slight increase in the number of candidacies per election cycle.
Table 6.1 counts the number of major-party candidacies per election cycle
from 1960 to 1996 (divided according to in-party and out-party candidacies) and, with the exception of 1984 and 1992 when a popular incumbent president (Reagan in 1984, Bush in 1992) was running for
re-election, shows a slight increase. The increase becomes more apparent
when we compare the elections from 1960 to 1972 and afterward. This

is because 1972 was when the number of direct primaries and the committed delegates chosen from those primaries began to rise, beginning the transition to what is known as the "new" nominating system in presidential politics.

In addition to an increase in the number of candidacies, the pool of modern presidential candidates increasingly consists of entrepreneurial-style candidacies. By this we mean: (1) "unconnected outsiders," or candidates with few party ties prior to the campaign (e.g., Steven Forbes in 1996); (2) "movement" candidates, or those representing factions off the mainstream of the party (e.g., Barry Goldwater in 1964);[7] and (3) "independent" candidates, those not affiliated with a political party (e.g., Ross Perot in 1992) or representing third parties (e.g., Ross Perot and the Reform Party in 1996). Table 6.2 demonstrates that while there has not been a dramatic increase in the number of entrepreneurial-style candidacies since the 1970s, they are now fairly common.

It should be noted that although there has been an increase in non–party-related candidacies, party service still matters and seems to matter more for Republicans, especially of late. For example, it was widely recognized (though still somewhat contentious) that it was Robert Dole's "turn" to receive the Republican party nomination in 1996 (similar to Ronald Reagan in 1980 and George Bush in 1988).[8] This, it must be stressed, does not mean that the party has any official role in the selection of its candidate but affects other intangibles like endorsements, fundraising, and so on.

Candidate Recruitment in France and Russia

Some pattern can be seen in the political background of French presidential candidates. Prior government service, usually at the ministerial level, is important in a run for the presidency; over half of the 15 prime ministers (eight) from 1958 to 1995 have run for the presidency. Party plays a big role in recruitment: indeed, almost all of the second-round candidates and all of the elected presidents have been party leaders (in 1981 the candidate from each of the four main parties was also the party leader). Most candidates from the major parties also come from one of the country's select educational institutes.[9] The more successful candidates have also been prominent in local politics (most often as mayor) and were involved in Fourth Republic politics as well. Almost 20 percent of the candidates (eight) have run for the presidency more than once (see Table 6.3).

How are individuals recruited into presidential politics in France? The phenomenon of "unconnected outsiders" is fairly unknown, but at first glance this seems hard to understand since French presidential candidates exercise a great deal of independence in their decisions to run.

Table 6.2
Entrepreneurial-style Candidacies, 1960–96*

Year / Candidate	Party	Type	Total
1964			
Barry Goldwater	Republican	Movement Candidate	1
1968			
Eugene McCarthy	Democrat	Movement Candidate	1
1972			
George McGovern	Democrat	Movement Candidate	
George Wallace	Democrat	Unconnected Outsider	2
1976			
Ronald Reagan	Republican	Movement Candidate	
George Wallace	Democrat	Unconnected Outsider	
Jimmy Carter	Democrat	Unconnected Outsider	3
1980			
John Anderson	—	Independent Candidate	1
1984			
Jesse Jackson	Democrat	Movement Candidate	
Gary Hart	Democrat	Unconnected Outsider	2
1988			
Jesse Jackson	Democrat	Movement Candidate	
Pat Robertson	Republican	Movement Candidate	2
1992			
Patrick Buchanan	Republican	Unconnected Outsider	
Paul Tsongas	Democrat	Unconnected Outsider	
Edmund Brown	Democrat	Unconnected Outsider	
David Duke	Republican	Unconnected Outsider	
Ross Perot	—	Independent Candidate	5
1996			
Patrick Buchanan	Republican	Movement Candidate	
Steve Forbes	Republican	Unconnected Outsider	
Ross Perot	Reform	Independent Candidate	2

* "Movement candidate" and "unconnected outsider" categories from Andrew Busch (1997: 175).

François Mitterand, for example, was not a member of a political party until 1971. In 1965 he ran for president, "demanding" that groups and parties of the left trust him as a leader and welcoming their endorsement, provided that they not try to "control" him. Similarly, in 1969 Georges Pompidou, anointed by Charles de Gaulle as successor (at least by implication), announced and initiated his own candidacy. He was endorsed by the Gaullists the next day but refused to be bound by their program.[10]

As in the United States, the decision to run for president in France is a matter of political entrepreneurship. French presidential candidates

Table 6.3
Political Background of French Presidential Candidates

	Number of Candidates	Percentage of Candidates	Percentage of 2nd Round Candidates*	Percentage of Winners
Party Leader	22	54%	92%	100%
Parliament	19	46	75	80
Minister	15	37	75	60
Fourth Republic Politics	14	34	75	80
Mayor	13	32	75	60
Prime Minister	8	20	33	60
	(n = 41)	(n = 41)	(n = 12)	(n = 5)

* "2nd Round" is the percentage of times a characteristic was recorded from a total of 12
  second-round candidacies. Mitterand's "yes" scores were therefore counted four times;
  similarly, Chirac and Giscard d'Estaing were counted twice. See Jody Baumgartner
  (1998a:121).

generally "emerge" self-recruited. As one French scholar explains, there
are several strategies by which individuals "emerge" as a viable candidate: by "achieving distinctive electoral success; leading a successful
party revolt; resigning (or threatening to resign) a high position with
éclat; and exploiting one's personality and nonpolitical resources."[11] One
cannot seriously consider running for president without the support of
at least one of the major parties, but increasingly, the party candidate is
also the party leader, placing a premium on influence and position
within the party (see Chapter 4); on the other hand, having a *presidential*
quality helps in becoming party leader.

As in the United States, polling plays an increasingly important role
in candidate recruitment in France. This is probably no accident. Recall
that Theodore White's account of John Kennedy's 1960 campaign, the
first to make systematic use of polling data, was translated into French
in 1961. Since then polling has become a major industry (see Table 5.10).
Alain Poher consulted the SOFRES polling firm before deciding to run
in 1969.[12] The power of polling in the recruitment process was evident
in 1995. The immensely popular Jacques Delors, former head of the European Union Commission and long considered a prime presidential candidate for the Socialists, was being encouraged by the party to run but,
in a situation very similar to that of Colin Powell in the United States in
1996, was eventually forced to publicly declare that he was *not* a candidate because of his immense popularity.[13] Subsequently Henri Emmanuelli (national secretary of the Socialists) lost in his bid to become
the party candidate because polling showed Lionel Jospin to be more

Table 6.4
Number of Major Presidential Candidacies in France, 1965–95

	1965	1969	1974	1981	1988	1995
Number of Candidacies	6	7	12	10	9	11

Note: See Appendix B.

popular. Finally, the RPR's Edouard Balladur, appointed Prime Minister as part of a deal between he and Chirac to *not* run for president in 1995, decided he would do so (as the candidate of the UDF) as the result of positive polling numbers.[14] The major French candidates (Chirac, Jospin, Balladur) reported expenditures of 2–3 percent of their 1995 campaign budgets on polling, a percentage similar to Clinton's and Dole's in 1996 (see Table 5.4).[15]

The number of first-round candidacies in France since 1965 has decreased from a high in 1974 (twelve), but overall shows an upward trend, especially considering that candidacy requirements (mainly in the petition phase) were made more stringent in 1976 (see Table 6.4).

With only one election in Russia to examine no patterns can be discerned with respect to candidate recruitment. However, it is notable that of the 11 candidates in 1996, six were members of the State Duma and nine belonged to a political party. Three candidates were leaders of a major political party (Zyuganov, Yavlinski, and Zhirinovsky), and almost all of them, including Yeltsin, had been members of the Communist Party of the Soviet Union. Examining the field further reveals

- two celebrities (a famous weightlifter, Yuri Vlasov, and a renowned eye surgeon, Svyatoslav Federov);
- a millionaire businessman (Vladimir Bryntsalov);
- an academic (Martin Shakkum);
- a prominent local government official (Aman Tuleev);
- a former chairman of the former Communist Party of the Soviet Union (Gorbachev); and
- a prominent military figure (Lebed).[16]

Candidate Recruitment: The Importance of Early Organization

Candidates must start their electioneering efforts increasingly early in order to obtain the party nomination in the United States. Why? The primary season is becoming ever-shorter.[17] In 2000 the nomination could be decided after the New York and California primaries on March 7. In

Table 6.5
**Early Starts: Out-party Candidates Announcing before June 30 of the Year
before the Presidential Election**

Year	1976	1980	1984	1988	1992	1996	2000
Early Candidacies (Number)	6	5	6	10	1	8	12
Early Candidacies (Percentage of Total)	43%	50	67	71	20	80	—

Source: James Davis (1997:37). Election 2000 data includes all candidates who were listed
   with the FEC as of July 15, 1999; see <http://www.opensecrets.org>.

the modern era, serious presidential aspirants start organizing or planning for the presidential race run immediately after the previous election
is over. Posturing and positioning for election 2000 began immediately
after the 1996 returns between Democrats Richard Gephardt and Al
Gore; Republican Steve Forbes was campaigning virtually non-stop from
January of 1996 on and by January of 1999 had visited all 50 states, given
more than 400 speeches, paid for 60 radio campaigns, and "deluged journalists across the land with tiresome press releases."[18] For most, the race
begins in earnest after the mid-term congressional elections (press coverage of election 2000 early favorites Al Gore and George W. Bush began
appearing as early as November of 1998).[19]

   As noted in the previous chapter, early fund-raising efforts are crucial
to a successful primary season. Since 1980 the amount of money raised
during the year prior to the presidential election year is an almost perfect
predictor of who will become the party nominee (see Table 5.2). Candidates are also announcing their candidacies earlier and earlier. Table 6.5
shows the number and percentage of out-party candidates announcing
their candidacy before June 30 of the year before the presidential election.
In fact, in the modern era, announcing one's candidacy has become a
media story in itself, and relatedly, the importance of early media coverage has led to a new phenomenon, namely, "announcing the announcement" of the candidacy. It is now regular practice to hold a press
conference to announce when the announcement to run will be made,
which generates additional news coverage.[20]

   One final aspect of the pre-primary period are the non-binding straw
polls that parties conduct in some states in the year or two prior to the
election year. Not all states conduct them, but a certain few seem to hold
them with some regularity (Iowa's and Florida's are both regular and
prominent). Often taken at state party conventions, these events sometimes double as fund-raising events and are designed to allow party
faithful to see the presidential aspirants up close and to let potential
aspirants get a sense of how a candidacy might fare and show others
their strength. Since the news media takes these straw polls seriously,

most presidential aspirants do so as well, at least to the extent that they do not dismiss them lightly. However, their effect on the campaign is marginal.[21]

In sum, in the modern era, fund-raising, organization, and campaigning the year prior to the election year are highly correlated with candidate success in the primaries. Presidential candidates are now self-recruited, less connected to party, and starting their runs for the White House earlier. This of course reinforces the role of candidate organizations throughout the remainder of the selection process, a not insignificant fact. Early starts are also important in France. Many candidates, for example, were preparing for the (scheduled) 1976 election (held in 1974) as early as 1970.[22] Jacques Chirac started his 1995 effort immediately after his failed 1988 bid, and although he did not announce his candidacy until November of 1994, he had headquarters and staff in place by 1992. This helped the campaign effort immensely.[23] Conversely, Lionel Jospin, his second-round opponent, did not start his campaign until three and a half months before the election; Prime Minister Edouard Balladur also started late, occupied as he was with running government.[24]

NARROWING THE FIELD OF ASPIRANTS: CANDIDATE SCREENING

The United States: Primaries and Caucuses

Recall that in the traditional era of presidential electioneering, screening, or the narrowing of the field of presidential aspirants was done rather informally by party notables and the selection of the party nominee was done at the national convention. The process, although complex and often rife with intrigue, was such that the eventual decision was firmly in the hands of the party. This has changed. Simply put, at the presidential level, the party has almost no control over its main product: its label. In the modern era the convention ratifies the nominee who has already been selected in the various state primaries and the much less numerous caucuses. There are several types of primaries (closed, open, blanket), but what is important to understand in terms of electioneering is that primaries and caucuses are the principal means by which pledged delegates are selected for the national convention.[25] In other words, the politics of the party nomination are played out in the various states, long before the national convention begins.

The first presidential primary was held in Wisconsin in 1905. By 1916 a total of 25 states held them, but that number declined to about 14 in 1936 and remained relatively stable until 1968. During this period primaries were used selectively and strategically, typically for a candidate

Table 6.6
Increase in the Number of Direct Primaries and the Percentage of Pledged Delegates Chosen from Those Primaries, 1968–96

	1968	1972	1976	1980	1984	1988	1992	1996
Democrats								
Number of Primaries	17	23	29	35	25	34	36	36
Percent Delegate Votes	37.5%	60.5%	72.6%	71.8%	62.1%	66.6%	69.6%	62.8%
Republicans								
Number of Primaries	16	22	28	34	30	35	39	43
Percent Delegate Votes	34.3%	52.7%	67.9%	76%	71%	76.9%	79.1%	88.3%

Source: Paul Beck (1997:222, Table 10.1). Figures include Washington, D.C., American Samoa, Guam, Puerto Rico, the Virgin Islands, and Democrats abroad, but do not include those states which hold non-binding preference primaries (the so-called "beauty contests). Democratic percentages exclude "superdelegates."

to demonstrate to party leaders that he was capable of garnering popular support. This was Kennedy's purpose for entering the primary in heavily Protestant West Virginia in 1960.[26] As the result of party reforms in the 1960s and early 1970s,[27] a "new" nominating system of selecting the majority of (pledged) convention delegates by way of direct primaries and caucuses was largely in place for the 1972 campaign.[28] Presidential aspirants now have no alternative but to compete in primaries. Table 6.6 illustrates this by showing the number of states holding direct primaries and the percentage of delegates chosen from those states since 1968.

The candidate screening process seems to have a certain "rhythm" which starts long before the first events are held in New Hampshire and Iowa.[29] The media begins forecasting and handicapping the race many months before based on candidates' ability to accumulate resources (monetary and otherwise), their campaign activity, and early polling results. As early as March of 1999, for example, *U.S. News & World Report* was calling George W. Bush "The Man to Beat."[30] These early forecasts are a big factor in primary success. Most agree that there is a "bandwagon" effect in the primary season, whereby early and favorable media coverage, added to other resources, enhances the chance of winning early primaries. This positive momentum in turn attracts more resources and more coverage, which helps perpetuate the cycle.[31] To put it another way, there seems to be a certain additive nature to the acquisition of campaign resources (including media coverage) before and during the primary season, meaning that the more one has, the greater one's ability to acquire more.[32] This seems to enhance the probability of electoral success. Conversely, unfavorable media attention combined with lack of resources and poor polling creates a negative momentum, depressing a candidate's overall (electoral and non-electoral) success.

By tradition the official race begins with the Iowa caucus, followed shortly afterwards by the New Hampshire primary. Although these two events do not absolutely determine the outcome of the nomination race they have in the past made or broken many presidential aspirations. Doing well in either state can greatly enhance the visibility of a lesser-known candidate. A good example was Gary Hart's second-place finish in Iowa in 1984 when he received 16.5 percent of the Democratic vote compared to front-runner and eventual nominee Walter Mondale's 49.5 percent. This example brings the role of pre-primary efforts and press expectations into sharp relief. Having done far better than expected, Hart immediately became the recipient of a great deal of favorable media coverage. Mondale on the other hand was expected to do well, and while he too received media coverage he was forced to share the limelight with the lesser-known Hart. Similarly, Pat Robertson's campaign received a boost in 1988 with his surprise second-place finish in front of Vice-President George Bush in Iowa.

Although some candidates choose to forgo entering the Iowa caucus, soon afterwards comes the New Hampshire primary, and historically, all aspirants participate in this event.[33] The formula of performance versus expectations and the resultant media coverage is more evident in New Hampshire. Eugene McCarthy's strong second-place finish in New Hampshire was a major factor in Lyndon Johnson's bowing out of the 1968 race. George McGovern in 1972 and Jimmy Carter in 1976 both gained tremendous amounts of visibility and credibility after their New Hampshire showings, as did Bill Clinton in 1992, whose second-place showing was considered especially strong in light of already rampant allegations of his draft dodging and marital infidelity on his part. In 1996 Pat Buchanan's early success in the Louisiana and Iowa caucuses and his win in the New Hampshire primary almost gave him the power to hold Robert Dole's nomination (one which most observers recognized was inevitable) hostage.

Serious presidential aspirants, especially front-runners, have no real alternative to participating in these two early events, but strategically that participation is almost a no-win proposition. To not enter risks not being taken seriously; to enter and not do as well as expected puts a pall over the entire campaign effort; to do poorly can end the campaign. In 1996 Lamar Alexander, after finishing third in Iowa and New Hampshire, was forced to pull out soon afterwards. To live up to expectations merits no special attention from the press, not least because there is always the chance that another aspirant will do better than expected and steal the spotlight. And even though aspirants who do better than expected receive a boost, it typically does not last long. The week after Buchanan won in New Hampshire he placed third in Arizona which made the idea of a Buchanan nomination much less credible.

The amount of attention paid to the Iowa caucus and the New Hamp-

Table 6.7
**Front-loading: The Number and Percentage of Primaries Held before April,
1968–96**

	1968	1972	1976	1980	1984	1988	1992	1996
Total Number of Primaries	17	23	30	37	31	37	39	43
Number of Primaries before April	1	3	6	11	10	22	17	30
Percentage of Primaries before April	6%	13	20	30	32	59	44	70

Source: Larry Sabato (1997:56, Figure 3).

shire primaries serves to underscore the importance of early money and
organization in modern presidential electioneering and far outweighs
their states' relative electoral importance (a combined total of 11 electoral
votes). Of the total amount of evening news election coverage prior to
March 15, 1996 (when the Republican nomination had been secured by
Dole), roughly 55 percent was devoted to Iowa and New Hampshire.[34]
Thus, in spite of the low probability that either (or both) of these events
will help the campaign effort much, not only must serious aspirants enter, they typically devote a disproportionate amount of resources to the
campaign effort in these states. In 1988 candidates from both parties
spent an average of 50 days in Iowa and 37 days in New Hampshire in
the year preceding the election year; in 1996 they spent 30 days in Iowa
and 26 in New Hampshire.[35]

Once these two events are over, the primary season is under way in
earnest. Increasing numbers of states, in an attempt to gain political advantage and highlight their importance, have been scheduling their primaries earlier and earlier. This increases the importance of the invisible
primary as well as the Iowa and New Hampshire events. The plain fact
is that the process of winnowing the field of presidential aspirants down
to one candidate per party is now very tightly compressed, starting and
ending within the space of about two months in the early spring of the
election year. In 1996, 73 percent of the Republican delegates were chosen
by the end of March.[36] Increased front-loading is illustrated in Table 6.7,
which shows the total number and percentage of primaries held before
April from 1968 to 1996.

In sum, the system of screening or winnowing the field of presidential
aspirants and selecting the eventual nominee demands that candidates
be increasingly reliant on themselves, their organizations, and their hard-
won resources throughout the primary season in order to secure the
party nomination. Since the majority of pledged convention delegates
are selected by way of presidential primaries, candidates have little
choice but to contest the majority of those races. The compressed nature

of the process demands that candidates make tough decisions about where to allocate their time and resources, and it also means that weaker candidates are forced to drop out of the race earlier than they otherwise may have been inclined. A few short weeks after the 1996 New Hampshire primary, Republicans Lamar Alexander and Richard Lugar withdrew from the race; Steven Forbes followed shortly thereafter. And although Pat Buchanan never officially withdrew, Dole had (all but officially) won the nomination by March 26. The point is that many aspirants are now winnowed out much earlier than they might be otherwise.

The United States: Party National Conventions

To the chagrin of many political observers (such as journalists and scholars nostalgic for "brokered" conventions of the past), party national conventions are far less contentious affairs than previous conventions. Conventions are still the forum in which parties debate and adopt their internal rules, but in terms of the election effort, only a few decisions of any consequence are left to be made at the convention. One is the selection of the vice-presidential nominee, a second, the adoption of the party platform; both of these decisions revolve around the candidate. One unintended consequence of this development is that the national convention has become an ill-concealed "infomercial" for the party nominee.[37] Paradoxically, as a result of this development, public interest in, and thus, media coverage of, the convention has declined. What began in 1956 as gavel-to-gavel coverage of the conventions by the three major networks evolved by 1992 to one or two hours of prime-time coverage; this may be reduced even further in the year 2000. The reason for this is fairly straightforward. With the presidential nominee already decided, conventions are fairly boring, neither newsworthy (as defined by the news profession) nor good entertainment.

The party makes several choices before the four-day convention begins (typically between mid-July and late August). Hoping to gain publicity and some momentum, the out-party usually holds their convention first; the in-party, quite naturally, works around the incumbent president's schedule. On the recommendation of the national party chair and the site selection committee, the party national committee chooses where the convention will be held, selects temporary and permanent convention officials (typically members of Congress and other prominent national party leaders), and decides who will be speaking at the convention.

Several factors go into the selection of the site, including the size, configuration, condition, and accessibility (for delegates and the television networks) of the convention hall as well as accommodations in the city. Most major cities are qualified in this respect, so the decision typically rests on the political climate of the state (e.g., is the state governor or the city's mayor from the party?) and financial inducements offered by the city. The big story in 1996 was the selection by the Democrats of Chicago as their site, traditionally a Democratic stronghold and host to two dozen conventions since 1860. This was significant because it was the first time either party has held their convention in Chicago since the turbulent Democratic convention of 1968, where the major story of the convention was the civil unrest outside the convention hall and the manner in which Mayor Daly handled these disturbances.[38]

Who attends party conventions? Much has been made about the 1968 and 1972 Democratic party reforms which were supposed to make the party more representative of the electorate. To some extent this has happened, at least with respect to the demography of convention delegates if only because since 1980 the party has mandated that state delegations be comprised of 50 percent women. Democrats also have a slightly higher representation of blacks and Latinos than do Republicans, but in both parties, delegates are mainly upper-income and better educated individuals. The reforms were also intended to move delegations back toward the ideological center, but since politically active people tend to be more ideologically extreme, attainment of this goal has by and large been unsuccessful.[39]

For the purposes of electioneering the most salient fact about delegates is that most are selected by way of the primary system. This means that most come to the convention already committed to a particular candidate. Thus, if the primary season is decisive, the convention as a whole is more unified which helps immeasurably in the campaign effort. An unintended consequence of moving to the primary system of delegate selection is that representation at the convention by elected officials has declined, this because they can only be represented if they are committed in advance to a particular (and winning) candidate. In the 1980s the Democrats sought to reverse this trend by introducing into the convention what are known as "superdelegates." These party notables (in 1996, all Democratic members of Congress, governors, and members of the DNC) arrive at the convention officially uncommitted, comprising a substantial minority. Their presence has re-introduced party voice into the convention, as well as some excitement, since they are asked not to discuss their choice for nominee. The Republicans have followed suit.[40]

The structure of the convention revolves around four major committees. The credentials committee is responsible for deciding on contested delegations and seating delegates (and their alternates). In the past it held a great deal of power, especially in divisive conventions where the outcome rested on seating blocs of delegates known to be favorable to one candidate or another. Since delegate selection is now a fairly institutionalized process, the power of this committee has waned of late. The permanent organization of the convention, including the chair, secretary, and sergeant at arms, is selected on the first day and is officially responsible for running the convention. The rules committee schedules events and speeches as well as setting rules and procedures for future conventions; this latter is often the cause of great controversy. Finally, the platform committee drafts the party platform, increasingly important of late because of intra-party struggles over particular issues (e.g., abortion).[41]

The business of the first two days of the convention is devoted to speeches and debate over the party platform. This is (and always has been) important because it sets the tone for both the convention and the general election, but since the 1980s it has become particularly important since the convention is used as a national "launch pad" for the general election campaign.[42] Conventions have always been managed, but since the party nomination is decided long before the convention begins, it is now more accurate to say that they are staged. Parties go to great lengths to schedule important speeches to ensure that they are seen by those (few) television viewers who are watching. The goal is to present a picture of a unified party, optimistic in their assurance of impending victory. Parties also try to highlight rising stars in the party (e.g., the Republican J. C. Watts in 1996) or other key candidates.

Historically, the opening day keynote speech is extremely important and is always given by a very well-known party figure. In 1984, for example, then-Governor of New York Mario Cuomo delivered the keynote speech at the Democratic national convention; in 1996 the Democrats turned to Indiana Governor Evan Bayh. Representative Susan Molinari of New York was chosen for the 1996 Republican convention to try and combat the image that the party is less open and sensitive to women. The keynote speech can often set the tone for the remainder of the convention and, by extension, the campaign. Cuomo's speech in 1984, for example, was memorable for his indictment of Reagan's policies, which he claimed were serving to widen the income gap. In the recent past, other speeches besides the keynote speech have been equally as important, if not more so. For example, in 1996 Hillary Clinton's speech came before Bayh's and generated as much enthusiasm as (if not more than) his. Elizabeth Dole's Phil Donahue-style performance at the Republican convention was equally uplifting. Other notable (and newsworthy) speeches are ones that do *not* get made, for example Pat Buchanan's in 1996.

The debate over, and writing of, the party platform begins long before the convention begins, and in the first two days the convention takes up the draft platform for adoption. Although theoretically the document is the party's official policy document, the reality is that it has always been, to some greater or lesser degree, a candidate-centered document. In fact, party platforms originated in 1832, when the

first Democratic National Convention . . . convened not so much to nominate Andrew Jackson for a second term, but to mobilize the party behind a decision that
had been rendered elsewhere. Jackson had already been "endorsed" by several
state legislatures, consequently, the party met to formulate measures to re-elect
an incumbent. . . . To that end Democrats drafted an "address" (known today as
the party platform) congenial to Jackson's candidacy.[43]

Even during the heydays of political parties, candidates (and sitting presidents, even if they were not seeking re-election) were prominent in the
platform-drafting process.[44]

But the reality is that "the party platform has become more of a presidential campaign document than in prior years,"[45] simply because of
the fact that the nomination is decided long before the convention begins.
In 1988 platform writing for the Democrats was dominated by Dukakis'
team; in 1992 the Republican platform panel was chosen by Bush's organization; in 1996 Clinton and the Democratic Leadership Council dominated the Democratic platform process. Perhaps the most contentious
intra-party issue faced by the Republicans in 1996 was abortion, and
here, platform language was agreed to by Dole.[46] In spite of all this,
platforms are largely ignored by candidates. Dole, for example, readily
admitted to not having read the very Republican platform he was instrumental in drafting.[47]

On the third day of the convention ballots are cast for the presidential
nominee, though this is now largely a formality, and on day four the
vice-presidential nominee is chosen.[48] In the modern era he or she is the
choice of the presidential candidate, typically chosen to balance the ticket
and add something to it by way of electoral support. This often means
reaching out to a particular region and/or one of the ideological wings
of the party. Dan Quayle was chosen as George Bush's running mate in
1988 in order to add a Midwestern appeal Bush did not have, to balance
Bush's age (Bush was 64, Quayle, 41), as well as to reach out to the more
conservative wing of the Republican Party. A similar but opposite tact
was taken by Clinton in 1992, who chose Albert Gore to emphasize his
own youth, centrist positions, and Southern roots.[49] The last order of
business is to introduce the ticket to the convention, at which point the
candidates make their acceptance speeches (a practice started by Franklin
Roosevelt in 1936, a further illustration of candidate non-involvement in
electioneering in the traditional era) in order to initiate the general election campaign with unity, energy, and the promise of victory.

Screening and Selecting the Aspirants in France and Russia

The process of winnowing the field of presidential aspirants in France
is different than in the United States, but the two-ballot electoral system

creates the same institutional effect: the field is narrowed to two candidates and their parties. In fact, many French refer to their two-ballot
system as *"primaires."*[50] In France, although parties are in nominal control
of who will represent them, the major French parties have no formal
nomination mechanisms to speak of. This contrasts with the situation in
the United States, where parties must comply with a bevy of state laws
in a variety of matters, not least, delegate selection procedures.[51] As
might have been evident from the section on candidate recruitment in
France, while the party nomination is officially in the hands of the party,
it is in actuality a process of candidate self-designation which often involves quashing the presidential ambitions of others in the party. It is
generally understood in France that presidential candidates "cannot be
'nominated,' . . . they must 'emerge' self-nominated, and . . . all political
parties can and should do is endorse that emergent candidate of whom
they most approve."[52] In fact, in 1981 François Mitterand was the first
major candidate to actually ask for his party's nomination,[53] but that
nomination, as well as those of the other three major parties, had been
decided long before.[54]

There are exceptions. For example, the withdrawal of Jacques Delors
in 1994 and the poor showing of the Socialists in the legislative elections
of 1993 left the party in such disarray that they eventually held a party
(not a direct, or popular) primary which pitted Lionel Jospin against First
Secretary Henri Emmanuelli, which Jospin won overwhelmingly (65 percent to 35 percent).[55] But there is no set path to the Élysée: it has always
been a personal process. While not the sole determinant, party ties seem
to be increasingly important in the decision to run for president but this
cannot be viewed in isolation from the fact that becoming party leader
is helped by one's perceived ability to win the presidency. Harmon Zeigler probably summed up the French "system" of nomination best:

Because the political parties are, in essence, vehicles for personal power, their
presidential nomination processes are vague. . . . [Socialists endorse] candidates
in full-party conferences, but the UDF and RPR just take it for granted that their
leader will compete. . . . The tradition [of the Right] is for self-selection and strong
personality. . . . and depends more upon personality than organization. There is
no clearly understood method of securing a party's nomination for president![56]

Given the relationship between French political parties and their presidential candidates, it should come as no surprise that the responsibility
for the party platform (or program) is generally in the hands of the candidate, and parties are generally reluctant to make their policies binding
on their candidates.[57] Once they have endorsed their candidate, that person has a "latitude of action which goes far beyond the letter of the party
constitution and sometimes goes quite against the party's traditions."[58]

François Mitterand's "110 Proposals" in 1981 is a case in point. Although ratified by the Socialists, it was very different from the ideologically charged Socialist program of 1972. In fact, there is increasingly less emphasis on ideological content in the platforms of all of the mainstream French parties. Lately they are putting forward "bare-bones platforms" based mainly on the pragmatic program of their presidential candidate.[59] According to one analyst, there was an "extreme simplification" of the issues in 1995.[60]

In Russia the only story of real interest with respect to party nominating procedures is that of the Communist Party (recall that President Yeltsin is not a member of a political party). In one sense the 1995 election to the Duma was their "unofficial primary."[61] Immediately afterwards, Gennadi Zyuganov negotiated a deal with the Agrarian Party's Mikhail Lapshin and former Soviet Prime Minister Nikolai Ryzhkov to ensure that each would support his nomination and then convened a party plenum in a successful attempt to preempt other prospective challengers.[62] In early February, on the same day that Yeltsin announced his candidacy, the Communists held their fourth party conference to nominate Zyuganov as their candidate.[63] The entire process was similar to the French "system" of parties ratifying candidates who have won the nomination by other means. Other Russian parties are more personalized, so it was natural to expect that their leaders also would be their candidate (Grigori Yavlinski of Yabloko, Vladimir Zhirinovsky of the Liberal Democrats).

Given what has been said about the Yeltsin and Zyuganov campaigns, it should come as little surprise that the crafting of their respective campaign platforms was oriented around their bases of power. In President Yeltsin's case this meant the state. His platform, published and released in early June, centered around a list of 49 presidential decrees which made all of his campaign promises "official."[64] Survey research was important in guiding the president's hand in this (and can probably be interpreted as indirect proof that the American campaign professionals had at least some influence on the campaign). In Zyuganov's case, intraparty struggles over the electoral program and controversy over a socalled "secret" hard-line party agenda increased as the campaign wore on.[65] In the end, a more pragmatic, less ideologically charged platform won out, not least because by then the power of the Party had been diluted by its alliance in the Popular-Patriotic Bloc.

In short, in the United States and France, individuals "recruit" themselves for presidential candidacy and rely on their own efforts to secure "their" party's nomination; a similar situation prevailed in Russia in 1996. This is evident throughout the entire process of candidate selection in both countries and perhaps to be expected, since in a very real sense the selection process in both countries is very unstructured. It is, in fact, quite generous to call the process by which individuals go from citizen to presidential candidate in the United States, France, or Russia a "system."

THE GENERAL ELECTION CAMPAIGN: PRESIDENTIAL SELECTION

Campaign Activity

After the national convention in the United States, the general election begins and the candidates square off in earnest. Each will have made every effort to heal any wounds that may have been incurred in the battle for the nomination and will now be in a position to focus their efforts on the opposition. This section discusses the activities involved in those efforts. We can conceptualize the variety of campaign activities as being one of two types; campaign management, including the crafting and implementation of strategy and tactics, polling, issue and opposition research, fund-raising, and grassroots activities such as get-out-the-vote (GOTV) drives; and communication. This latter is probably what most of us think about when we think of political campaigns and includes political advertising, press relations, and efforts directed toward staging "news" events.

We have discussed some of these activities already. Issue and opposition research, fund raising, and press relations were covered in Chapters 4 and 5. These activities, perhaps obviously, continue throughout the general election season but will not be discussed in any great depth here. This section will focus on strategy and tactics, polling, grassroots activities, political advertising, and attracting news coverage. These activities are also ongoing prior to the general election season, albeit with a different goal in mind (securing the party nomination).

Campaign Management: Strategy and Tactics

A presidential campaign, like a military campaign, relies on sound strategy. Although electioneering in this century has become far more sophisticated, it was not until the 1952 campaign of Dwight Eisenhower that a formal blueprint, or strategy, was crafted and adopted for the campaign; it is now standard practice. Campaign professionals are, by and large, the ones responsible for crafting and implementing campaign strategy. Though candidates retain the final say regarding the direction of the campaign, most are "neither very involved nor influential in the day-to-day tactical operation of the campaign."[66] Sound strategy must account for and anticipate environmental (electoral, media, campaign finance systems, etc.), technological, and situational (the mood of the country, major current events) factors, as well as the candidate's style, expertise, background, and so on.

The main questions include how the campaign is to be organized and what regions and groups should be targeted. Since campaigning is not a science, a natural tendency might be to campaign everywhere. Indeed, since 1960 when Kennedy made use of his own aircraft in the campaign, travel to virtually all 50 states has been the norm for a presidential campaign. In 1996 candidates (with their own leased planes) flew more and paid less for that travel than any previous year's crop of presidential aspirants.[67] Incumbents with access to Air Force One generally enjoy an advantage in this regard. For example, George Bush's estimated transportation costs during a three-month period in 1992 was less than $1 million; Bill Clinton, on the other hand, spent roughly $600,000 per week to keep a fleet of five planes in the air during the same period.[68]

But in a country as vast as the United States, decisions still have to be made about when and where to focus time and resources, so the first element of a sound strategy is the "where and when" of the campaign. Each party (and by extension, their candidate) can generally count on certain regions for electoral support; one element of campaign strategy is to reinforce this base. Conversely, other regions will most likely be casting their vote for the opponent; energy spent wooing these voters is typically wasted. Lately, the Republicans have started with a considerably larger electoral base than their opposition. In seven of the past eight elections, 16 states have voted Republican, giving them a total of 128 electoral college votes; during the same period Democrats could count on only one state and the District of Columbia for a total of 13 electoral college votes (recall that it takes 270 votes to win). In spite of this, Democrats can generally count on support in the Northeast and the Midwest and, prior to the 1960s, the South. Since then, the South has largely been a Republican region, who also do well in the West. Thus, a winning electoral combination for the Democratic party seems to be a candidate from the South (e.g., Carter and Clinton) or the West, since it cuts into the Republican geographic base.[69]

Because the electoral college awards all of a state's electoral votes to the winner of that state,[70] another guideline in targeting the campaign is to focus on large states, sometimes even if the candidate has little chance of victory in them. The strategy of a geographic coalition consists of identifying key states—larger states where the candidate has a chance of victory—and focusing most of the campaign effort on them; additional time is spent bolstering support in areas where the candidate is likely to do well; and little attention is paid to the smallest states or to those where the candidate is almost sure to lose. This means that the "big seven" states (California, Florida, Illinois, New York, Pennsylvania, Ohio, Texas) almost always receive a great deal of attention from candidates of both parties.[71] So, for example, seven of the eight states Jimmy Carter and Gerald Ford targeted in 1976 were the same.[72] Dole, although he knew he had virtually no chance of winning California (which has 54 votes, a full 10 percent of the electoral college) in 1996, spent much of the last three weeks of his campaign there (and roughly $4 million). But it is generally pointless to spend much time in states where the candidate has little chance of winning.

Thus, in 1964 Barry Goldwater virtually ignored the Northeast, where he stood little chance. He spent a little time in the South where he was sure to win, and he concentrated most of his effort in the Midwest and the West where he thought he could win some support. In addition to the "big seven," the Nixon team of 1968 went after three states where he had a chance of beating Hubert Humphrey (New Jersey, Wisconsin, and Missouri) as well as five border-South states in order to cut into George Wallace's (Southern) base. The Reagan (in 1980 and 1984) and Bush (in 1988) strategy was to focus on the Republican South and West as well as to try to swing the Midwest industrial states of Michigan, Illinois, and Ohio. Bush's strategy in 1992 and Dole's in 1996 had to contend with the fact that they were badly behind; Bush opted to focus on the Midwest and Dole on the Northeast. Neither strategy paid off. Clinton, on the other hand, started each of his campaigns ahead in five of the "big seven" states, and thus targeted these states and 15 others where he led.[73]

After targets are identified schedules must be made. By this time the candidate campaign team (now consisting of several hundred people) includes several dozen people responsible for scheduling visits by the presidential and vice-presidential candidates and their family members as well as arranging press relations, accommodations, travel, and so on, for these visits. This is no small task. One well-known Democratic poll-ster (Peter Hart) takes an approach that illustrates how systematic this complex effort is. Hart breaks the campaign season into 80 campaign days which consist of four potential events per day. The scheduler, then, has 320 total units with which to work.[74] Carter's campaign manager Hamilton Jordan reduced campaign scheduling to a formula which awarded points to each state for size, previous Democratic support, existing Democrat support (based on control of elective offices), and turn-out. After defining the important states, each day's campaign effort was worked out mathematically according to the score of the state as well as the pre-determined value of a visit by Carter, Mondale, or a family member.[75] As an example of just how precise these schedules are formulated, Carter's scheduler Eliot Cutler, convinced that Ohio was the key to the race, scheduled 65 percent of vice-presidential candidate Walter Mondale's time there in the last two weeks of the campaign (Carter won Ohio by 8,000 votes).

Concurrent with scheduling is the work of the advance teams, which includes arranging security, housing, and transportation needs and making sure that placards, buttons, and banners (with the candidate's theme) are on hand and ready to be distributed. It requires physical preparation of the site where the candidate is to appear, ensuring that the press is notified and has the types of access they need, equipment feeds are in order, electricity needs are adequate, and so on. Great efforts are taken to make sure that there is a sympathetic, enthusiastic crowd at the event, and conversely, that hecklers and the like are not. In short, the work of the advance teams is to make sure that the candidate's appearance goes exactly as planned. The goal? To have the event produce a news story that night which puts the candidate in a favorable light. Much stock is placed in the work that these teams do, because in spite of all the preparation, things can and do go wrong. For example, in spite of all the preparation, a 1984 Labor Day parade in New York City in which Walter Mondale was appearing to help kick off his campaign was so sparsely attended that the news story that evening consisted of Mondale walking down virtually deserted city streets.[76]

Campaign Management: Polling

Public opinion polling has been part of presidential politics in the United States since 1916, used by parties, candidates, and the media for a variety of purposes. The well-known magazine *Literary Digest* correctly predicted the outcomes of the 1924 through the 1932 elections but fatally forecast an Alfred Landon victory in 1936. The *Digest* relied on a large (roughly 2 million ballots), rather unrepresentative national sample drawn from its readership. Others, among them George Gallup and Elmo Roper, were developing and perfecting more scientific polling methods based on much smaller, random samples. They correctly predicted Roosevelt's 1936 victory and the winners in 1940 and 1944; an incorrect forecast of a Thomas Dewey victory in 1948 did little to deter the growth of the fledgling industry. Sampling procedures continued to improve and polling became big business.[77] The bigger firms now include Gallup, Harris, Yankelovich, *The Wall Street Journal*/NBC, *Washington Post*/ABC, the *Los Angeles Times*, and *New York Times*/CBS. The polls of these major firms serve a variety of functions during the presidential selection process, not least to provide the mass media stories for their gristmills.

As polling techniques became more sophisticated candidates began using polling data to aid the campaign effort in various ways. Over time pollsters became more central to the campaign effort and they now comprise a core component of the strategic team. One noted pollster, Richard Wirthlin, summed it up simply: "There's no question that our role has changed from collector of facts to interpreter and strategist."[78] For example John Kennedy's decision to enter what was to be the pivotal West Virginia primary (as well as Wisconsin's) in 1960 was based on Louis Harris' polling data which showed that Democratic rival Hubert Humphrey might be vulnerable there. Since then it has been unthinkable to even consider a run for the presidency without commissioning a bevy of polls.

Presidential aspirants use private pollsters who now have their own trade association, the National Association of Political Pollsters (NAPP), founded in 1972 by well-known presidential pollsters Patrick Caddell, Peter Hart, Robert Teeter, and Richard Wirthlin (mostly as a response to election laws and FEC guidelines concerning polling).[79] Polls are used by candidates to help decide if a run for the presidency is viable, to identify a potential base of donors, volunteers, and voters, to bolster their viability in the media and with supporters, to help develop an effective image and public appeal, and to determine how to best respond to attacks from opponents. In short, from the earliest stages of recruitment through the end of the campaign (and beyond, but that is a story for a different book), polling is central to presidential electioneering.[80]

Several types of polls are used throughout the campaign. One general type, preference polls, are taken to show the candidate or aspirant how he or she is faring. They include "benchmark polls," taken before the primary season begins in order to test the political waters and to determine in a general way which candidates are favored by which parts of the electorate and why. They also provide a baseline to determine campaign effectiveness and effects in order to see if adjustments are necessary as the campaign wears on. "Trend" polls are preference polls taken at various intervals, for example just after the primary season and just before the general election campaign begins. The goal of trend polls is to see if respondents' preferences have changed. "Tracking polls" are basically overnight trend polls used as the campaign wears on, especially in the closing weeks. Reagan's pollster Richard Wirthlin was the first to use daily tracking polls in 1980,[81] and since then their use has become standard practice.[82]

Another type of poll is that which tests to see how the campaign should present itself. Based on an initial reading of the political climate and a reading of which issues may be salient, various themes, messages, and candidate images are tested with various groups to see which will resonate with which voters. More sophisticated and complex than preference polls, they are by and large responsible for the content of the campaign (e.g., advertisements, speeches, how or if the candidate should respond to attacks, and more). They are taken more or less continuously throughout the campaign in order to see how well these various aspects of the campaign are working, and are typically planned to complement the candidate's geographic strategy as well as to target groups within various regions. In short, they drive campaign content.

Several new types of polls are becoming increasingly popular and are used to complement the more standard polls. "Focus group" polling is a technique which brings together a dozen or so socially homogenous people for a fairly lengthy (one and a half to three hours) moderated discussion about issues relevant to the campaign. Participants are usually drawn from an area which is representative of a constituency the candidate's team thinks is critical. Since the samples are not random, focus group polls are not scientific. They are, however, invaluable in complementing other polling data, helping to "put the flesh on the bones," so to speak.[83] Perhaps the most highly touted use of focus group polling in recent memory was the 1992 Clinton campaign's "Manhattan Project," designed to revive his faltering, post-primary campaign. Here, focus group polling of white, middle-class voters provided data which showed that although voters viewed him with some skepticism (as a "typical" politician) they also responded to other aspects of the candidate positively, in particular his empathy. This information convinced Clinton that he needed to tell voters more about himself and his past, which guided much of the remainder of the campaign.[84]

"Dial group" polling, a technique also used in the Manhattan Project, is a way for candidates to elicit instantaneous feedback. Here, respondents listen to or watch a number of prepared presentations (speeches, sound bites) from the candidate with their hands on a dial. The respondents are asked to twist the dial according to how positively they are feeling about the message (image, etc.) being presented at the moment, and the scores (from 1 to 100) are transmitted through a computer to a graphic readout which dynamically displays the results.

Finally, a new technique, "push-polling" is used more as a way to attack the opponent rather than as a method of collecting data. It is, to put it mildly, an extremely controversial technique and considered unethical by most, in part because it masquerades as something it is not. Here, respondents are asked to react to negative statements or questions about the opponent and the idea is not so much to analyze data collected from the responses, but rather to create the negative image itself. So, for example, in 1996 the Dole campaign conducted a telephone campaign against Steve Forbes in which the caller would present the respondent with Forbes' position on a variety of issues that the respondent was likely to disagree with (abortion, gays in the military) and then ask if this knowledge made them more or less likely to vote for Forbes.[85]

It would, in sum, be difficult to overestimate the place of polling in modern presidential electioneering. Strategy and tactics revolve around good polling data and virtually every decision throughout the campaign is guided to some greater or lesser degree by these data. The fact that pollsters are accorded such high positions in the campaign (and afterwards) is a testament to their importance in the electioneering process.

Campaign Management: Grassroots Activities

Although we have for the most part ignored voters in our story, they do, of course, have the final say in who takes up residence at 1600 Pennsylvania Avenue. And, as fundamental as this may sound, the campaign effort will do little good if voters do not turn out at the polls. Low voter turnout, due to a variety of factors, is a fact of American political life (turnout in 1996 was 49 percent of the voting-age population). All things being equal, turnout tends to be higher in more competitive races, but neither side can afford to take turnout for granted. One of the important activities of the general election campaign is the get-out-the-vote (GOTV) effort each side makes to ensure that the party faithful register and turn out to cast their ballot.[86]

This effort, mainly funded by the national party, is typically carried out by state and local party organizations. Get-out-the-vote efforts of each party reflect the differences between their core constituencies. Generally speaking, Democratic party identifiers, many of whom come from the lower end of the socio-economic scale, are typically less active in politics and less likely to vote. Therefore, considerable effort is made to get these people registered, arrange for their transportation to the polls, sometimes providing for child care. Advertising campaigns are mounted and targeted for those areas where turnout is expected to be low (based on turnout in prior elections). These ad campaigns are non-partisan, encouraging all citizens to register and vote, but the hope is that they will reach and mobilize more people who identify with and will vote for the party who is paying for the effort.

Party efforts to increase turnout often make the critical difference in the election. And, similar to electioneering efforts in the traditional era, in large part they depend on how unified the party is after the convention. For example, in 1968 the Democratic Party was so divided that it took until late October for them to come together and mobilize behind Hubert Humphrey. Unfortunately this was too late to register many voters who might have made a difference. Carter's 1976 win has been attributed in large part to the successful voter registration drive coordinated and funded by the DNC and aided by organized labor (who typically play an important role in the Democratic GOTV effort). Similarly, the Republican Party in 1984 mounted an exceptionally sophisticated, and for them, successful, effort to increase turnout.[87]

Communications: Communications Consultants

It is perhaps in the communications aspect of presidential electioneering that we see the culmination of professionalization and sophistication in the modern era. Much of what guides strategy and content of political communication in the modern era has not changed. What differs is the way in which communication is crafted and carried out. Now, in what Robert Dinkin refers to as the "Mass Media Age" of political campaigning (1952 to the present), political communication is "a science, relying on detailed statistical information and complex analytical tools . . . candidates [are] sold to the public in an increasingly systematic fashion."[88]

To this end, candidates rely on the services of a variety of communications consultants.[89] At the presidential level these consultants work for very large firms, most often their own. Starting with polling research, different consultants develop a theme, crafting several stock speeches that will be used with slight variations (based on the audience) throughout the campaign. Others take responsibility for coaching the candidate on style and presentation, working on cadence, rhythm, volume, eye contact, body language, and hand gestures. Others help negotiate terms of the presidential debates and coach the candidate in debate skills,[90] deal with press relations, and handle the purchasing of media time and space.[91] Last, but certainly not least, are the consultants responsible for crafting political advertisements.

Consultants, in short, are in one sense the true communicators in the presidential campaign. The candidate's role is fairly simple: he or she is expected "only" to be enthusiastic every day, in spite of the fact that the same speech is being delivered over and over again, and to stay "on the message," both in prepared speeches and any impromptu remarks. This, of course, is no small task, but the message they convey, by and large, is a product of campaign professionals.

Communications: Substance and Content

A few fundamental rules guide the development of the candidate's message. First, since the opposition is now the other party as opposed to others in the same party, the focus changes. Since they are designed to appeal mainly to party activists, messages during the campaign for the nomination tend to be more extreme. The general election campaign is waged among the entire population, so candidate messages tend to become more moderate. The second main rule is to keep the message simple. Based on polling results, the issues of the day, the candidate's style, and what the opposition is doing, the main objective is to develop a single theme, one that the candidate can repeat to audiences around the country that will be printed on campaign paraphernalia, posted on the candidate's Web site, and so on. Here, simplicity is the key. Reagan's 1980 "Are you better off than you were four years ago?" theme illustrates this perfectly.

Beyond these two guidelines several decisions need to be made. How much, for example, should the party be stressed? This depends in large part on who controls the White House and Congress, as well as the prevailing mood of the country. It also depends on whatever happen to be the salient issues. As a general rule Republicans tend to do better with foreign policy, capitalizing on the perception that they are better equipped to defend America and her interests. For example, the 1980 Reagan campaign centered around criticism of Carter's handling of the Iran hostage crisis and the Soviet invasion of Afghanistan. Republicans have also tended to capitalize on divisive social issues such as government involvement in school bussing, affirmative action, welfare problems, and so on, which many liberal Democrats tend to favor. Democrats, on the other hand, have tended to do better stressing economic issues, drawing on their history as the party who led the country out of the Great Depression and the party of the average worker. Democrats, in other words, do well when the economy is not, stressing "bread-and-butter" issues such as jobs, wages, benefits, and so on. With the country in recession in 1992, James Carville's constant admonition to the Clinton campaign team was to remember their main issue: "It's the economy stupid."[92]

Trying to craft a "presidential" image is as difficult as trying to define stature. Still, some general comments can be made about what the public is drawn to in a leader and it is these characteristics that the campaign team will try to build on and emphasize. Presidents are expected to be strong and assertive leaders, and individuals who are perceived as being otherwise are usually penalized at the ballot box. Carter in 1980 and Mondale in 1984, for example, were viewed as indecisive and weak, while Reagan, by keeping his rhetoric simple and tough, was perceived as being strong. For challengers this is often more difficult since they have no presidential record to run on. Their best bet is to stay upbeat and positive, projecting assurance and a willingness to take action. This was the "take-charge" approach of Kennedy in 1960 and Nixon in 1968.

Being seen as someone qualified to do the job is also important. Here again, an incumbent generally has at least a slight advantage, but this does not mean that challengers are without ammunition of their own. In 1992 Ross Perot challenged George Bush's presidential experience with his record as a highly successful businessman, and Bill Clinton brought his gubernatorial experience into the battle with him. Empathy, or the impression that the aspirant can identify with the American people is an indispensable trait of presidential aspirants. Here again, Clinton excels;

conversely, Dole was seen by most as cold and distant. Finally, people want to feel as if they trust their president, so integrity and honesty are important as well. This is especially important for challengers, since the experience of Nixon in 1972 and Clinton in 1992 suggest that a good record in office matters less for incumbents who may have character flaws.[93]

Perhaps as important as stressing the positive aspects of a candidate's image is downplaying negative aspects and stressing the negative in the opponent. In the same way that positive impressions help a candidate, negative perceptions can spell political death. In fact, regardless of how high a presidential candidate's polling numbers might be, it is generally accepted that "negatives" of higher than 30–40 percent are fatal to a campaign.[94] A large part of the 1988 Bush strategy, for example, was based on turning Michael Dukakis' vague image into a negative one.

Candidates must also determine if and how they will respond to attacks from the opponent. This is a strategic choice, resting on whether the candidate can afford to ignore the attacks, thus creating the impression that he or she is above them. The other alternative is to respond, and here, the 1992 Clinton team virtually re-defined "rapid response," responding to each Bush attack before daily news deadlines had passed. This ensured that any "attack" story was either killed or that their side of it was presented, and in this way the criticism was diffused. Thus, they could stay focused on *their* issue.[95]

Communications: The Medium

Although most of us associate modern political communications with television, candidates and parties in the modern era of presidential electioneering make use of a variety of media, print, electronic, and otherwise to convey their message. While the amount of printed campaign material has waned in the modern era, other electronic media are becoming more popular. For example, production costs are such that a 10-minute videocassette with a well-designed introduction can be packaged in an attractive mailer and sent out to targeted groups for under $2 apiece.[96] Clinton, for example, distributed almost 30,000 video biographies to New Hampshire Democrats before the 1992 primary.[97] Direct mail and telephone banks are also effective ways to target particular groups of voters. Richard Nixon in 1960 was the first presidential candidate to extensively use telephones in his campaign and with advances in telephony and database management the use of this medium has become increasingly sophisticated, accessible, and popular.[98]

Another increasingly popular medium employed by campaigns is cable television (local or national). There are two good reasons for a campaign to consider using cable. The first is rather obvious: increasingly

144 Modern Presidential Electioneering

more people watch cable television. In 1996 roughly 70 percent of American households subscribed to cable, and cable accounted for almost 30 percent of the prime-time audience.[99] Secondly, cable television allows candidates to target their messages, both geographically and demographically. In 1992 the Clinton campaign made heavy use of cable television to advertise in New Jersey, a state which is mainly served by expensive New York City or Philadelphia stations. During the last three days of the 1992 campaign the DNC advertised heavily on several cable networks known for older audiences (e.g., Lifetime) in Florida and Ohio in both a geographic and demographic targeting of what it perceived to be a critical bloc of voters.[100] Finally, World Wide Web sites are now "mandatory" for candidates for all public office,[101] and by the spring of 1999 all of the major presidential aspirants were maintaining sites. Many were also offering automated email campaign updates from these sites.

Paid advertising on broadcast television is beyond the scope of this book (see Chapter 1), but "unpaid advertising," or news coverage, is not. In the modern age, getting your candidate on the evening news is considered by many to be the highest of political art forms—the *sine qua non* of modern presidential campaigning.[102] The idea is to stage an event such that it, and by extension the candidate, will be newsworthy. Incumbents have a built-in advantage in this regard, the epitome being the "Rose Garden strategy." Here, ordinary (and some unordinary) daily activities of the president are staged against the backdrop and grandeur of the presidential office and its trappings such that the incumbent is cast in a favorable light. Taking a page from the 1984 Reagan playbook, Clinton and his staff employed this strategy in 1996, "[staging] an endless series of events designed to capture favorable television coverage around-the-clock."[103]

To sum up about political communications, little by way of the content and substance of candidate appeals has changed in the modern era of presidential electioneering. Party, issues, and image have always been important. What has changed is the way these positions and images are researched, developed, and crafted, and how they reach the public. Modern presidential aspirants rely on trained and skilled professional consultants for virtually every utterance and appearance, and a variety of media to transmit their appeals.

Campaigns in France and Russia

Targeting is less important in a country as small as France and more difficult in Russia since Russian electoral geography is still somewhat amorphous (Communists tend to do better in rural areas; reform Democrats in the cities; beyond this it is hard to say). In addition, the official campaign season is considerably shorter in France than in the United

States, and in both France and Russia is broken up into first- and second-round campaigns. Strategy, in other words, must anticipate another push to build and solidify the second-round coalition.

Beyond this, campaign management in France is very similar to that in the United States. First, campaign professionals are involved in the decision-making process each step of the way. Second, polling is a very important part of that strategy (recall that polling is such a fact of French presidential politics that it is banned for the two weeks preceding the election). Polling gained credibility in France when a major polling firm predicted that Charles de Gaulle would be forced to a second ballot in 1965; since then, aspirants commission polls months in advance of the election season.[104] French presidential campaign themes contain more by way of partisan imagery, but they too, like in the United States, have become extremely simplified; Chirac's "France for You" is a prime example of this. In fact, most see American style campaigning, or the "conscious and unconscious importation of North American political communication techniques" on the rise in France.[105]

In France, there is no political advertising on television, but the televised second-round debate is increasingly important, as are efforts directed toward attracting unpaid media. There is, like in the United States, increasingly greater attention paid to the staging of TV-oriented political events (called "political coups") and personal rallies in France.[106] Several analysts, in fact, have complained that the media hype surrounding modern presidential elections has transformed French politics for the worse.[107] The far-right candidate of the National Front, Jean Marie Le Pen, has certainly proven adept at attracting media attention. Le Pen's racist rhetoric did for him what money did for Ross Perot in the United States, attracting a great deal of media coverage and gaining him entrance to presidential politics. From the late 1970s to the mid-1980s he skillfully took advantage of this exposure, in the process transforming his notoriety into a credibility of sorts, and the newfound credibility into respectability.[108]

President Yeltsin's use of campaign professionals and his almost total control of the media in 1996 have been mentioned. To the surprise of many, the infirm president found the strength (or will) to be a vigorous and active campaigner. His animated dancing at the "Vote or You Lose" rock concerts which were staged with state funds to turn out the youth vote was one example of his vitality.[109] In addition to rock concerts, his campaign included television ads sponsored and produced by the Central Election Committee, but designed by ad executive Sergei Lisovski (one of the Yeltsin aides detained in the Kremlin money scandal). These fifteen-minute programs (ads), not surprisingly, bordered on advocacy for Yeltsin.[110]

Zyuganov ran a far more traditional campaign, stressing party themes and relying on the party to conduct what, in the main, was a grassroots campaign. He and his party eschewed television advertising (until the evening prior to the day of second-round voting, when they were denied air time), relying exclusively on printed campaign material.[111] One party activist was explicit about the campaign techniques and methods of the party: "We do not need to waste money on American-style electioneering."[112] With the exception of the Zyuganov effort, the campaign efforts of all of the major candidates were very similar to American presidential campaign efforts, including their use of political advertising (Vladimir Zhirinovsky, the Russian Le Pen, is nothing if not skillful in his use of television) and heavy reliance on campaign professionals.

SUMMARY

Party was paramount in the traditional era of presidential campaigning. Candidate selection and campaign activities were the sole domain of party professionals. In the United States, candidates, their large organizations, with the assistance of their paid surrogates (campaign professionals), are now the central element of both the selection and campaigning dimensions of presidential electioneering.

In the United States, the process of candidate selection is now completely dominated by candidates and their organizations; parties are virtually absent. Presidential aspirants are now self-selected, the smart ones beginning their efforts several years in advance of the primary season by building large and powerful campaign organizations. The direct primary method of candidate selection can fairly be characterized as a self-reliant, Darwinian "survival of the fittest" process. The successful nominee and his or her organization then becomes the dominant and driving force of and during the party national convention. While party is more visible during the general election season (especially during GOTV drives), the candidate continues to rely on his organization, most notably his hired campaign professionals—the new electioneers—for campaign management and communication (as well as other activities discussed earlier).

A similar situation for the most part prevails in France and Russia as well. There are several institutional differences between the candidate selection process in France, Russia, and the United States (and within the parties of each country as well), but the net effect of these differences is minimal. The process is strikingly similar in all three countries, meaning that in each the process could fairly be characterized as one of "candidate *self*-selection." In France we referred to the process as one of political party entrepreneurship, meaning that a presidential aspirant must commandeer a major political party in order to win that party's nomination. The process in Russia is perhaps more chaotic, and here differences between parties are perhaps more evident, although it is obviously far too early to make many meaningful statements about the process. As in the United States, in both countries campaign professionals are a major force in the conduct of political campaigns.

In the last chapter we will summarize our picture of modern presidential electioneering and discuss what these various changes, separately and together, might mean for the political systems of these countries.

7

Conclusions: Modern Presidential Electioneering

PRESIDENTIAL ELECTIONEERING: FROM PARTY- TO CANDIDATE-CENTERED

There is a wealth of scholarship devoted to what has become a less partisan electorate in the United States and elsewhere in the latter part of the twentieth century. Much of this work also details an increased "candidate-centeredness" in modern political campaigns, this in reference to how citizens decide how to cast their vote and the content of political messages.[1] This book has added to our understanding of what "candidate-centered" campaigns mean by separating out the organizational dimensions of the campaign—the electioneering.

The model we associate with traditional presidential electioneering is party-centered, meaning that candidates were involved but minimally in the process. Presidential aspirants were recruited and selected based mainly on their party ties and what they could bring to the party; parties were for the most part responsible for footing the bill of the campaign; and it was the party organization itself which carried out most of the activities associated with the presidential campaign. This has changed and, as we have seen, presidential electioneering has undergone a revolutionary transformation since 1960. Parties have not been displaced in the process, but their organizational contribution to the campaign effort has been marginalized or subordinated to the efforts of candidate organizations.

The picture of electioneering painted in this book is not new. As early as 1976 Robert Agranoff cited four developments (now largely familiar) in political campaigning which he asserted had given rise to a "new style" of campaign politics in the United States:

- The candidate rather than the party has become the chief focus of the campaign;
- The campaign is no longer run by party professionals but by campaign professionals, media specialists, etc.;
- These professionals apply their prior experience in markets to electorates;
- A variety of media, not just political parties, is used to communicate the campaign message.

The modern mode of modern presidential electioneering also prevails in countries other than the United States; in this book we have seen it in the cases of France and Russia. A recent and growing body of scholarly literature, anticipated by Agranoff's study, speaks to the notion that candidate-centered electioneering practices and campaigns are spreading to other countries[2] and is often referred to as an "Americanization" of campaign politics. Although this work is focused on parliamentary elections, to a greater or lesser degree it describes modern electioneering in other countries as a more candidate-centered process in which party has become increasingly marginalized and where the use of sophisticated technology and campaign professionals has become more and more commonplace.[3] These conclusions parallel Agranoff's. In short, what is happening to electioneering practices in the United States is not unique.

This chapter will pull together the various strands of what we have learned about presidential electioneering in the modern era in the United States, France, and Russia. In the first section we will briefly review the factors which have contributed to the personalization of presidential electioneering. Following that, we revisit the various elements of modern presidential electioneering, highlighting the roles of political parties and presidential candidates. Finally, we will examine some of the implications of a more personalized mode of presidential electioneering.

WHAT HAPPENED?

A variety of not-unrelated factors have contributed to the organizational personalization of presidential electioneering. Many are familiar to students of party politics and are often discussed in what has become a perennial "decline of parties" debate.[4] Most social change is multicausal and the personalization of presidential electioneering is no exception. What follows does not pretend to be an in-depth analysis but is intended to highlight institutional and societal factors associated with the personalization of presidential electioneering.

The first and perhaps most obvious institutional factor associated with personalized presidential electioneering is the nature of the office itself, namely, its unitary structure. This is not to suggest that personalized presidential electioneering is inevitable with a unitary executive, but simply than the potential exists. Regardless of the electoral system chosen to select the president, only one will be selected and this all but demands an individual focus. Other variations in the institutional design of the office do not seem to have much effect on the process. Specifically, the presence or absence of a second-in-command, length of term of office, or provisions for re-eligibility, do not seem to have made much difference in the personalization of presidential electioneering when we compare the experiences of the United States and France.

Similarly, in spite of the differences in media systems and restrictions (or lack thereof) on television advertising in the three countries we examined in this book, there seems to be little difference in the amounts of time and energy put into producing television appearances (paid or otherwise) by candidates. In particular, France's fairly restrictive media access system (government-sponsored television access only with no paid advertising) does not seem to have abated the personalization process, rising costs, or the individual focus of the campaign. Finally, the nature of the party system, type of political parties, or their maturity and complexity seem to make little difference in whether presidential electioneering in the modern era is more candidate or party-centered.

We can, however, point to three institutional factors which may facilitate personalized presidential electioneering. The first, specific to the United States, is the movement toward convention delegate selection by way of direct primaries. The effect of this development on the personalization of presidential electioneering has been profound. Control of the recruitment, screening, and selection of the party nominee has shifted such that the party has virtually no say in who will carry its banner in the November election. Furthermore, since securing the party nomination is dependent on a candidate's own efforts, presidential aspirants are building large, well-financed campaign organizations earlier and earlier, and these organizations play a prominent role throughout the remainder of the election season. Comparison with France suggests that primaries cannot be the singular cause of the personalization of electioneering practices since French political parties have nominal control over the selection of their presidential nominee. What makes the French system similar to the United States' is the lack of regularized, party-controlled nomination procedures. The net result is the same, namely, that candidates rely on self to secure the party nomination.

The second institutional factor which fairly can be associated with personalized presidential electioneering is campaign finance laws which, by whatever the specific arrangement, put money directly into the hands of candidates as opposed to channeling campaign funds through political parties. This is no less significant than the direct primary system in terms of its effect on the process since it has the formal effect of de-coupling parties and candidates. Put another way, candidates have less incentive to align with and rely on parties if they are largely dependent on their own efforts to fund the campaign effort. However, here again we must exercise caution in attributing too large of an effect on personalized presidential electioneering to campaign finance laws. The pre-reform period of the modern era in the United States (1960 through 1976) suggests that candidates could and would seek out (and find) other sources of campaign funding on their own. Therefore, campaign finance laws which put money directly into the hands of candidates rather than parties probably only formalize what might otherwise be informal practice.

The final institutional factor involved in the personalization of presidential electioneering practices is the existence of fairly open media systems, meaning at least some private ownership of mass media outlets and a constitutionally guaranteed freedom of the press. Together these allow candidates access to channels of mass media, enabling them to convey their message to the public without the assistance of their party (if any).

There are several societal factors associated with the personalizing trend in presidential electioneering as well, many of which are related. First, technological advancements, both in transportation and communication, have reduced candidates' reliance on their parties for political communication. Modern jet travel, in conjunction with what seems to be perpetual progress in communications technologies, continues to make the world a smaller place. It would be unimaginable for an individual to carry a campaign (of any sort) across the expanse of the United States without these developments. In the pre-aviation and pre-electronic age the practical utility of a political party was evident: political communication was virtually impossible without one. In addition to these considerations, many of the newer communications technologies, in particular television, are far more amenable to an individual focus. The effect of this on presidential electioneering is perhaps clearer if one tries to imagine how a political party might portray itself to the public on television. Television simply is not well suited to conveying complex messages or covering complex processes: there are no party "sound bites."

Television's role in political campaigning, while not trivial, is hardly the whole story here, since the "broadcasting" of political messages has been increasingly supplemented by "narrowcasting" technologies and techniques or the targeting of specialized messages to particular groups. This has been facilitated by advances in computer technology. From the advent of the first mainframe computers to increasingly powerful desktop computing devices, this development has been of incalculable (no pun intended) value in information management. Record keeping, analysis of polling data, database management and use, and more have all been facilitated (indeed, in some cases made possible by) the increased availability of modern computers. Concomitant with this, in what may be referred to as other scientific developments, have been advances in survey methodology and information management as well as a body of knowledge dealing with marketing and marketing techniques (recall that the first campaign professionals, after all, were drawn from marketing agencies). In sum, we might think of technology and knowledge as part of an overall forward march in the realm of science and the crafting and targeting of political messages is increasingly sophisticated because of this. Some have referred to this development as a "scientification" of politics.[5]

Sophisticated marketing and technology calls for specialists, and the history of political election campaigning suggests that candidates will be ever conscious of, and anxious to deploy, the latest in communication and campaign management technology (e.g., the use of World Wide Web sites in 1996 and 2000 in the United States). It was probably not inevitable that a "scientification" of politics would come at the expense of displacing political parties in the electioneering effort. Indeed, the personnel of party organizations could have become proficient at these skills (and increasingly, many are). But they did not, at least not immediately. Candidates, in short, began to look elsewhere (originally in marketing or polling firms) for people who knew how to use these technologies.

Enter campaign professionals, a class of individuals whose emergence and viability (perhaps even vitality) as an industry may have been to some extent inevitable, given the rather diffuse but no less evident process of social modernization.[6] Approaches to defining "modernization" differ widely, but one of the less controversial aspects of the process is an increased division of labor (or specialization) in the economy along with which comes a certain professionalization and an accumulation and diffusion of knowledge.[7] The plain fact is that presidential candidates came to rely on a growing and increasingly specialized and professional class of individuals to conduct their campaigns, and that reliance continues to grow unabated, not least because advances in marketing, polling, and communications technologies continue. The point? Campaign professionals do for the candidate what the party used to do, namely, conduct the campaign. Traditional party elites have been displaced as strategists, tacticians, and conveyors of the candidates' message in presidential campaigns.

Two other societal factors are relevant to a discussion of the personalization of presidential electioneering. First, although we have avoided discussion of the electorate in this book, it should at least be mentioned that in terms of the electioneering effort, the less partisan electorate of the modern era provides little (if any) incentive for candidates to align too closely with party. This has affected the crafting of candidate images and appeals, where in the extreme cases candidates have deliberately campaigned as party and Washington "outsiders" (e.g., Jimmy Carter). In addition, an electorate less mobilized along partisan lines, along with an increase in cognitive skills and a greater availability of political information, has contributed to a "new politics" of greater levels of previously "unconventional" political participation, including issue- and candidate-oriented mobilization that often takes group form. This is one factor in the increased involvement of independent groups in the electoral process.[8]

In short, differences in the institutional design of the presidency seem to have made little difference in whether or not there has been a personalization of presidential electioneering practices in the United States, France, and Russia. Three aspects of the institutional environment of the selection process have aided in the personalization of presidential electioneering, namely, unstructured party nomination procedures, campaign finance laws which put money directly in the hands of presidential aspirants, and open media systems (at least some private ownership and constitutionally guaranteed freedom of the press). We have also identified a set of societal factors that has aided in this development which can best (if cautiously) be summed up as part of the process of social modernization, in particular, an increased body of scientific knowledge and economic specialization.

The modern mode of presidential electioneering may not be universal, but from what we have seen here we can speculate that organizational candidate-centeredness could be expected in presidential campaigns and elections elsewhere given certain conditions, namely:

- Unstructured party nomination procedures;
- Fairly ready access by candidates to finances which are unconnected to political parties;
- Fairly ready access by candidates to media exposure;
- Fairly ready access by candidates to the fruits of modern technology and the specialists who know how to use those technologies.

PRESIDENTIAL ELECTIONEERING IN THE MODERN ERA

Political parties are by no means irrelevant in modern presidential electioneering. Although we have not discussed this dimension of political parties in this book, it should be remembered that at minimum a party label functions as an information shortcut, providing the electorate with an initial understanding of where a candidate stands on certain

Conclusions   155

issues and thus simplifying political communication. As we have seen
throughout the book, parties in both the United States and France are
more capable electioneering machines than in 1960. By virtually any definition they are now stronger organizations. However, their role in the
presidential selection process has changed. At the risk of over-
simplifying, where once they were in control of the campaign and ran
the candidate of their choice, they now attempt to be of service to the
candidate who wins the party nomination by other means.

The Personnel of Modern Presidential Electioneering

In Chapter 4 we saw that in both France and the United States, particularly throughout the 1980s, party organizations have grown and are
continuing to grow. The size of both major party organizations in the
United States has increased roughly tenfold since 1972. Both parties now
maintain a year-round national staff of several hundred people, a staff
which expands considerably during election years, and staffing in both
state and local party organizations has increased. In addition to having
more hands to perform electioneering tasks, specialization within party
organizations has increased; this trend would be consistent with the
growth and institutionalization of any organization, as would the increased professionalization of party staffers. Electioneering personnel increasingly move from party to candidate to private practice, illustrating
their increased professionalization.[9] In short, party national chairpersons
preside over increasingly specialized and capable electioneering machines.

Some evidence also suggests that American political parties are more
cohesive units. Intra-party leadership and ideological factional struggles
continue, but are being managed better (at least at the national convention when they are in the public eye). Like in the traditional era, this has
a positive effect on the electioneering effort; unlike in the traditional era,
this is probably the result of the fact that the nomination is decided long
before the convention begins. The real change in party orientation is the
fact that they seem to have embraced their new role as service organizations to "their" presidential candidate. This role reversal probably
comes as an almost natural result of the fact that they lost (abdicated?)
their control over the process of candidate selection. It also reflects the
fact that they were slow to adapt to newer electioneering practices; in
other words, the shift can be seen as an institutional response to ensure
their own survival.

French political parties, like most European parties, have always been
more centralized and more organizationally proficient than those in the
United States but have become more so since the inception of the Fifth
Republic. Much of this increased strength has been driven by presiden-

tial campaign politics. Although mass membership in most French parties has declined, the major parties now have larger and more professionalized staff and an increased division of labor within their organizations. The real story of interest with respect to the personnel aspect of French political parties is found in the personalities of those parties. Personality and party factionalism (a logical extension) play a dominant role in French politics, especially in French presidential politics. If French party leaders are not the party's main presidential aspirant (and they often are), they typically take a back seat to the individual who is.

While personality is arguably more important in French presidential selection than ever, so too is a strong party. Trying to parse the relationship between party, party factions, party leaders, and presidential aspirants in French politics is exceedingly difficult. Increased personalization of French presidential politics takes a form which may be referred to as political *party* entrepreneurship. In order to win the top national office, viable presidential candidates must either build or overthrow, and then maintain and lead a major political party. The history of presidential campaign politics in the Fifth Republic is one of notable political personalities jockeying for position within their party and effectively taking control of it, or, simply starting their own party.

Little accident then that overall party cohesion in France seems increasingly driven by electoral considerations. This is reflected in the increasingly pragmatic candidate platforms and the non-binding nature of ideologically-oriented party platforms. This may not sit well with party activists, but there is little evidence that the pattern of growing electoral pragmaticism is abating.

There has been some progress by way of party development in Russia, but there are numerous obstacles. The fact that Russia does not allow a party name on the presidential ballot beside a candidate's name unless that party has collected the signatures necessary for registering the candidate and specifically nominated the candidate would appear to be a good sign for the future of party politics. Of the main political parties in Russia in 1996, only the Communist Party displayed signs of being organizationally mature. They were well staffed and organized with branch offices throughout the country. However, they were deeply divided over basic policy (and regime) questions and this affected the campaign effort. Other Russian parties are young and personalized, but some are already fairly well developed, including the Liberal Democrats. The party is a vehicle for neo-fascist Vladimir Zhirinovsky, but this by itself should not preclude organizational development. Other Russian parties are also developing fairly well, including Our Home is Russia, Yabloko, Russia's Democratic Choice, and the Agrarian Party. It would be foolish to prognosticate about the future of party politics in Russia, but there are several parties which were registered for the Duma elections of 1999 and could prove to be a force in the coming years. These include the pro-Kremlin Unity Party, founded by several dozen regional leaders in late September 1999, and the center-left electoral alliance of Fatherland-All Russia, which boasts of, among others, political luminaries Moscow Mayor Yuri Luzhkov and former prime minister Yevgeni Primakov, both very popular and considered prime presidential candidates for the 2000 election.[10]

Candidate organizations are a phenomenon new to the modern era of presidential electioneering. Although systematic evidence on their size and composition is sketchy, it is safe to say that the staff of candidate organizations in the United States, at least those of the more successful candidates, number in the hundreds. That number may be lower based on differences in how aspirants for the nomination allocate their resources and how competitive that struggle is, but when the general election season starts the organizations of the major party candidates are fully staffed with several hundred full-time staff. During the primary season, candidates who have won favor with a particular state's political leaders can sometimes count on the support of that state's organization staff; during the general election season this is certainly the case for candidates of both parties in all states.

Similar to electioneering in the traditional era, candidates in all countries often place great stock in the advice of close family members and retain final decision-making power. Candidate organizations differ with respect to their hierarchical structure but virtually all of the top positions are filled with campaign professionals (see Text Boxes 4.2 and 4.3), the new electioneers. Employing sophisticated techniques and offering a wide array of services, it is virtually unthinkable to run a presidential campaign without a team of these high-priced professionals. However, because of their involvement, candidate organization cohesion often suffers; probably because of their high degree of professionalism (as well as their egos), there is often infighting within candidate organizations, most frequently over the direction in which the campaign should go.

Although the formal politics of selecting the party nominee in France and Russia differ from the process in the United States, we have seen similar developments in the growth and professionalization of candidate organizations in those countries. Candidates in both countries build and rely on their own organizations throughout the campaign, retaining the services of campaign professionals, both "imported" (American) and "home grown" (importantly, the proliferation of campaign professionals in France seems to have been influenced by electioneering practices and practitioners in the United States, which supports the notion that electioneering practices in other countries have been, or are becoming, "Americanized").

Even before we move the discussion to the resources involved in modern presidential electioneering one thing becomes apparent. Since a political party is an organization whose main purpose is to place their representatives into positions of government (see Chapter 3, note 46), it is clear that with one difference, modern candidate organizations bear a striking resemblance to political parties. That difference, the fact that they are only temporary organizations, is not insignificant. But with candidate organizations forming earlier and earlier, their "temporary" status becomes increasingly less so, and the tendency for highly placed members of candidate organizations to follow elected presidents into appointed office further blurs the distinction, since these officials are ostensibly appointed to help pursue the president's (not the party's) policy agenda.

The Resources of Modern Presidential Electioneering

In addition to being better staffed, political parties in the United States are financially more viable than even a decade ago. By way of smaller donations from direct mail programs as well as larger donations from fund-raising events, parties have more money at their disposal to engage in electioneering activities. Campaign finance laws have allowed political parties to raise and spend increasing amounts of money and they have done just that. American political parties are now allowed to raise and spend more "hard money" relative to candidates than when the campaign finance reform laws of the 1970s were enacted, but they play little formal role during the primary season and a minimal one in financing the general election campaign. The funding of the national convention, of course, is totally their domain, and here funding by major corporations through convention host committees (especially in 1996) reminds one of the "fat cat" days of campaign finance.

Presidential aspirants are using a variety of means to raise increasing amounts of money for their electioneering efforts prior to the start of the primary season. Their most common strategy to do this while circumventing campaign finance laws is to form technically independent leadership PACs which allow them to raise unlimited amounts of money, the bulk of which goes to the building of the aspirant's campaign organization. Although direct mail remains a popular method of fund-raising, developing and relying on a network of large donors is more efficient; often the same donors are solicited more than once. An increasingly popular way for candidates to raise large donations is the practice known as "bundling," where an individual or an organization collects donations from a variety of sources and then presents the "bundled" total, technically a collection of smaller donations, to the campaign effort. George W. Bush's Pioneers were so effective at this method that by the summer of 1999 he had raised $37 million and had announced he would not seek federal matching funds in 2000.

In France the picture of campaign finance is less clear because data concerning campaigns held before 1988 are largely speculative. Reforms of the late 1980s and early 1990s have regularized campaign finance in France and made it more transparent. Presidential electioneering has certainly become more expensive in France, but the fact that television advertising is banned has probably contained the cost somewhat, at least by comparison with the United States. Parties rely on a variety of sources for their funding, including dues from elected officials and members as well as direct mail programs inspired by American parties. Parties and candidates can now solicit donations from private individuals but the rules are structured such that candidates have, and use, a variety of options (private donations, the state, and their party) to fund their campaign efforts.

Perhaps what stands out most in all three countries with respect to campaign finance is that the expense of modern presidential electioneering (combined with the stakes involved) drives participants to circumvent campaign finance laws. This is probably most apparent in Russia, where President Yeltsin (and his team) made no attempt to comply with spending limits in 1996. In France anecdotal evidence suggests that illicit funding of political campaigns has not been completely eliminated by campaign finance reform. The fact that great sums of money are reportedly (but unofficially) spent by candidates prior to the official campaign probably supports this suspicion and is similar to the situation in the United States where the increased importance of raising large amounts of money before the primary season begins has made candidates far more "creative" in their compliance with campaign finance laws. In addition, the explosion in the raising and spending of soft money in the United States suggests an almost complete disintegration of the spirit (and in some cases the letter) of the campaign finance reform laws of the 1970s.

Non-monetary resources have assumed greater importance in presidential electioneering as well. In the United States and France both parties maintain permanent headquarters in the national capitol as well as in states and regions, replete with the fruits of modern communications technology, research divisions to collect and analyze information, and data sets which aid in fund-raising and communication. Evidence also suggests that links between parties and other groups are becoming more institutionalized, adding even more muscle to the campaign effort. Candidates' organizations are acquiring and using greater amounts of non-monetary resources as well; they are increasingly guarded about press access in an attempt to control information about their selves; air travel has become mandatory (particularly in the United States and Russia); finally, candidates are directly allying with independent groups and other political leaders. These ties are especially important since they provide additional hands for the campaign effort as well as often furnishing physical resources (e.g., state headquarters).

Controlling resources in politics typically (though not always) translates into greater strength for those who control them. Modern presidential electioneering places a growing premium on the acquisition and control of electoral resources, to the extent that in all countries candidates and parties seem to be willing to risk breaking the law to procure them. Only a few decades ago party played a much larger role in the supply of these critical resources to candidates. Now, they are increasingly in the hands of candidates. Indeed, if we consider how much money leadership PACs raise and spend, how they spend it (on their presidential candidate, but also contributing to the campaign efforts of others), and the number of years these organizations operate, it is striking how similar they are to political parties in terms of their resource base.

The Processes of Modern Presidential Electioneering: Choosing Candidates and Campaign Activity

In the traditional era of presidential electioneering parties were central in the process of candidate selection; they now play only a minimal role.[11] Though party ties are still important, especially so in France, we saw that candidates play the dominant role in all aspects of the selection process in all three countries examined in this book. Choosing candidates, meaning the recruitment, screening, and selection of the eventual party nominee is now a matter of political entrepreneurship. One report notes that after seeing the movie "The Candidate," Dan Quayle concluded that he was better looking than Robert Redford and with the help of campaign professionals he could make a successful bid for the White House.[12] The process of recruitment and selection has been opened up to individuals with few or no party ties and even to those with no prior political experience (e.g., Steve Forbes, Ross Perot). In addition, recruitment and organization-building efforts are starting increasingly earlier; it seems foolish to consider a run for the presidency without preparing for the effort at least a few years in advance.

In the United States, political parties are now almost entirely absent from the nomination process; the nomination of French and Russian presidential candidates is actually a "system" of candidate self-designation and self-promotion. In all three countries it is a rather unstructured system of self-reliance which rewards early and efficient self-starters. Candidates must begin building large and efficient organizations early and their reliance on these organizations continues after the party nomination has been won. Thus party nominees, with an organizational power structure similar to that of their party, play a large role in managing the party national convention (in the United States) and in the drafting and adoption of the party platform.

The activities associated with political campaigns in the modern era are not entirely dissimilar from their traditional counterparts. Campaign management, for example, still involves crafting and implementing a strategy designed to secure the support of 50 percent plus one of the electorate and taking steps to implement that strategy. Decisions are made about where best to deploy resources (including the candidate, his running mate, and his family members) based on pre-existing bases of support, which key blocs of votes may be contestable, the prevailing political and economic climate, whichever issues may be salient at the moment, and many other factors. Typically the strategy centers around devoting most of the resources to large states where the candidate has some chance of winning. Implementation of the strategy, in other words scheduling and arranging the candidate visits, is the next step, and involves taking care of many details such that the candidate visit (the event) goes off as planned, hopefully attracting favorable news coverage in the process.

Political communications in the modern era, like in the traditional era, is still driven by considerations of partisan and issue content as well as candidate imagery. Finding the theme, preferably a singular and simple one which will resonate positively with the majority of voters, is still key. What is distinctive about political communications and campaign management in the modern era can be summed up in two words: campaign professionals. In all three countries, it is the members of this growing and increasingly specialized industry who are the new electioneers. They are the ones who take the polls and analyze the data which drive strategic considerations of where to target the campaign as well as identifying which appeals are most likely to resonate with voters and why. They occupy top positions in the candidate organization, making (many, if not most) decisions about the campaign, and directing its implementation. They craft the campaign messages, arrange for their production, purchase the media spots to air or print, and take care of media relations. This does not exhaust the list of tasks for which they are responsible. Policy and opposition research, data management, the production and distribution of campaign literature, paraphernalia, posters and signs, and audio-visual advertisements, technical-legal work to insure that the organization is in compliance with various electoral and campaign finance laws, fund-raising, and more, are their domain as well.

In the past all of these tasks were carried out by political parties. In fact, it might be argued that presidential campaign activity was the original raison d'être for political parties in the United States. Quite simply,

candidates needed the expertise, connections, and organizations of political parties to nationalize their message and mobilize support. This has
changed. Indeed, that may be the understatement of this study. One of
the major themes in any account of modern political campaigning is the
proliferation of campaign professionals, professionals who, as a rule,
work for candidate organizations. To be sure, political parties also employ campaign professionals, but it is candidates who, on the whole, take
advantage of their services. And since advances in communications and
information technology continue, the demand for the array of specialists
who have mastered these technologies will as well. This is true in the
United States as well as in France and Russia.

It would be reductionist to claim that parties no longer play a role in
the process dimension of presidential selection but their role has been
minimized. Moreover, modern presidential candidates are increasingly
less dependent on political parties in the conduct of general campaign
activity. Put another way, candidates and their surrogates have, by and
large, replaced parties as the campaigners, and parties have little say
over who shall bear their party name. This in turn affects other activities
in the process (e.g., the organization and operation of party conventions,
the content of party platforms). Parties are still important throughout the
process, but their relationship with presidential aspirants has changed.
To re-state the obvious, parties are less in control of the campaign effort.
The shift to more candidate-centered presidential electioneering has implications for both the future of parties and governance, as will be discussed in the final section.

IMPLICATIONS

This examination of presidential electioneering practices is suggestive
of several things. First, and perhaps obviously, it suggests that modern
political campaigns, at least at the presidential level, are no place for
amateurs. Presidential aspirants must start their efforts early; they must
be well organized and well funded; they must be, or become, nationally
known; and to be successful, they must rely on campaign professionals
to run their campaign. What this says about normative questions like
the nature of modern democratic elections and representation is another
matter. The role of the citizen seems, at the least, greatly reduced, somewhat analogous to a fan at a sporting event. Fans are important in sports
(e.g., in the case of a "home field advantage"), but in the end, teams win
or lose based on their ability to play the game. Fans are, at best, ancillary
to the process. It may be that we are in, or are entering, an era where
the winning presidential aspirant is that individual who can best work
the system, regardless of what the citizenry might want. This overstates
the case but it does so to make a point: modern presidential electioneer-

ing practices might be such that citizens are increasingly marginal to the election outcome.

Another striking feature of modern presidential electioneering that this book has brought to light is how similar candidate organizations, at least those of the better-funded candidates, are to party organizations. They are often in operation for several years; they are staffed with large, specialized, and professional staff who are committed to getting their candidate elected; they are extremely well funded; they also boast of a wealth of other resources, including direct association with independent groups which formerly allied with political parties and state party organizations; and of course, they do much of the campaigning themselves. Moreover, many of the top individuals in the organization are retained from one year to the next and in the case of an elected president, follow the candidate into office, working with the president to pursue his (not the party's) policy agenda.

This comparative look at electioneering in three countries may also contain a lesson for would-be reformers. For example, a great deal of energy is expended in both the scholarly community and in Washington, D.C. over the subject of "real" campaign finance reform. The constitutional difficulties of this issue aside, the experience of all three countries suggests that when election politics are expensive, candidates and parties will find ways to get more money. This is most emphatically not to suggest that reform efforts are a waste of time. However, the root of the problem is not necessarily avarice on the part of over-ambitious candidates but rather the expense of elections themselves. Similarly, the experience of France suggests that banning political advertising (a constitutional impossibility in the United States) would not by itself drive the costs of elections down completely, since candidates would still spend great sums on the production of their government-sponsored media spots. Finally, to demonstrate the axiom that changes in one part of a system produce (often unintended) changes in another part of the system, while campaign finance laws which were in part intended to reduce the power of business interests in campaign politics have arguably accomplished that, they have also institutionalized the role of interests in electoral politics.

The remainder of this section is devoted to two main questions. First, how have modern presidential electioneering practices affected the kinds of individuals who run, are successful in, and can win presidential elections? Second, what effect have they had on president-party ties, both before and after the election, and how does this affect policy?

164 Modern Presidential Electioneering

Aspirants, Candidates, and Presidents in the Modern System

Presidential evaluation is practiced by journalists, historians, political scientists, and citizens alike. Does the modern system produce good presidents? Does it test or teach the qualities that presidents should have? Are capable but uncharismatic people disadvantaged in the modern system? Asking this question immediately runs the risk of placing the researcher (and his or her analysis) into heated debate. In the end, the difficulty is both empirical and normative, since the criterion by which we judge, or should judge, presidents is far from clear. Here, Bert Rockman's observation is apt: "How can we select presidents who are both temperate and competent? How can we . . . select presidents who are apt to be successful by whatever reasonable criteria we employ? The answer, despite a good bit of inveighing to the contrary, is pretty simple. No one knows."[13]

To state the obvious, rules matter. The structure of the process of presidential selection advantages some and disadvantages others. This includes what kinds of people, with what kind of qualities get on the ballot, and the kind of president the process eventually produces. Modern presidential electioneering clearly produces different kinds of candidates. First of all, it probably affects who decides *not* to run for president. Increased media attention probably repels some (e.g., Colin Powell in 1996), and the front-loaded primary season has had a profound "scare-off" effect for many potential, some probably capable, presidential aspirants. In 1996 the front-loaded primary season and the prospect of intensive fund-raising efforts (combined with media attention) led to ten Republican "declarations of noncandidacy" from August 1994 to late November 1995, including Jack Kemp, Dick Cheney, Dan Quayle, and Newt Gingrich.[14]

One of the biggest faults of the modern nominating system is its failure to deal adequately with political ambition, since the ability to build party support is no longer a prerequisite for success in modern presidential electioneering.[15] It is here that we find the answer to an unanswered riddle from Chapters 5 and 6: if stature and the relative chance of success matters more in the recruitment process (and there is little reason to believe it does not) and the chances of nominating a long-shot candidate are increasingly less (there are no dark horses in the modern age), why are there more candidacies and more extreme candidacies (e.g., Pat Buchanan in the United States, France's Jean Marie Le Pen, Russia's Vladimir Zhirinovsky) per election cycle? In fact, why do "extreme" candidates run at all? The simple answer is that since parties have less, if any, control over choosing their candidate, their ability to moderate extreme elements (to channel ambition) is lessened. Actually, the recent emergence and success of extreme candidates should come as no surprise at all, since anyone who knows how to work the electioneering system and has (or can gain access to) the resources to do so can emerge as a "viable" candidate—theoretically, entirely independent of party (à la Ross Perot).[16] In fact, a bombastic personality capable of attracting media attention can gain access to the presidential arena without a tremendous amount of money (as in the cases of Pat Buchanan, Jean Marie Le Pen, and Vladimir Zhirinovsky.)

From what we have seen in this book, those individuals with the following qualities, not all of which are unrelated, would seem to be especially well suited to be successful at modern presidential electioneering. The individual should:

- Have the independent ability to raise a great deal of money;
- Have the ability to build and maintain public support;
- Have the ability to organize a campaign well, or have the good sense to delegate this task to someone who can;
- Have a certain charismatic (at the minimum, telegenic) style, meaning appearance and speaking ability;
- Have an impeccable family background, as well as very thick skin;
- Be nationally known and/or well connected; and
- Be extremely comfortable with newer technologies.[17]

Many of these qualities were helpful, if not essential, in the traditional era of presidential electioneering (e.g., being nationally known and well connected), but in the modern era they seem to be indispensable to success.

What skills are brought to, or learned from, the campaign? Does the process help elected presidents govern more effectively? Most of the work which addresses this issue is found tangentially in party scholarship. One noted scholar claimed that in the modern system, "what it takes to achieve the nomination differs . . . sharply from what it takes to govern effectively."[18] Knowledge of national government seems to be of little importance in presidential electioneering but certain campaign skills help in governing. The ability to build and maintain public support can be of some use in office, although public support is notoriously difficult to translate into influence in office (President Clinton discovered this in his health care reform bid in 1994).[19] Organizational skills, which ostensibly are not task-specific, are important during campaigns and thus also useful in governing. And a successful candidate must be able to build coalitions, though these no longer need be strictly party coalitions (this is addressed in more detail below); this also helps in governance. However, as one analyst noted in a comparison of executive (presidential and prime ministerial) selection and learning systems in the modern era, presidents generally "learn to campaign" rather than govern.[20] This leads to a discussion of president-party ties.

President-Party Ties in the Modern System

It is arguably in this category, which is admittedly not-unconnected to the previous one, that the most serious implications of a more personalized presidential selection process can be seen. This area cuts to the heart of the matter, namely, the relationship between party and candidate. One of the main assumptions of this book is that although the existence of political parties by no means guarantees democracy, they are vital for the functioning of a healthy democratic political order. In the strictest sense this is only an assumption, albeit one with which most political scientists would agree. The relationship between a stable party system and a healthy democracy seems well established.[21] Larry Diamond's observation is apt:

Political parties remain important if not essential instruments for presenting political constituencies and interests, aggregating demands and preferences, recruiting and socializing new candidates for office, organizing the electoral competition for power, crafting policy alternatives, setting the policy-making agenda, forming effective governments, and integrating groups and individuals into the democratic process.[22]

That being said, in an era when the role of political parties is rapidly changing and direct political communications between the elite and the citizenry are increasingly facilitated by modern technologies, the possibility that democracy can exist without political parties ought to be allowed. Having allowed for that possibility, this book assumes that it is highly unlikely, and further, explicitly questions the viability of a democratic order without political parties.

There are serious implications for political parties, the party system, and governing in a more personalized presidential selection system. To echo Juan Linz's warning, it is especially important in countries making the transition to democracy, many of whom are choosing presidential government.[23] Parties are a mediating influence, a stable channel for the marshaling of disparate political forces, and without that mediating influence, messianic and self-reliance tendencies in a president may be encouraged or exacerbated and the potential for abuse of power becomes greater. Therefore, strong president-party ties are critical for the system; probably to the surprise of no one, all strong-party theorists line up against the personalization of presidential selection since it weakens party influence over, and ties with, the executive.

Some analysts claim that all successful presidents in American history have been effective party leaders, and indeed, there is nothing inherent in the modern system which precludes strong president-party ties.[24] Ronald Reagan was, according to most, a successful party leader.[25] The fact is, however, that in the modern era the gap between presidential candidates and their party is increasing, not least because candidates have less of a need for their parties to win office. Moreover, the increased prominence of independent groups in electoral politics suggest that coalition building during the campaign is increasingly done outside conventional party bounds. This surely affects party ties afterwards. The increased distance between candidate and party is more easily seen in the case of the United States than in France, where how one judges the relationship between party and candidate may depend on the view one takes of who has "won the prize." In other words, is the presidency won by the candidate or the party? It is difficult to see how president-party ties in Russia will develop since the current president has no party; in the United States president-party ties are generally tenuous at best.

This said, how do president-party ties affect policy direction and, given political campaign styles, can elected officials be held accountable for policy success or failure? Party lends a certain stability to the direction and course of policy, insulating it to some degree from the whims of the public. In the extreme, a candidacy unconnected to a political party runs a danger similar to that which the founders feared, namely, demagogic or populist politics. Moreover, a less partisan citizenry is more volatile, and a president's ability to maintain long term public support suffers as a consequence.

Presidential electioneering practices affect how, and with whom, a president sets out to accomplish his policy agenda.[26] It must be stressed, and most emphatically, that a successful presidential candidate cannot ignore his party organization. The issue here is whether or not personalized campaigns marginalize the party such that coalition-building efforts after the election are compromised. Charles Jones notes that party linkages are especially "needed under conditions of distributed power" in the United States.[27] An "extraordinarily self-centered" election process has the potential (as per Juan Linz) to exacerbate messianic and self-reliance tendencies in a new president, leading to party exclusion afterwards.[28] Many, in fact, have noted that presidents find it increasingly difficult to translate electoral support into governing support and that alliances between presidents and parties are now both shorter and more volatile.[29]

Short-term, electoral considerations of personalized campaigns increasingly seem to drive policy direction and may also raise false expectations about presidential performance. In this sense, the modern selection process may be increasingly deficient. Electoral considerations have driven down the ideological content of campaign platforms in France; in the United States, ideological content has probably remained constant (in others words, minimal). Theodore Lowi claimed that all modern presidents eventually fall victim to a cycle of high expectations that they can never fulfill;[30] similarly, James Ceaser noted an increase of less-than-principled appeals by candidates in the modern nominating system.[31] Others note that because the American selection process is loosely structured, pollsters may encourage candidates to adopt policy stands which diverge from the party line.[32] Bill Clinton's constant use of focus group polling in the formulation of policy is a clear, though by no means the first, example of this.

In this respect, Nelson Polsby wondered how and if a "new elite" of campaign professionals can be held accountable to the public.[33] Indeed, presidential accountability in the new selection environment suffers as well in the modern selection process. Without party, how can the president be held accountable for his or her policy initiatives? While some research suggests that elected presidents generally keep (or try hard to keep) their campaign promises, this does not guarantee accountability, theoretical or otherwise.[34] As part of, but by no means the sole leader of, the Democratic party, can Clinton be held accountable for Democratic defections in Congress (on, for example, the rejection of presidential fast-track trading authority in 1997)?

How we select presidents has serious consequences for the type of individual who becomes president, as well as having effects on political parties, policy, and the political system as a whole. Understanding the process of presidential selection is perhaps more important now since many countries in this "Third Wave" of democracy seem to be showing a "preference for presidentialism."[35] There are, simply, more presidential systems than ten years ago. Do voters still matter? Are they more than pawns in an electioneering game which is waged among a select few elite? Certainly. After all, they retain control of the ultimate electioneering resource, namely, the vote. However, modern electioneering practices increasingly shape the choice that is presented to them, and thus, what is politically possible after the election. In this general sense, electioneering practices fundamentally shape modern politics.

Appendix A
Presidential Candidates and Their Parties in the United States, 1960–96

Election of 1960 (8 Candidacies)

Goldwater, Barry (R, AZ)
Humphrey, Hubert (D, MN)
Johnson, Lyndon (D, TX)
Kennedy, John (D, MA)
Morse, Wayne (D, OR)
Nixon, Richard (R, NY)
Rockefeller, Nelson (R, NY)
Symington, Stuart (D, MO)

Election of 1964 (9 Candidacies)

Goldwater, Barry (R, AZ)
Johnson, Lyndon (D, TX)
Lodge, Henry Cabot (R, MA)
Nixon, Richard (R, NY)
Rockefeller, Nelson (R, NY)
Scranton, William (R, PA)
Smith, Margaret Chase (R, ME)
Stassen, Harold (R, PA)
Wallace, George (D, AL)

Election of 1968 (9 Candidacies)

Humphrey, Hubert (D, MN)
Kennedy, Robert (D, NY)
Maddox, Lester (D, GA)
McCarthy, Eugene (D, MN)
McGovern, George (D, SD)
Nixon, Richard (R, NY)
Reagan, Ronald (R, CA)
Rockefeller, Nelson (R, NY)
Romney, George (R, MI)

Election of 1972 (16 Candidacies)

Ashbrook, John (R, OH)
Chisholm, Shirley (D, NY)
Harris, Fred (D, OK)
Hartke, Vance (D, IN)
Humphrey, Hubert (D, MN)
Jackson, Henry (D, WA)
Lindsay, John (D, NY)
McCarthy, Eugene (D, MN)
McCloskey, Paul (R, CA)
McGovern, George (D, SD)
Mills, Wilbur (D, AR)
Muskie, Edmund (D, ME)
Nixon, Richard (R, NY)
Sanford, Terry (D, NC)
Wallace, George (D, AL)
Yorty, Sam (D, CA)

Election of 1976 (16 Candidacies)

Bayh, Birch (D, IN)
Bentsen, Lloyd (D, TX)
Brown, Edmund (D, CA)
Byrd, Robert (D, WV)
Carter, Jimmy (D, GA)
Church, Frank (D, ID)
Ford, Gerald (R, MI)
Harris, Fred (D, OK)
Jackson, Henry (D, WA)
McCormack, Ellen (D, NY)
Reagan, Ronald (R, CA)
Sanford, Terry (D, NC)
Shapp, Milton (D, PA)
Shriver, Sargent (D, MD)
Udall, Morris (D, AZ)
Wallace, George (D, AL)

Election of 1980 (13 Candidacies)

Anderson, John (R, IL)
Baker, Howard (R, TN)
Brown, Edmund (D, CA)
Bush, George (R, ME)
Carter, Jimmy (D, GA)
Connally, John (R, TX)
Crane, Phillip (R, IL)
Dole, Robert (R, KS)
Fernandez, Benjamin (R, CA)
Kennedy, Edward (D, MA)
LaRouche, Lyndon (D, NY)
Reagan, Ronald (R, CA)
Stassen, Harold (R, NY)

Election of 1984 (10 Candidacies)

Askew, Reubin (D, FL)	Jackson, Jesse (D, IL)
Cranston, Alan (D, CA)	LaRouche, Lyndon (D, NY)
Glenn, John (D, OH)	McGovern, George (D, SD)
Hart, Gary (D, CO)	Mondale, Walter (D, MN)
Hollings, Ernest (D, SC)	Reagan, Ronald (R, CA)

Election of 1988 (15 Candidacies)

Babbit, Bruce (D, AZ)	Haig, Alexander (R, PA)
Biden, Joseph (D, DE)	Hart, Gary (D, CO)
Bush, George (R, ME)	Jackson, Jesse (D, IL)
Dole, Robert (R, KS)	Kemp, Jack (R, NY)
du Pont, Pierre (R, DE)	LaRouche, Lyndon (D, NY)
Dukakis, Michael (D, MA)	Robertson, Pat (R, VA)
Gephardt, Richard (D, MO)	Simon, Paul (D, IL)
Gore, Albert (D, TN)	

Election of 1992 (12 Candidacies)

Agran, Lawrence (D, CA)	Harkin, Tom (D, IA)
Brown, Edmund (D, CA)	Kerrey, Bob (D, NE)
Buchanan, Patrick (R, VA)	LaRouche, Lyndon (D, NY)
Bush, George (R, ME)	Tsongas, Paul (D, MA)
Clinton, William (D, AR)	Wilder, Douglas (D, VA)
Duke, David (R, LA)	Woods, Charles (D, NV)

Election of 1996 (13 Candidacies)

Alexander, Lamar (R, TN)	Keyes, Alan (R, MD)
Buchanan, Patrick (R, VA)	LaRouche, Lyndon (D, NY)
Clinton, William (D, AR)	Lugar, Richard (R, IN)
Dole, Robert (R, KS)	Specter, Arlen (R, PA)
Dornan, Robert (R, CA)	Taylor, Maurice (R, IL)
Forbes, Steve (R, NJ)	Wilson, Pete (R, CA)
Gramm, Phil (R, TX)	

HOW CANDIDACIES WERE COUNTED

Drawing on *Congressional Quarterly* (1997), candidacies were counted and recorded according to the following rules: (1) if a candidate entered one-third of the total number of primaries, or (2) if a candidate was entered in more than one primary and received 1 percent of the combined vote in all primaries. The first rule was formulated to make a judgement on how to consider candidacies based on write-in votes. The stipulation that the candidate be entered in more than one primary was formulated to deal with "favorite-son" candidacies as in the case of James Rhodes (R, OH) in 1968 whose 100 percent of the Ohio votes (where he was unopposed) gave him 13.7 percent of the combined Republican vote. This, however, was the only primary in which he was entered. Finally, some common sense combined with knowledge of general accounts of campaigns was used in determining the candidate field of 1960 and 1964. Other candidacies were determined according to those recorded by Richard Stanley and Harold Niemi (1998:61–62).

Appendix B
Presidential Candidates, Their Parties, and Their Share of the First-round Vote in France, 1965–95

Election of 1965 (6 Candidacies)

de Gaulle, Charles	Union for the New Republic	43.7%
Mitterand, François	Federation Democratic & Socialist Left	32.2
Lecanuet, Jean	Popular Republican Movement	15.8
Tixier-Vignancour Jean-Louis	(No Party)	5.3
Marcilhacy, Pierre	(No Party)	1.7
Barbu, Marcel	(No Party)	1.2

Election of 1969 (7 Candidacies)

Pompidou, Georges	Union for Defense of Republic	44%
Poher, Alain	Progress and Modern Democracy	23.4
Duclos, Jacques	Communist Party of France	21.5
Defferre, Gaston	French Section Worker's International	5.1
Rocard, Michel	Unified Socialist Party	3.7
Ducatel, Louis	(No Party)	1.3
Krivine, Alain	Trotskyites	1.1

Election of 1974 (12 Candidacies)

Mitterand, François	Socialist Party	43.3%
Giscard d'Estaing, Valéry	Independent Republicans	32.6
Chaban-Delmas, Jacques	Union for Defense of Republic	15.1
Royer, Jean	Gaullists	3.2
Laguiller, Arlette	Trotskyites	2.3
Dumont, René	Environmentalists	1.3
Le Pen, Jean Marie	National Front	.8
Muller, Emile	Socialist Democratic Movement of France	.7
Krivine, Alain	Trotskyites	.4
Renouvin, Bertrand	New French Action	.2
Sebag, Jean Claude	European Federalist Movement	.2
Heraud, Guy (Federalist)	European Federalist	.1

Election of 1981 (10 Candidacies)

Giscard d'Estaing, Valéry	Union of French Democrats	28.3%
Mitterand, François	Socialist Party	25.8
Chirac, Jacques	Rally for the Republic	18.0
Marchais, Georges	Communist Party of France	15.3
Lalonde, Brice	Ecologists	3.9
Laguiller, Arlette	Trotskyites	2.3
Crépeau, Michel	Left-radical Movement	2.2
Debré, Michel	Gaullists	1.6
Garaud, Marie-France	Gaullists	1.3
Bouchardeau, Huguette	Unified Socialist Party	1.1

Election of 1988 (9 Candidacies)

Mitterand, François	Socialist Party	34.1%
Chirac, Jacques	Rally for the Republic	19.5
Barre, Raymond	Union of French Democrats	16.5
Le Pen, Jean Marie	National Front	14.4
Lajoinie, André	Communist Party of France	6.8
Waechter, Antoine	Vertes (Greens)	3.8
Juquin, Pierre	Renovators (Communist, hard-line splinter)	2.1
Laguiller, Arlette	Trotskyites	2.0
Boussel, Pierre	Trotskyites	.4

Election of 1995 (11 Candidacies)

Jospin, Lionel	Socialist Party	23.3%
Chirac, Jacques	Rally for the Republic	20.8
Balladur, Edouard	Union of French Democrats	18.6
Le Pen, Jean Marie	National Front	15.0
Hue, Robert	Communist Party of France	8.6
Laguiller, Arlette	Trotskyites	5.3
de Villiers, Phillippe	Movement for France	4.7
Voynet, Dominique	Vertes (Greens)	3.3
Cheminade, Jacques	Federation for New Solidarity	.3
Waechter, Antoine	Movement of Independent Ecologists	—
Lalonde, Brice	Generation Ecology	—

Note: For 1965–88, see Alistair Cole and Peter Campbell (1989:99, 106, 115, 125, 151); 1995 data from Cristophe Texier (1996).

Appendix C
Presidential Candidates, Their Parties, and Their Share of the First-round Vote in Russia, 1996

Candidate	Party	Vote
Boris Yeltsin	(No Party)	35.3%
Gennadi Zyuganov	Communist	32.0
Aleksander Lebed	(No Party)	14.5
Grigori Yavlinski	Yabloko	7.3
Vladimir Zhirinovsky	Liberal Democrat	5.7
Svyatoslav Fedorov	Worker's Self-Government	.9
Mikhail Gorbachev	International Fund for Socioeconomic & Political Research	.5
Martin Shakkum	Socioeconomic Reform	.4
Yuri Vlasov	National Patriotic Party	.2
Vladimir Bryntsalov	Russian Socialist Party	.2
Aman-Geldy Tuleev	Communist*	< .01
"Against All"	—	1.5

*Tuleev withdrew from the race at the last minute in favor of Zyuganov but was still included in published accounts as the result of early voting in the eastern regions of Russia.

Source: From Stephen White, Richard Rose, and Ian McAllister (1997:260, 267).

Notes

CHAPTER ONE

1. George Stephanopoulos, *Newsweek* (February 8, 1999): 34. This work draws liberally from Jody C Baumgartner, "Electing Presidents and Other Potentates," in Ryan Barilleaux, ed., *Presidential Frontiers: Underexplored Issues in White House Politics* (Westport, CT: Praeger, 1998).

2. An excellent history of political campaigning in America can be found in Robert Dinkin, *Campaigning in America: A History of Election Practices* (Westport, CT: Greenwood, 1989); on the role of television in American politics, see Steven E. Frantzich, *Political Parties in the Technological Age* (London, UK: C. Hurst, 1989); on campaign finance, see Herbert Alexander, *Financing Politics: Money, Elections, and Political Reform* (Washington, DC: CQ Press, 1992); one of the many good accounts of the modern nomination process is James Ceaser, *Presidential Selection: Theory and Development* (Princeton, NJ: Princeton University Press, 1979); for accounts and implications of the rise of political consultants, see Robert V. Friedenberg, *Communication Consultants in Political Campaigns: The Ballot Box Warriors* (Westport, CT: Praeger, 1997).

3. Michael Nelson, "Sentimental Science: Recent Essays on the Politics of Presidential Selection," *Congress and the Presidency* 9(1982):99–106.

4. Dwight Eisenhower was actually the first to use television advertising in his 1952 campaign; see Judith Trent and Robert Friedenberg, *Political Campaign Communication: Principles and Practices* (Westport, CT: Praeger, 1995), p. 11.

5. The Ken-Air Corporation, formed by the Kennedy family, bought a $385,000 Convair airplane which they then leased to the Kennedy campaign at $1.75 per mile. See James Davis, *Presidential Primaries: Road to the White House* (Westport, CT: Greenwood, 1980), p. 221.

6. Quoted in Friedenberg, *Communication Consultants in Political Campaigns*, pp. 20–21.

7. Dinkin, *Campaigning in America*, p. 160.

8. The masculine form of the third-person used throughout much of this book simply reflects the fact that we have yet to elect a woman president.

9. Richard Niemi and Herbert Weisberg, *Controversies in Voting Behavior* (Washington, DC: CQ Press, 1984), offer a succinct summary of the history of voting and election studies; see, especially, pp. 7–9 for the genesis and subsequent development of the National Election Studies. Bernard Susser, "From Burgess to Behavioralism and Beyond," in *Approaches to the Study of Politics* (New York: Macmillan, 1992), offers a similarly concise account of disciplinary development and the rise of the so-called behavioralist movement.

10. This review cannot possibly do justice do the enormous volume of work done in this area. Those with even a passing familiarity of the subject will recognize this claim for the understatement that it is.

11. White's latest effort was *The Making of the President, 1972* (New York: Atheneum, 1973); for the latest from the *Newsweek* team, see Peter Goldman et al., *Quest for the Presidency, 1992* (College Station: Texas A&M University Press, 1994); see also Jack Germond and Jules Witcover, *Mad as Hell: Revolt at the Ballot Box* (New York: Warner Books, 1993).

12. These phrases are from, respectively, Hunter S. Thompson's *Fear and Loathing: On the Campaign Trail '72* (New York: Warner Books, 1973) and Timothy Crouse's *The Boys on the Bus* (New York: Random House, 1973), well-known accounts of the Nixon campaign. Recently Bob Woodward, in *The Choice* (New York: Simon & Schuster, 1996), contributed an account of the early days of President Bill Clinton and Senator Bob Dole's 1996 campaigns.

13. Trent and Friedenberg, *Political Campaign Communication*, p. 12.

14. The political communications literature is voluminous. A good overview can be found in Doris Graber, "Political Communication: Scope, Progress, Promise," in *Political Science: The State of the Discipline II* (Washington, DC: APSA, 1993).

15. Of course, if there were any truly conclusive evidence demonstrating how to influence voting behavior, this entire book could be a footnote.

16. Kathleen Hall Jamieson's *Packaging the Presidency: A History and Criticism of Presidential Campaign Advertising* (New York: Oxford University, 1992), dealing with paid political advertisements, stands out as a fairly comprehensive discussion; see also Matthew McCubbins, *Under the Watchful Eye: Managing Presidential Campaigns in the Television Era* (Washington, DC: CQ Press, 1992), or Marion Just, *Crosstalk: Citizens, Candidates, and the Media in a Presidential Campaign* (Chicago: University of Chicago Press, 1996).

17. Dan Nimmo, "Politics, Media, and Modern Democracy: The United States," in David Swanson and Paolo Mancini, *Politics, Media, and Modern Democracy: An International Study of Innovations in Electoral Campaigning and Their Consequences* (Westport, CT: Praeger, 1996).

18. See Tom Rosenstiel, *Strange Bedfellows: How Television and the Presidential Candidates Changed American Politics, 1992* (New York: Hyperion, 1993), who charges that television and candidates are "strange bedfellows"; Edwin Diamond and Robert Silverson assert that because of television, "the old lines dividing insider and outsider, politics and entertainment, news and talk, have not blurred

as much as they have been obliterated" (*White House to Your House: Media and Politics in Virtual America* [Cambridge, MA: MIT, 1995] p. 7).

19. These include edited volumes by Gerald Pomper (1976–96; the latest, *The Elections of 1996: Reports and Interpretations* [Chatham, NJ: Chatham House, 1997]), Paul R. Abramson et al. (1980–96; the latest, *Change and Continuity in the 1996 Elections* [Washington, DC: CQ Press, 1998]), and Michael Nelson (1984–96; the latest, *The Elections of 1996* [Washington, DC: CQ Press, 1997]).

20. A phrase taken from Arthur Hadley, *The Invisible Primary* (Englewood Cliffs, NJ: Prentice Hall, 1976), referring to the pre-primary phase; other labels include the "early days," from John Kessel, *Presidential Campaign Politics* (Pacific Grove, CA: Brooks/Cole, 1992) or the "exhibition season," from Rhodes Cook, "The Nominating Process," in Michael Nelson, *The Elections of 1988* (Washington, DC: CQ Press, 1989).

21. Thomas E. Patterson, in *Out of Order* (New York: Vintage Books, 1994), claims the media is "out of order" in their coverage of presidential campaigns, noting that the predominant mode of campaign coverage is more oriented to the game, or horse-race aspects of the campaign, as opposed to issues or governing.

22. See, for example, studies by John Kessel on the races of 1980 through 1992 (the latter, Kessel, 1992), and Joseph A. Pika and Richard A. Watson for the races of 1980 through 1996 (the latest, *The Presidential Contest, with a Guide to the 1996 Presidential Race* [Washington, DC: CQ Press, 1996]).

23. For the most recent of each of these volumes, see Stephen Wayne, *The Road to the White House: The Politics of Presidential Elections* (New York: St. Martin, 1997), and Nelson W. Polsby and Aaron Wildavsky, *Presidential Elections: Strategies and Structures in American Politics* (Chatham, NJ: Chatham House, 1996), respectively.

24. Gerald M. Pomper, "Campaigning: The Art & Science of Politics," *Polity* 2(4) (1970):533–39; more recently, see James A. Thurber, "The Study of Campaign Consultants: A Subfield in Search of a Theory," *PS: Political Science and Politics* 31(2) (1998):145–49.

25. David Lee Rosenbloom, *The Election Men: Professional Campaign Managers and American Democracy* (New York: Quadrangle Books, 1973). Actually, political consultants have been assisting in presidential campaigns since the early part of this century; more on this in the next chapter.

26. Joseph Napolitan, *The Election Game and How to Win It* (Garden City, NY: Doubleday, 1972).

27. See Charles T. Royer, *Campaign for President: The Managers Look at '96* (Hollis, NH: Puritan, 1997), for the latest of these.

28. Larry J. Sabato's *The Rise of Political Consultants: New Ways of Winning Elections* (New York: Basic Books, 1981) is a dated, but extremely thorough collection of essays by practitioners and consultants and is an outstanding review of this field; similarly, Ron Faucheux's *The Best of the Best from Campaigns & Elections: The Road to Victory: The Complete Guide to Winning in Politics* (Dubuque, IA: Kendall/Hunt, 1995) is culled from *Campaigns & Elections*, the magazine of political consultants. Also worthy of note is a book by well-known Republican consultant Frank Luntz (*Candidates, Consultants, and Campaigns*, [Oxford, UK: Basil Blackwell, 1988]). Though academics are largely absent from this field, exceptions to the rule are Robert Friedenburg; *Communication Consultants in Political Campaigns*, Daniel Shea, *Campaign Craft: The Strategies, Tactics, and Art of Political Campaign*

Management (Westport, CT: Praeger, 1996), who conjoins campaign management techniques with (mainly political communications) theory; and Barbara G. and Stephen A. Salmore, *Candidates, Parties, and Campaigns: Electoral Politics in America* (Washington, DC: CQ Press, 1989), who attempt to reconcile academic and practitioner accounts of congressional and presidential campaigns and elections.

29. See, for example, Robin Kolodny and Angela Logan, "Political Consultants and the Extension of Party Goals," *PS: Political Science and Politics* 31(2) (1998): 155–59, on consultants and their relationship with political parties; David A. Dulio, Candice J. Nelson, and James A. Thurber, "Campaign Elites: The Attitudes and Roles of Professional Political Consultants" (Paper presented at the Annual WPSA Meeting, 1999), on how consultants see themselves in the campaign process; or David A. Dulio, "Just Win Baby! Campaign Consultants, Ethical Standards, and Campaign Reform" (Paper presented at the Annual MPSA Meeting, 1999), on ethics and methods in the industry.

30. Paul Herrnson, *Party Campaigning in the 1980s* (Cambridge, MA: Harvard, 1988).

31. The approach taken here bears conceptual similarities to scholarship which looks at political party organizations. Specifically, the framework draws conceptually from the work of Andrew M. Appleton and Daniel S. Ward, "Party Response to Environmental Change: A Model of Organizational Innovation," *Party Politics*, 3(3) (1997): 341–62, who organized their work on party organizational innovation along four dimensions. In their research, "personnel" included the structure and functions of party committees, division of labor among party staff, the creation of new staff positions, and the shift from voluntary to paid staff. Party "organization activities" embraced electoral mobilization, recruitment, candidate services, polling, newsletter publication, and affiliations with other organizations. The "finance" aspect of party organization included fund-raising sources and techniques, the implementation of subventions, and subvention procedures and formulas. Finally, they looked at "physical resources," meaning headquarters and satellite offices as well as technology. In the present study, the personnel and activities categories are retained, and the physical and monetary resource categories are collapsed into a singular resource category. All are expanded.

32. See Paul Allen Beck, *Party Politics in America* (New York: Longman, 1997), pp. 59–63, 85–105, and Alan Ware, *Political Parties and Party Systems* (Oxford, UK: Oxford University, 1996), pp. 93–112, for a general discussion of personnel and cohesion of party organizations; Wayne, *Road to the White House*, pp. 203–14 deals with this aspect of candidate organizations.

33. See Samuel P. Huntington's classic work *Political Order in Changing Societies* (New Haven: Yale, 1968) which deals with, among other subjects, institutional development and maturity.

34. Ibid.

35. See Beck, *Party Politics in America*, pp. 270–300, and Ware, *Political Parties and Party Systems*, pp. 296–312, for a (primarily) party perspective; Wayne, *Road to the White House*, pp. 27–63, and Polsby and Wildavsky, *Presidential Elections*, pp. 36–50, 65–96, approach this aspect mainly from the candidate point of view.

36. Beck, *Party Politics in America*, pp. 196–269, and Ware, *Political Parties and Party Systems*, pp. 257–316, cover this very broad area with regard to both party

and candidate; Wayne, *Road to the White House*, pp. 97–284, and Polsby and Wildavsky, *Presidential Elections*, pp.119–260, focus more, but not exclusively on, presidential aspirants.

37. See Dinkin, *Campaigning in America*, pp. 164–74, for a summary; see also Frantzich, *Political Parties in the Technological Age*.

CHAPTER TWO

1. James Bryce, *The American Commonwealth*, vol. 2 (Indianapolis: Liberty Fund, 1995), p. 884 (emphasis added).

2. Though scholars debate actual dates, the 1820s are generally accepted as the beginning of the two-party system in America. Dinkin refers to the years 1824–52 as the "Jacksonian Period" of political campaigning. During this time the power and influence of political parties was in its formative stages; he dates the Golden Age from 1854–88 (Dinkin, *Campaigning in America*).

3. See Joel H. Sibley, "From 'Essential to the Existence of Our Institutions' to 'Rapacious Enemies of Honest and Responsible Government': The Rise and Fall of American Parties, 1790–2000," in L. Sandy Maisel, *The Parties Respond* (Boulder, CO: Westview, 1998), for a concise summary of the evolution of American political parties, especially during this era. Wilfred E. Binkley's history of American political parties, *American Political Parties: Their Natural History* (New York: Alfred E. Knopf, 1962), is far more detailed. William Riordon's *Plunkitt of Tammany Hall* (New York: Meridian, 1991) is an insightful and delightful look at New York City's Tammany Hall political machine in the Golden Age as seen through the eyes of its boss, George Washington Plunkitt.

4. See James C. N. Paul's *Rift in the Democracy* (Philadelphia: University of Pennsylvania, 1951) for an account of the rise and fall of the Democratic Party (the Regency) of New York State. This section draws heavily on Jody C Baumgartner, "Hunker Democrats (1848)," in Ronald Hayduk et al., *Encyclopedia of American Third Parties* (M. E. Sharpe, 1999).

5. Speaking in the United States Senate, January, 1832 (quoted in Ivor D. Spencer, *The Victor and the Spoils: A Life of William L. Marcy* [Providence, RI: Brown University, 1959], pp. 59–60).

6. Dinkin, *Campaigning in America*, p. 74.

7. Leonard Dinnerstein, "Election of 1880," in Arthur Schlesinger, Jr. and Fred Israel, *History of American Presidential Elections, 1789–1968* (New York: Chelsea House, 1971), pp. 1509–10.

8. Allan Peskin, *Garfield* (Kent, OH: Kent State, 1978), p. 512.

9. George Brown Tindall and David E. Shi, *America: A Narrative History* (New York: W. W. Norton, 1996), p. 787.

10. Peskin, *Garfield*, p. 452.

11. Ibid., p. 454.

12. Ibid., pp. 454, 477.

13. Ibid., p. 462. Planning spontaneous shows of support was a common strategy at national party conventions in the traditional era, nor is it uncommon in the modern era.

14. Dinnerstein, "Election of 1880," p. 1495.

15. Peskin, *Garfield*, p. 471.

16. Ibid.

17. Garfield's convention managers were active in "buttonholing" delegates throughout the convention, but turning the tide by convincing the Wisconsin delegation to vote for Garfield was their biggest accomplishment (ibid., p. 477).

18. Dinnerstein, "Election of 1880," p. 1495.

19. Peskin, *Garfield*, pp. 475–76.

20. Dinnerstein, "Election of 1880," p. 1497.

21. Garfield did not actually see Conkling, but placated his lieutenants to the point that they agreed to support Garfield's effort wholeheartedly. Because of this, Conkling himself had to agree to help, though his personal support was, in the end, shaky (Peskin, *Garfield*, p. 480).

22. While overstated, in late July Garfield complained that he still had no organization or money (ibid.).

23. Ibid., p. 488.

24. Dinnerstein, "Election of 1880," p. 1507.

25. Peskin, *Garfield*, p. 495.

26. Standard Oil also helped by mobilizing its 2,000 Indiana workers, while Garfield was able to draw valuable support from over 25,000 fellow church members (Peskin, *Garfield*, p. 504). At this time the various states still had different election days; see Dinkin, *Campaigning in America*, pp. 70–71.

27. This according to one biographer (Peskin, *Garfield*, p. 482).

28. Dinnerstein, "Election of 1880," pp. 1506–7.

29. Those interested in further reading in the history of political campaigning in America should consult Dinkin's *Campaigning in America*; Schlesinger and Israel's edited four-volume *History of American Presidential Elections, 1789–1968* is a thorough and comprehensive examination of the history of presidential elections.

30. James A. Reichley, "The Rise of National Parties," in John Chubb and Paul Peterson, *The New Direction in American Politics* (Washington, DC: Brookings Institution, 1985), pp. 175–77; Reichley's discussion centers on the rise of national party organizations in the United States. In addition to their respective national committees, both parties have maintained congressional campaign committees since just after the Civil War (the Democratic Congressional Campaign Committee and the National Republican Congressional Committee) and senatorial campaign committees since 1913 (the Democratic Senatorial Campaign Committee and the National Republican Senatorial Committee) when direct election of senators became law; see Beck, *Party Politics in America*, p. 94.

31. Dinkin, *Campaigning in America*, p. 50.

32. For example, George Washington Plunkitt; see note 3.

33. Bryce, *The American Commonwealth*, pp. 868–69.

34. Dinkin, *Campaigning in America*, p. 64.

35. Ibid., for accounts of the 1856 Republican "Wide Awakes," the Democratic "Douglas Guards," and more.

36. Ibid., p. 65.

37. Bryce, *The American Commonwealth*, p. 872.

38. Ibid., p. 869.

39. Theodore J. Lowi, *The Personal President: Power Invested, Promise Unfulfilled* (Ithaca, NY and London, UK: Cornell, 1985), pp. 72–73.

40. Dinkin, *Campaigning in America*, p. 178.

41. This discussion draws heavily on Herbert Alexander's chapter on pre-1972 campaign finance in *Financing Politics*, pp. 9–14.

42. Francis Russell's *The President Makers: From Mark Hanna to Joseph P. Kennedy* (Boston: Little, Brown, and Company, 1976) is an informative and interesting treatment of eight of the most well-known "president makers" of the past century.

43. This term, coined in 1888 by publisher Henry Stoddard (referring to John Forster, president of the League of Young Republican Clubs), was popularized in 1928 by Frank Kent of the *Baltimore Sun* (Alexander, *Financing Politics*, p. 12).

44. Dinkin, *Campaigning in America*, p. 100.

45. Ibid., p. 133.

46. Ibid., p. 132.

47. Bryce, *The American Commonwealth*, p. 852.

48. Ibid., p. 853.

49. Dinkin, *Campaigning in America*, p. 9.

50. Bryce, *The American Commonwealth*, p. 852; see also his chapter on "Types of American Statesman."

51. The first national nominating convention was held by the Anti-Masons in 1831.

52. Van Buren, Clay, and Grant were nominated by acclamation.

53. Bryce, *The American Commonwealth*, p. 849.

54. Ibid., p. 854.

55. Ibid., p. 856.

56. A focus on crafting a "presidential image," it should be remembered, is not new to the television age. Keith Melder, *Hail to the Candidate: Presidential Campaigns from Banners to Broadcasts* (Washington, DC: Smithsonian Institution, 1992), illuminates what has been a long history of crafting "presidential imagery"; in a similar vein, Gil Troy, *See How They Ran: The Changing Role of the Presidential Candidate* (Cambridge, MA: Harvard, 1996), discusses the history of "merchandising" presidential candidates in political campaigns.

57. Dinnerstein, "Election of 1880," pp. 1509–10.

58. See, for example, Peskin's account of Garfield's 1880 general election campaign (Peskin, *Garfield*, pp. 482–513).

59. Dinkin, *Campaigning in America*, p. 67.

60. Ibid.

61. Ibid., p. 68.

62. E. E. Schattschneider, *Party Government* (New York: Farrar and Rinehart, 1942), p. 1.

CHAPTER THREE

1. This discussion draws heavily on Ryan J. Barilleaux, *American Government in Action: Principle, Process, and Politics* (Upper Saddle River, NJ: Prentice Hall, 1996), pp. 246–47; for a more detailed and complete examination of the intellec-

tual roots and practical considerations involved in creating an American presidency, see Forrest McDonald, *The American Presidency: An Intellectual History* (Lawrence: University Press of Kansas, 1994). Thomas Cronin's *Inventing the American Presidency* (Lawrence: University Press of Kansas, 1989) is a more pointed look at the actual work of the Constitutional Convention.

2. Alexander Hamilton handled most of the chores in writing on various aspects of the presidency in *The Federalist*; see Numbers 68 (on presidential selection), 71 (on tenure in office), and 72 (on re-eligibility).

3. Barilleaux, *American Government in Action*, p. 247.

4. American presidents who won more than one election were George Washington (1789, 1792), Thomas Jefferson (1800, 1804), James Madison (1808, 1812), James Monroe (1816, 1820), Andrew Jackson (1828, 1832), Abraham Lincoln (1860, 1964), Ulysses Grant (1868, 1872), Woodrow Wilson (1912, 1916), Franklin Roosevelt (1932, 1936, 1940, 1944), Dwight Eisenhower (1952, 1956), Richard Nixon (1968, 1972), Ronald Reagan (1980, 1984), and William Clinton (1992, 1996).

Nine men have served as president of the United States without having been elected: John Tyler (1841–45, after the death of William Harrison), Millard Fillmore (1850–53, after the death of Zachary Taylor), Andrew Johnson (1865–69, after the death of Abraham Lincoln), Chester Arthur (1881–85, after the death of James Garfield), Theodore Roosevelt (1901–05, after the death of William McKinley), Calvin Coolidge (1923–25, after the death of Warren Harding), Harry Truman (1945–49, after the death of Franklin Roosevelt), Lyndon Johnson (1963–65, after the death of John Kennedy), and Gerald Ford (1974–77, after the resignation of Richard Nixon). Of these, four subsequently won elections in their own right: Theodore Roosevelt (1904), Calvin Coolidge (1924), Harry Truman (1948), and Lyndon Johnson (1964).

5. General de Gaulle's polemic on France's need for a strong executive can be found in Charles de Gaulle, "The Bayeux Manifesto," in Arend Lijphart, *Parliamentary Versus Presidential Government* (Oxford, UK: Oxford University, 1992); Nicholas Wahl, "The French Constitution of 1958: The Initial Draft and Its Origins," *American Political Science Review* 53 (June 1959), examines the drafting and design of the Constitution of the French Fifth Republic; and Maurice Duverger, "A New Political System Model," Lijphart, *Parliamentary Versus Presidential Government*, looks at the theoretical and empirical issues involved in classifying France's political system. The French Constitution itself is reprinted in S. E. Finer, Vernon Bogdanor, and Bernard Rudden, *Comparing Constitutions* (Oxford, UK: Clarendon, 1995).

6. The dual-executive setup in France has been the source of much scholarly debate over how to classify the French Fifth Republic (e.g., parliamentary, presidential, semi-presidential). The prevailing wisdom, particularly since France is in the midst of its third period of "cohabitation" (when president and prime minister are from different parties), is that the French system is none of these, nor is it a synthesis. Rather, it is an "alternation," depending upon whether the president enjoys a parliamentary majority. Arend Lijphart's "Introduction" in *Parliamentary Versus Presidential Government* provides a succinct synthesis of this debate.

7. Ibid.

8. This discussion draws heavily on Stephen White et al., *How Russi.: Votes*

(Chatham, NJ: Chatham House, 1997). The 1993 Russian Constitution can be found online at <http://www.bucknell.edu/departments/russian>; Carla Thornson, "Russia's Draft Constitution," *RFE/RL Research Report* 2(48) (1993): 9–15 does a good job of looking at the provisions of the constitution (though at the time still in its draft stages), as does Isaak I. Dore, "The Distribution of Governmental Power Under the Constitution in Russia," *Parker School Journal of East European Law* 2(6) (1995): 673–705.

9. Several hundred deputies and their supporters had barricaded themselves in the Russian "White House," their legislative home. Yeltsin had set an October 4 deadline for their dispersion and an evening of violence on October 3 in the streets of Moscow led to a military attack the following morning. One hundred forty-five people died in the violence and over 800 were wounded; see White et al., *How Russia Votes*, pp. 92–94.

10. See, for example, Steven Fish, "The Pitfalls of Russian Superpresidentialism," *Current History* 96(612) (1997): 326–31.

11. The results, specifically the reported turnout, are widely believed to have been doctored.

12. The two-term limit was a reaction to Franklin Roosevelt's four terms in office and is embodied in the Twenty-second Amendment to the United States Constitution (1951, on the "Number of Presidential Terms"). See Cronin, "Presidential Term, Tenure, and Re-eligibility," in *Inventing the American Presidency*, for more on the historical origins of "term, tenure, and re-eligibility" of the American presidency.

13. In both 1969 (after de Gaulle's resignation) and 1974 (after the death of Georges Pompidou) Alan Poher assumed this role.

14. In the United States, the House of Representatives impeaches, while the Senate tries the impeachment with the Chief Justice of the Supreme Court presiding; two-thirds of the Senate must vote for the president to be removed. In France the president must be indicted by a majority vote in each house of the legislature and then must be tried by the High Court of Justice. The impeachment procedure in Russia is the most complex and exacting. The charges against the president must be confirmed by a ruling of the Supreme Court; the Constitutional Court must then confirm that the procedure of bringing charges has been observed; at least one-third of the deputies of the State Duma must initiate the charges in the presence of a special commission of the Duma; finally, two-thirds of the members of each house of the legislature must vote to impeach (there is also a three-month time limit for the motion to pass the upper house Federation Council).

15. By way of contrast, Russia imposes a requirement of 21 years of age for the deputies of the State Duma, their lower house, and in the United States a candidate for the House of Representatives must be 25 years old, a citizen for seven years, and a resident of the state in which he or she is running. See Roy Pierce, *Choosing the Chief: Presidential Elections in France and the United States* (Ann Arbor: University of Michigan, 1995), pp. 3–16, 214–32, for more on the electoral environment in France, and White et al., *How Russia Votes*, Chapters 1, 3, and 7, for the same in Russia.

16. Anne Stevens, *The Government and Politics of France* (New York: St. Martin, 1996), p. 69.

17. White et al., *How Russia Votes*, p. 94.

18. See Larry J. Sabato, "Presidential Nominations: The Front-loaded Frenzy of '96," in *Toward the Millennium: The Elections of 1996* (Boston: Allyn and Bacon, 1997), pp. 6–7, for 1996 laws.

19. John F. Bibby and L. Sandy Maisel, *Two Parties— Or More? The American Party System* (Boulder, CO: Westview, 1998), p. 62.

20. Shlomo Slonim, "Designing the Electoral College," in Cronin, *Inventing the American Presidency*, discusses the factors which went into designing the electoral college. Wayne, in *Road to the White House*, provides a very succinct overview of its evolution, including a discussion of the 1804 Twelfth Amendment to the United States Constitution. These are interesting historical details, but not pertinent to the present electoral environment.

21. Technically George Washington is an exception to this rule.

22. Due to Charles de Gaulle's resignation and Georges Pompidou's death, 1981 was the first year the presidential election was held at the regular (i.e., seven-year interval) time.

23. Scott Mainwaring, and Matthew S. Shugart, "Juan Linz, Presidentialism, and Democracy: A Critical Appraisal," *Comparative Politics* 29(4) (1997): 449–72; or, John M. Carey, "Institutional Design and Party Systems," in Larry Diamond, et al., *Consolidating the Third Wave Democracies* (Baltimore: Johns Hopkins, 1997), p. 78.

24. Carl Bernstein and Bob Woodward, *All the President's Men* (New York: Simon and Schuster, 1974).

25. Ira Chinoy, "In Presidential Race, TV Ads Were Biggest '96 Cost By Far," *Washington Post*, March 31, 1997, p. A19.

26. See, for example, Craig R. Whitney, "Common Currency: Do Francs and Yen Corrupt? Absolutely," *New York Times*, March 16, 1997, sec. 4, pp. 1, 4.

27. Bernstein and Woodward, *All the President's Men*.

28. In brief, the statutes were the Federal Election Campaign Act of 1971, which among other things repealed the Federal Corrupt Practices Act of 1925; the Revenue Act of 1971 set up the Presidential Election Fund which allows citizens to contribute money to presidential campaigns via their tax returns; the Federal Election Campaign Act of 1974 was a set of sweeping amendments to the 1971 act, many of which were declared unconstitutional, including the formation of the bipartisan Federal Election Commission. The amendments of 1976 reconstituted the FEC. All of these laws and amendments dealt with contribution and spending limitations as well.

The FEC opinion referred to was the "Sun Oil" opinion of 1975. At Sun Oil's request the FEC rendered an opinion (a 4–2 decision) which paved the way for the growth of corporate Political Action Committees. Finally, the case of *Buckley v. Valeo* (1976) upheld the Sun Oil opinion as well as laws limiting individual and group donations to candidate campaigns, but overturned the laws limiting spending on behalf of a candidate, declaring it protected speech (this also in0cludes candidates who contribute to their own campaign). For a good summary of these laws and decisions see Wayne, *Road to the White House*, pp. 33–37.

29. Only two major party candidates have rejected federal spending limits (and thus federal funds) so far, namely, John Connally in 1980 and Steve Forbes in 1996; the latter spent close to $38 million of his own money in pursuit of the

1996 Republican nomination. Ross Perot, running as an independent, did so as well, spending over $63 million in his 1992 campaign (ibid., p. 39).

30. There are other provisions to be met, notably the "10 percent rule," which states that aspirants must receive at least 10 percent of the vote in two consecutive primaries in which they are entered in order to remain eligible for funding. If they lose their eligibility they must then garner at least 20 percent of the vote in a subsequent primary to requalify (ibid., p. 44).

31. Ibid., pp. 48–49.

32. Ibid., p. 44.

33. See ibid., pp. 50–52, Text Box 2.3, for a very concise yet thorough explanation of soft money.

34. Brooks Jackson, "Financing the 1996 Campaign: The Law of the Jungle," in Sabato, *Toward the Millennium*. We will return to the subject of soft money in Chapter 5.

35. This section draws liberally from Thomas Drysch, "The New French System of Political Finance," in Arthur Gunlicks, *Campaign and Party Finance in North America and Western Europe* (Boulder, CO: Westview, 1993), and Pierre Avril, "Regulation of Political Finance in France," in Herbert Alexander and Rei Shiratori, *Comparative Political Finance Among the Democracies* (Boulder, CO: Westview, 1994).

36. Whitney, "Common Currency: Do Francs and Yen Corrupt?"

37. Michael McFaul, *Russia's 1996 Presidential Election: The End of Polarized Politics* (Stanford, CA: Stanford, 1997, p. 13). More accurately, candidates were allowed to collect up to 19 billion rubles during the campaign and could spend up to 14.3 billion rubles.

38. Government-sponsored media is minimal in the United States, restricted mainly to the foreign broadcast services (e.g., the Voice of America program) which are not permitted by Congress to air in the United States. Even so-called "public" broadcasting in the United States is actually a joint venture with many partners: the federal, state, and local governments; universities; business; private sponsors; and foundations. This section draws heavily on Doris Graber, *Mass Media and American Politics* (Washington, DC: CQ Press, 1997), Chapters 2 and 3.

39. Members are appointed by the president and confirmed by the Senate and serve five-year terms (ibid., p. 47).

40. Ibid.

41. An FCC ruling in 1992 mandated that the lowest rates stipulation applies only to candidates for federal office; see Friedenberg, *Communication Consultants in Political Campaigns*, p. 177.

42. It was John Kennedy's skillful use of television in 1960 that supposedly ushered in the television age of presidential politics.

43. Wayne, *Road to the White House*, pp. 252–54.

44. Candidates who feel they have been unfairly excluded from the debates (like Ross Perot in 1996) can appeal to the FCC. The appeal goes to that agency because of their involvement in lifting (or otherwise circumventing) equal time constraints for presidential debates (Graber, *Mass Media and American Politics*, p. 61).

45. Polsby and Wildavsky, *Presidential Elections*, p. 233.

46. Peter J. Humphreys, *Mass Media and Media Policy in Western Europe* (Manchester, UK: Manchester University, 1996). This section draws liberally from

Jacques Gerstlé, "Election Communication in France," in Frederick Fletcher, *Media, Elections, and Democracy* (Toronto: Dundurn, 1991), and Anne Johnston and Jacques Gerstlé, "The Role of Television Broadcasts in Promoting French Presidential Candidates," in Lynda Kaid, *Political Advertising in Western Democracies: Parties & Candidates on Television* (Thousand Oaks, CA: Sage, 1995).

47. The government pays for the printing and distribution of campaign platforms. In addition, to help keep costs down, certain forms of advertising are banned until three months prior to election (all commercial bill posting, press advertising, and campaigning via free phone or telematic numbers).

48. All candidates also received free radio time on both national and regional state-run radio stations. This section draws liberally from reports by various authors found in the Open Media Research Institute's (OMRI) *Daily Digest* and *Russian Presidential Election Surveys* (both published at <http://www.rferl.org/>) from the spring and early summer of 1996.

49. What we mean by a political party should be defined here; Kenneth Janda's definition is an excellent start. According to Janda, a political party is "an organization that pursues a goal of placing its avowed representatives in government positions" ("Comparative Political Parties: Research and Theory," in Ada Finifter, *Political Science: The State of the Discipline II* [Washington, DC: APSA, 1993], p. 166); it is probably fair to specify that placing their "avowed representatives in government positions" should be the primary goal, not simply a goal. This amendment to Janda's definition helps distinguish between political movements and interest groups who have been increasingly active in electoral politics in the past 20 years.

A party system is the structure of party competition in a given political system and is defined primarily by the number of competitive parties, competitiveness defined as their relative capacity to play a significant role in mobilizing support (securing votes) and/or to translate those votes into seats in the legislature; see Ware, *Political Parties and Party Systems*, pp. 147–83.

50. For further reading on political parties and party system theory, see Ware, *Political Parties and Party Systems*, pp. 147–83.

51. As noted, this book draws very heavily from material found in Beck, *Party Politics in America*, a comprehensive text on party politics in America. Though somewhat dated, the classic text on American party politics is V. O. Key, Jr., *Politics, Parties, & Pressure Groups* (New York: Crowell, 1964); Binkley, *American Political Parties*, explores the history and development of parties in America, as does James Reichley, *The Life of the Parties: A History of American Political Parties* (New York: Free Press, 1992); Walter Dean Burnham's *Critical Elections and the Mainsprings of American Politics* (New York: Norton, 1970) is a look at parties through electoral eyes; Leon D. Epstein, *Political Parties in the American Mold* (Madison: University of Wisconsin, 1986), addresses American parties in light of Maurice Duverger's claim in *Political Parties: Their Organization and Activity in the Modern State* (New York: Wiley, 1965) that European-style parties would be the way of the future; finally, John Aldrich's *Why Parties? The Origin and Transformation of Political Parties in America* (Chicago: University of Chicago, 1995) is a recent and important work on the development of parties in the United States.

A good summary of French party politics can be found in Alistair Cole, "The Presidential Party and the Fifth Republic," *West European Politics* 16(2) (1993): 49–

66; see also his edited volume, *French Political Parties in Transition* (Aldershot, UK: Dartmouth, 1990). Readers might also be interested in Howard Machin's treatment of the "Stages and Dynamics in the Evolution of the French Party System," *West European Politics* 12(4) (1989): 59–81; David S. Bell's edited volume is a dated but informative look at French parties (*Contemporary French Political Parties* [London, UK: Croom Helm, 1982]), as is J. R. Frears, *Political Parties and Elections in the French Fifth Republic* (London, UK: C. Hurst, 1977). The most comprehensive book on Russian party politics at this early stage is still White et al., *How Russia Votes*, but M. Steven Fish, "The Advent of Multipartism in Russia, 1993–95," *Post-Soviet Affairs* 11(4) (1995): 340–83, and Ian McAllister and Stephen White, "Democracy, Political Parties and Party Formation in Postcommunist Russia," *Party Politics* 1 (1995): 49–72, do a good job of surveying the early development of party politics in Russia as well.

52. Maurice Duverger, *Political Parties.*

53. Beck, *Party Politics in America*, p. 70, Figure 3.1.

54. Ibid., p. 103. The Democrats have a more centralized organization than the Republicans, but like the Republicans are very dependent on their constituent state and local parties.

55. See Ware, *Political Parties and Party Systems*, pp. 93–123, for a good discussion of political party organizations in France, Germany, Great Britain, Japan, as well as the United States.

56. Again, for more on party politics in the United States, see Epstein, *Political Parties in the American Mold*, which is a more theoretically oriented volume, or Beck, *Party Politics in America*, which pays a bit more attention to the detailed empirical reality of party politics in the United States.

57. Michael McFaul, "Russia's Rough Ride," in Larry Diamond et al., *Consolidating the Third Wave Democracies* (Baltimore: Johns Hopkins, 1997), p. 83.

58. See, for example, Russell J. Dalton, *Citizen Politics: Public Opinion and Political Parties in Advanced Industrial Democracies* (Chatham, NJ: Chatham House, 1996).

59. Richard Sakwa, "Parties and the Multiparty System in Russia," *RFE/RL Research Report* 2(31) (1993): 7–15.

CHAPTER FOUR

1. The presidential aspirants associated with these leadership PACs are Bill Bradley (Time Future Inc.), Dan Quayle (Campaign America), Al Gore (Leadership '98), Lamar Alexander (Campaign for a New American Century), George W. Bush (America First PAC), and Steve Forbes (Americans for Hope, Growth & Opportunity).

2. Huntington, *Political Order in Changing Societies*. This section draws heavily on Beck, *Party Politics in America*, pp. 59–63, 85–105.

3. Reichley, "The Rise of National Parties."

4. Beck, *Party Politics in America*, pp. 79–80.

5. John Bibby, "State Party Organizations: Coping and Adapting to Candidate-Centered Politics and Nationalization," in L. Sandy Maisel, *The Parties Respond* (Boulder, CO: Westview, 1998).

6. Paul S. Herrnson, "National Party Organizations at Century's End," in L. Sandy Maisel, ed., *The Parties Respond* (Boulder, CO: Westview, 1998), p. 62.

7. Paul S. Herrnson, *Congressional Elections: Campaigning at Home and in Washington* (Washington, DC: CQ Press, 1998), p. 75.

8. The following discussion of national committee chairpersons draws heavily on Beck, *Party Politics in America*, pp. 89–92.

9. See Sidney M. Milkis, *The Presidency and Political Parties: The Transformation of the American Party System Since the New Deal* (Oxford, UK: Oxford University, 1993), for a fuller exposition of the role of the president as national party leader.

10. The classic study of the new breed of amateur party activists is James Q. Wilson, *The Amateur Democrat* (Chicago: University of Chicago, 1962).

11. Dinkin, *Campaigning in America*, p. 163.

12. Ware, *Political Parties and Party Systems*, p. 113.

13. Pierce, *Choosing the Chief*, p. 12.

14. Andrew Knapp, *Gaullism since de Gaulle* (Aldershot, UK: Dartmouth, 1994), p. 261.

15. Lack of data is an obstacle to any non–French-speaking student of the French presidency, as there is little research available in the English language (Anthony King, "Foundations of Power," in George Edwards III et al., *Researching the Presidency: Vital Questions, New Approaches* [Pittsburgh, PA: University of Pittsburgh, 1993]). Unfortunately the paucity of English-language scholarship on foreign presidencies is not limited to the French presidency, perhaps because stable presidential systems are fairly uncommon. Even recent texts on party politics avoid the subject of presidential selection in France in any great detail; see, for example, Ware, *Political Parties and Party Systems*, or Harmon Zeigler, *Political Parties in Industrial Democracies* (Itasca, IL: F. E. Peacock).

16. Vincent Wright, *The Government and Politics of France* (New York: Holmes and Meier, 1989), p. 196.

17. Knapp, *Gaullism since de Gaulle*, p. 274.

18. Ibid., p. 242. It should be noted that by 1998 there was considerable dissent in Chirac's Rally for the Republic over leadership, at least partly attributable to their rout in the snap parliamentary elections of 1997. In short, many (party leader Jacques Séguin and party notables Jacques Toubon and Jean Tiberi) were unhappy with President Chirac's leadership and were making their dissatisfaction known ("France's Right: New Name, Old Confusion," *Economist*, May 23, 1998, p. 47).

19. Cole, "The Presidential Party and the Fifth Republic," p. 59.

20. For the French Communists, see Howard Machin,"The President, the Parties and Parliament," in Jack Hayward, ed., *De Gaulle to Mitterand: Presidential Power in France* (New York: New York University, 1993), p. 140. For the Socialists, see William Safran, *The French Polity* (New York: Longman, 1995), p. 71, Gino Raymond, "The Decline of the Established Parties," in *France During the Socialist Years* (Brookefield, VT: Dartmouth, 1994), p. 94; and Machin,"The President, the Parties and Parliament," p. 140. For the Union of French Democrats, see Ella Searls, "The Giscardians and Party Politics," in David Bell, *Contemporary French Political Parties* (London, UK: Croom Helm, 1982), p. 18, and Machin, "The President, the Parties and Parliament," p. 140. For the Rally for the Republic, see

Frears, *Political Parties and Elections in the French Fifth Republic*, p. 51, and Machin, "The President, the Parties and Parliament," p. 140. Finally, for the National Front, see Kay Lawson and Colette Ysmal, "France: The 1988 Presidential Campaign," in Shaun Bowler and David Farrell, *Electoral Strategies and Political Marketing* (New York: St. Martin, 1992), p. 118. It must be noted that official French party membership figures should be viewed with extreme caution, since parties have an incentive to inflate their reported numbers (to overstate their strength) and there is "no common or comparable definition" among parties of what constitutes membership (Cole, "The Presidential Party and the Fifth Republic," p. 59).

21. Quoted in Robert Orttung, *OMRI* (1996f).

22. Fish, "The Advent of Multipartism in Russia, 1993–95," p. 346.

23. Ibid., p. 342.

24. McFaul, *Russia's 1996 Presidential Election*, p. 46.

25. After the government banned the party they also confiscated its considerable assets (Stephen White and Ian McAllister, "The CPSU and Its Members: Between Communism and Postcommunism," *British Journal of Political Science* 26[105–22] [1996]: 106–7).

26. Joan DeBardeleben, *Russian Politics in Transition* (Boston: Houghton Mifflin, 1997), p. 188.

27. Michael McFaul, "Russia's 1996 Presidential Elections," *Post-Soviet Affairs* 12(4) (1996): 318–50.

28. David Remnick, "Letter from Russia: Gorbachev's Last Hurrah," *New Yorker*, March 11, 1996, p. 73.

29. Steve Boilard, *Russia at the Twenty-First Century: Political and Social Change in the Post-Soviet Era* (Fort Worth, TX: Harcourt Brace College, 1998), p. 64.

30. Fish, "The Advent of Multipartism in Russia, 1993–95," p. 360.

31. McFaul, *Russia's 1996 Presidential Election*, p. 57.

32. Penny Morvant, *OMRI* (1996).

33. In 1995 they claimed 170,000 members, which may be suspect, but evidence suggests that they can claim at least half that number (Fish, "The Advent of Multipartism in Russia, 1993–95," p. 359).

34. Sabato, *The Rise of Political Consultants*, pp. 285–86.

35. Data on candidate organization staffing and other expenses are in the form of the volumes of information collected and compiled by the FEC; of course it is only available from 1976 onwards.

36. We are concentrating on the out-party because it is there that the most intense primary battles typically are.

37. Ruth Marcus and Ira Chinoy, "Lack of Primary Season Foe Leaves Clinton in the Money; President Saved for August Spending Spree," *Washington Post*, August 24, 1996, p. A1.

38. Ira Chinoy, "In Quest for Presidency, Candidates Learned They Could Bank on Finance Laws," *Washington Post*, November 5, 1996, p. A17.

39. Dinkin, *Campaigning in America*, p. 170.

40. Thomas R. Marshall, *Presidential Nominations in a Reform Age* (New York: Praeger, 1981), p. 96.

41. Chinoy, "In Quest for Presidency, Candidates Learned They Could Bank on Finance."

42. Wayne, *Road to the White House*, p. 209; this section draws heavily on Wayne's discussion on pp. 208–11.

43. Ibid., p. 210.

44. Dinkin, *Campaigning in America*, p. 170.

45. Howard Machin, "The 1995 Presidential Election Campaign," in Robert Elgie, ed., *Electing the French President: The 1995 Presidential Election* (New York: St. Martin, 1996), p. 44.

46. James G. Shields, "France's Presidential Election: The Gaullist Restoration," *Political Quarterly* 66(4) (1995): 320–27.

47. Joseph Szarka, "The Winning of the 1995 French Presidential Election," *West European Politics* 19(1) (1996): 15–67.

48. Lawson and Ysmal, "France: The 1988 Presidential Campaign," pp. 109–10.

49. Dinkin, *Campaigning in America*, p. 170.

50. See Machin, "The 1995 Presidential Election Campaign," p. 45, and Philippe J. Maarek, "New Trends in French Political Communication: The 1995 Presidential Elections," *Media, Culture, and Society* 19 (1997): 357–68. Other academics have worked for candidates as well; for example, Jean-Luc Parodi and Roland Cayrol have worked for Rocard (Lawson and Ysmal, "France: The 1988 Presidential Campaign," p. 106).

51. Lawson and Ysmal, "France: The 1988 Presidential Campaign," p. 109.

52. Soskovets failed at his initial task as campaign head, almost missing the deadline for submitting the signatures required for ballot registration (McFaul, *Russia's 1996 Presidential Election*, p. 18).

53. Michael Kramer, "Rescuing Boris," *Time*, July 15, 1996, p. 30.

54. Robert Orttung, "Voters Face a Red-and-White Choice," *Transition*, 2(11) (1996): 6–17.

55. McFaul, *Russia's 1996 Presidential Election*, pp. 19–21.

56. Orttung, *OMRI* (1996e; 1996b).

57. Orttung, "Voters Face a Red-and-White Choice," p. 7.

58. Orttung, *OMRI* (1996b).

59. McFaul, *Russia's 1996 Presidential Election*, p. 51.

60. Illustrating the gap between candidate and party in the 1996 Russian presidential electioneering effort, in at least one region (Novosibirsk) both Yavlinski and Lebed picked people to head their campaign efforts based on campaigning skills rather than party. Yavlinski turned not to the local branch of Yabloko but rather to the head of rival party Democratic Russia (Yakov Savchenko); Lebed passed over Congress of Russian Communities' Alexander Lyulko (the party's number one Duma candidate in the region) in favor of Democratic Party of Russia leader Vladimir Shirikov (Orttung, *OMRI*, 1996c).

61. Huntington, *Political Order in Changing Societies*.

62. Denise Baer and David A. Bositis, *Politics and Linkage in a Democratic Society* (Englewood Cliffs, NJ: Prentice Hall, 1993), pp. 204–43, Appendix.

63. Norman J. Ornstein et al., *Vital Statistics on Congress, 1997–1998* (Washington, DC: CQ Press, 1998), pp. 211–12.

64. Larry Sabato, *The Parties Just Begun: Shaping Political Parties for America's Future* (Boston: Little, Brown, 1988), pp. 45–46.

65. Larry Sabato, "The Conventions: One Festival of Hope, One Celebration

of Impending Victory," in *Toward the Millennium: The Elections of 1996* (Boston: Allyn and Bacon, 1997a), p. 93.

66. Tindall and Shi, *America: A Narrative History*, p. 1474.

67. Sabato, "Presidential Nominations: The Front-loaded Frenzy of '96," pp. 99–100.

68. Herrnson, "National Party Organizations at Century's End."

69. *Colorado Republican Federal Campaign Committee v. FEC* (1996).

70. Herrnson, "National Party Organizations at Century's End," p. 69.

71. Machin, "Stages and Dynamics in the Evolution of the French Party System," p. 59.

72. Safran, *The French Polity*, pp. 82–83; see also Alistair M. Cole, "Factionalism, the French Socialist Party and the Fifth Republic: An Explanation of Intraparty Divisions," *European Journal of Political Research* 17 (1989): 77–94.

73. Cole, "Factionalism, the French Socialist Party and the Fifth Republic," p. 91.

74. Raymond, "The Decline of the Established Parties," p. 102.

75. Safran refers to this practice as "political wandering" (*The French Polity*, pp. 108–9).

76. Balladur's "velvet" takeover of Union of French Democrats meant that UDF's Raymond Barre and founder Valéry Giscard d'Estaing could not run for fear of totally fracturing the right, which in the worst-case scenario (for them) might have allowed the extreme-right Jean-Marie Le Pen and his National Front to advance to the second round. Giscard d'Estaing had his "revenge" on Balladur by supporting the RPR's Chirac in the election (Szarka, "The Winning of the 1995 French Presidential Election," p. 155).

77. Marie-France Toinet, "The Elections of 1981: Background and Legal Setting," in Howard Penniman, *France at the Polls, 1981 and 1986: Three National Elections* (Durham, NC: Duke, 1988), p. 13.

78. Daniel Singer, "Letters from Europe: The Mitterand-Chirac-Barre Show," *The Nation*, April 16, 1988, p. 525.

79. Howard Machin and Vincent Wright, "Why Mitterand Won: The French Presidential Elections of April-May 1981," *West European Politics* 5(1) (1982): 5–35.

80. Ibid., p. 16. This weakness is partly inherent, since the UDF is a weak-knit confederation of parties.

81. James G. Shields, "Barre, Chirac, Le Pen et al.: France's Fragmented Right," (*Contemporary Review* 254(1476) (1989): 1–6.

82. Machin, "The 1995 Presidential Election Campaign."

83. Searls, "The Giscardians and Party Politics," p. 12.

84. Jean Charlot and Monica Charlot, "France," in David Butler and Austin Ranney, *Electioneering: A Comparative Study of Continuity and Change* (Oxford, UK: Clarendon, 1992), p. 140.

85. Machin, "The President, the Parties and Parliament," p. 129.

86. Stevens, *The Government and Politics of France*, p. 239.

87. Fish, "The Advent of Multipartism in Russia, 1993–95," p. 346.

88. Orttung, *OMRI* (1996c).

89. Orttung, *OMRI* (1996e).

90. Nikolai V. Zlobin, "The Political Spectrum," in Alexander Dallin, *Political Parties in Russia* (Berkeley, CA: University of California, 1993), p. 64.

91. DeBardeleben, *Russian Politics in Transition*, p. 188.

92. Sabato, "Presidential Nominations: The Front-loaded Frenzy of '96," pp. 76–77.

93. David Remnick, "Letter from Russia: War for the Kremlin," *New Yorker*, July 22, 1996, pp. 40–57.

94. The two were apprehended leaving the Kremlin with $500,000 in cash. In what was reported to be an agonizing decision for Yeltsin, Korzhakov was fired immediately (White et al., *How Russia Votes*, p. 264).

95. Quoted in Dinkin, *Campaigning in America*, p. 161.

96. Jimmy Carter was the first president to appoint a political media consultant to his inner circle (Sabato, *The Rise of Political Consultants*, p. 116).

97. Pew Research Center, "The Views of Political Consultants: Don't Blame Us" (1998); James Thurber and David Dulio, "Industry Portrait: Political Consultants," *Campaigns & Elections* (July 1999) p. 28.

98. Friedenberg, *Communication Consultants in Political Campaigns*, pp. 17–18.

99. Ibid., p. 200.

100. Charles Clark, "Political Consultants: The Issues," *The CQ Researcher* 6(37) (1996): 867–73.

101. Ibid.

102. Nicholas O'Shaughnessy, *The Phenomenon of Political Marketing* (New York: St. Martin, 1990), p. 156.

103. David M. Farrell, "Campaign Strategies and Tactics," in Lawrence LeDuc et al., *Comparing Democracies: Elections and Voting in Global Perspectives* (Thousand Oaks, CA: Sage), pp. 176–77.

104. Sabato, *The Rise of Political Consultants*, p. 115.

105. Ibid., p. 146.

106. O'Shaughnessy, *The Phenomenon of Political Marketing*, p. 231.

107. Roger Simon, "Backstage at the Opening," *U.S. News & World Report*, June 28, 1999, pp. 20–21.

108. Six of these seven schools offer graduate credit; of these, four offer Masters degrees and one offers a Doctorate (in political communications). See *Campaigns & Elections* (1997a).

109. Pew Research Center, "The Views of Political Consultants"; see also Dulio, "Just Win Baby!" and for a more general picture of how consultants see themselves in the campaign process, see Dulio, Nelson, and Thurber, "Campaign Elites."

110. In Rosenbloom, *The Election Men*, p. 86.

111. Kolodny and Logan, "Political Consultants and the Extension of Party Goals."

112. John F. Harris, "Clinton's Campaign Consultants Reaped Millions from TV Ads," *Washington Post*, January 4, 1998, p. A4.

113. Searls, "The Giscardians and Party Politics," p. 14; see also Shaun Bowler and David M. Farrell, "Conclusion: The Contemporary Election Campaign," in *Electoral Strategies and Political Marketing* (New York: St. Martin, 1992), p. 227.

114. Sabato, *The Rise of Political Consultants*, p. 61. The IAPP now claims over 90 members (almost half of whom, interestingly, are Americans); see David Far-

rell, "Political Consultancy Overseas: The Internationalization of Campaign Consultancy," *PS: Political Science and Politics*, 31(2) (1998): 171–76.

115. Machin and Vincent Wright, "Why Mitterand Won," pp. 18, 30; Farrell, "Campaign Strategies and Tactics," p. 178.

116. Bowler and Farrell, "Conclusion," p. 228.

117. Machin, "The President, the Parties and Parliament," p. 139.

118. Lawson and Ysmal, "France: The 1988 Presidential Campaign," p. 108.

119. Shields, "France's Presidential Election," p. 322.

120. Irène Hill, "Financing the Presidential Campaign," in John Gaffney and Lorna Milne, *French Presidentialism and the Election of 1995* (Aldershot, UK: Ashgate, 1997), p. 95.

121. Orttung, "Voters Face a Red-and-White Choice," p. 7.

122. Kramer, "Rescuing Boris," p. 31.

123. Kramer ("Rescuing Boris") suggested that the Americans were critical to the campaign effort; Remnick ("Letter from Russia: War for the Kremlin," p. 46) disagreed, suggesting that the Russians were, in effect, humoring the Americans. The truth probably lies somewhere in between. Since Kramer's piece relied heavily on the accounts of the campaign professionals themselves, it is probably slightly skewed.

124. Hiring the Americans was part of the overall campaign management shift made when Chubais took over from Soskovets (McFaul, *Russia's 1996 Presidential Election*, p. 19).

125. Orttung, *OMRI* (1996d).

126. Nick Hayes, "Yeltsin Then and Now," *Star Tribune*, June 20, 1996, p. 24A.

127. Orttung, *OMRI* (1996g).

128. Bowler and Farrell, "Conclusion."

CHAPTER FIVE

1. "Washington Whispers: Sucker Punch," *U.S. News & World Report*, July 26, 1999, p. 8.

2. Wayne, *Road to the White House*, pp. 28–29.

3. Herrnson, "National Party Organizations at Century's End," p. 80.

4. Ibid., p. 59.

5. Ibid., p. 57.

6. For the quadrennial cost of living increases in hard money spending limits, see Wayne, *Road to the White House*, p. 49, Table 2.5.

7. Ibid., pp. 46, 49.

8. AT&T donated $2,653,226 and Amway Corporation, $1,320,000 to the San Diego Host Committee (Republicans); Ameritech and Motorola contributed $2,425,625 and $1,108,830, respectively, to Chicago's Committee for '96; see Jackson, "Financing the 1996 Campaign," p. 241.

9. Presidential candidates can spend as much as they like if they forgo public funding.

10. An excellent guide to presidential campaign finance can be found in Wayne, *Road to the White House*, pp. 27–63. In 1996 fewer than 20 percent of taxpayers donated to the presidential campaign fund. As the result, the fund ran

low and because of the way the law was written, many candidates had to wait for their money and find alternative ways to finance the all-important primary battles; see Beck, *Party Politics in America*, p. 289.

11. According to direct mail expert David Tyson, quoted in Anthony Corrado, "The Changing Environment of Presidential Campaign Finance," in William Mayer, *In Pursuit of the White House: How We Choose Our Presidential Nominees* (Chatham, NJ: Chatham House, 1996), pp. 228–29.

12. Ibid.

13. A direct mail campaign is also fairly expensive to administer. One study reported that on average, direct mail campaigns elicit a response rate of less than 3 percent and have an average contribution of roughly $25. See ibid., p. 251, note 31.

14. Wayne, *Road to the White House*, p. 41.

15. Corrado, "The Changing Environment of Presidential Campaign Finance," pp. 228–29.

16. Ibid., pp. 213, 228.

17. "Washington Whispers: Family Ties," *U.S. News & World Report*, June 21, 1999, p. 9.

18. Emmett H. Buell, "The Invisible Primary," in William Mayer, *In Pursuit of the White House: How We Choose Our Presidential Nominees* (Chatham, NJ: Chatham House, 1996), p. 12.

19. See, for example, Sheila Kaplan, "Campaign 2000, by the Numbers," *U.S. News & World Report*, January 18, 1999, pp. 20–21.

20. "Washington Whispers: Betting on Victory," *U.S. News & World Report*, August, 9, 1999, p. 8.

21. Corrado, "The Changing Environment of Presidential Campaign Finance," p. 246.

22. Wayne, *Road to the White House*, p. 43.

23. From the Center for Responsive Politics, <http://www.opensecrets.org>. Leadership PACs need not be, and often are not, associated with presidential candidates.

24. Corrado, "The Changing Environment of Presidential Campaign Finance," p. 24.

25. Wayne, *Road to the White House*, p. 42.

26. Corrado, "The Changing Environment of Presidential Campaign Finance," p. 241.

27. Wayne, *Road to the White House*, p. 42.

28. Written in early July 1999; see Nancy Watzman, "Virtual Fund-raising: Force for Democracy or a New Edge for Incumbents?" *Capital Eye* 6(3) (1999): 6.

29. For a review, see Mary Clare Jalonick, "Rating 2000 Presidential Campaign Web Sites," *Campaigns & Elections* (July 1999) p. 36.

30. David Dulio, Donald Goff, and James Thurber, "Untangled Web: Internet Use During the 1998 Election," *PS: Political Science and Politics* 32(1) (1999): 53–59; Paul Hendrie, "FEC May Revise Cyberspace Campaign Rules," *Capital Eye* 6(3) (1999a): 7, discusses the problems and possible FEC solutions to online giving in more detail.

31. Craig Varoga, "Campaign Doctor," *Campaigns & Elections* (July 1999) p. 77.

32. David Dodenhoff and Kenneth Goldstein, "Resources, Racehorses, and Rules: Nominations in the 1990s," in L. Sandy Maisel, *The Parties Respond* (Boulder, CO: Westview, 1998), p. 195; see also Buell, "The Invisible Primary."

33. Jackson, "Financing the 1996 Campaign," p. 235.

34. Wayne, *Road to the White House*, p. 48.

35. Anthony Corrado, "Financing the 1996 Elections," in Gerald Pomper, *The Election of 1996* (Chatham, NJ: Chatham House, 1997), p. 137.

36. Paul Hendrie, "Giving Double to Keep Gore out of Trouble," *Capital Eye* 6(3) (1999): 5.

37. Wayne, *Road to the White House*, pp. 50–52, Box 2–3.

38. Corrado, "Financing the 1996 Elections," p. 152.

39. See Jackson, "Financing the 1996 Campaign," p. 245, for a list of some three dozen donors, each of whom donated better that $350,000 to one or both parties.

40. "Big DNC Donations Linked to Coffees," *Washington Post*, January 28, 1997, p. A2.

41. Harris, "Clinton's Campaign Consultants Reaped Millions."

42. Wayne, *Road to the White House*, pp. 46–47.

43. Corrado, "Financing the 1996 Elections," p. 152.

44. Jackson, "Financing the 1996 Campaign," p. 237.

45. Hill, "Financing the Presidential Campaign," p. 87.

46. Ibid., p. 86.

47. Ibid., p. 87. Estimates for various campaigns in the 1980s range from $15 to $45 million.

48. Avril, "Regulation of Political Finance in France," p. 88. French francs converted by author using the June 1999 exchange rates (One franc equals $0.157).

49. Knapp, *Gaullism since de Gaulle*, p. 267.

50. Ibid., pp. 265–66.

51. Ibid., p. 261.

52. Whitney, "Common Currency: Do Francs and Yen Corrupt?"

53. Stevens, *The Government and Politics of France*, p. 239.

54. Avril, "Regulation of Political Finance in France," p. 87.

55. Drysch, "The New French System of Political Finance," p. 165.

56. Hill, "Financing the Presidential Campaign," p. 92.

57. Ibid., pp. 90–92.

58. Ibid., p. 94.

59. The costs in 1981 were estimated at $31.4 million each for Giscard d'Estaing and François Mitterand; see Avril, "Regulation of Political Finance in France," p. 87.

60. Lawson and Ysmal, "France: The 1988 Presidential Campaign," p. 104.

61. Hill, "Financing the Presidential Campaign," p. 87.

62. Ibid., p. 95.

63. McFaul, *Russia's 1996 Presidential Election*, pp. 50–52.

64. Ibid., p. 57.

65. Herrnson, "National Party Organizations at Century's End," p. 60.

66. James L. Gibson and Susan E. Scarrow, "State and Local Party Organi-

zations in American Politics," in Eric Uslaner, *American Political Parties: A Reader* (Itasca, IL: F. E. Peacock, 1993), p. 237.

67. Wayne, *Road to the White House*, p. 128.

68. Polsby and Wildavsky, *Presidential Elections*, p. 190.

69. Telephone conversation with Steve Donlin, owner, SD Associates (Hartford, CT), August 2, 1999.

70. Knapp, *Gaullism since de Gaulle*, p. 267.

71. Lawson and Ysmal, "France: The 1988 Presidential Campaign," p. 109.

72. Steven Griggs, "Candidates and Parties of the Left," in Robert Elgie, *Electing the French President: The 1995 Presidential Election* (New York: St. Martin, 1996), p. 113.

73. In many cases the physical plant of the Russian Communist Party is the state machinery from the previous regime.

74. McFaul, *Russia's 1996 Presidential Election*, pp. 37, 46.

75. Kramer, "Rescuing Boris," p. 31.

76. Daniel Treisman, "Why Yeltsin Won," *Foreign Affairs* 75(5) (1996): 64–77.

77. Remnick, "Letter from Russia: War for the Kremlin," p. 49.

78. Gary Selnow, *High-tech Campaigns: Computer Technology in Political Communication* (Westport, CT: Praeger, 1994, p. 68); see also Farrell, "Campaign Strategies and Tactics."

79. Telephone conversation with Steve Donlin, owner, SD Associates (Hartford, CT), August 2, 1999.

80. Dinkin, *Campaigning in America*, p. 139.

81. Wayne, *Road to the White House*, p. 211.

82. Polsby and Wildavsky, *Presidential Elections*, pp. 88–89.

83. Larry Sabato, "Open Season: How the News Media Covers Presidential Campaigns in the Age of Attack Journalism," in Doris Graber, *Media Power in Politics* (Washington, DC: CQ Press, 1994, p. 200).

84. Stephen Ansolabehere et al., *The Media Game: American Politics in the Television Age* (New York: Macmillan, 1993), p. 84.

85. Sabato, *The Rise of Political Consultants*, p. 195.

86. Ibid., pp. 238–41.

87. Drysch, "The New French System of Political Finance."

88. White et al., *How Russia Votes*, p. 251.

89. McFaul, *Russia's 1996 Presidential Election*, p. 34.

90. Igor Malashenko, the president of NTV; see Laura Belin, *OMRI* (1996a).

91. Remnick, "Letter from Russia: War for the Kremlin," p. 49.

92. Belin, *OMRI* (1996b).

93. Belin, *OMRI* (1996c).

94. White et al., *How Russia Votes*, p. 253.

95. Orttung, *OMRI* (1996a).

96. White et al., *How Russia Votes*, p. 250.

97. Corrado, "The Changing Environment of Presidential Campaign Finance," p. 226.

98. Herrnson, "National Party Organizations at Century's End."

99. Wayne, *Road to the White House*, pp. 50–53.

100. Dinkin, *Campaigning in America*, p. 163.

101. James Davis, *U.S. Presidential Primaries and the Caucus-convention System: A Sourcebook* (Westport, CT: Greenwood, 1997), p. 75.

102. Wayne, *Road to the White House*, p. 128.

103. Farrell, "Campaign Strategies and Tactics," p. 165.

104. Machin and Vincent Wright, "Why Mitterand Won," p. 18.

105. McFaul, *Russia's 1996 Presidential Election*, p. 27.

106. Ibid., pp. 33–34.

107. Ibid., p. 19.

108. Belin, *OMRI* (1996d).

109. McFaul, *Russia's 1996 Presidential Election*, p. 36. Komsomol, which once boasted millions of members, has since shrunk considerably to roughly 15,000 members (Bronwyn Donne, "Yeltsin Strikes Chord with the Young at Red Square Concert," *The Times*, June 11, 1996).

110. Orttung, "Voters Face a Red-and-White Choice," p. 10.

111. McFaul, *Russia's 1996 Presidential Election*, p. 37. Vladimir Zhirinovsky was the only major nationalist figure not invited to join the bloc.

112. Wayne, *Road to the White House*, p. 50.

113. Harold W. Stanley, "The Nominations: Republican Doldrums, Democratic Revival," in Michael Nelson, *The Elections of 1996* (Washington, DC: CQ Press, 1997), p. 31.

114. Kenneth T. Walsh, "The Man to Beat," *U.S. News & World Report*, March 15, 1999, pp. 18–21.

115. "Washington Whispers: Opponents Invited," *U.S. News & World Report*, June 28, 1999, p. 8.

116. Written in July 1999.

117. Dodenhoff and Goldstein, "Resources, Racehorses, and Rules," p. 191.

118. Remnick, "Letter from Russia: War for the Kremlin," p. 49; Treisman, "Why Yeltsin Won."

119. Morvant, *OMRI* (1996a).

120. Hayes, "Yeltsin Then and Now."

121. White et al., *How Russia Votes*, p. 259.

122. Szarka, "The Winning of the 1995 French Presidential Election," p. 155.

123. Farrell, "Campaign Strategies and Tactics," p. 166.

124. Dodenhoff and Goldstein, "Resources, Racehorses, and Rules."

CHAPTER SIX

1. Respectively, Goldman et al., *Quest for the Presidency, 1992*; Jules Witcover, *Marathon: The Pursuit of the Presidency, 1972–1976* (New York: Viking, 1977); Napolitan, *The Election Game and How to Win It*; Theodore H. White, *The Making of the President* (New York: Atheneum, 1960); Joe McGinniss, *The Selling of the President, 1968* (New York: Trident Press, 1969); and Wayne, *Road to the White House*.

2. This chapter draws heavily on Wayne, *Road to the White House*, pp. 159–283; and Polsby and Wildavsky, *Presidential Elections*, pp. 181–257.

3. Wayne, *Road to the White House*, pp. 182–83.

4. Bruce Buchanan, "The Presidency and the Nominating Process," in Michael Nelson, *The Presidency and the Political System* (Washington, DC: CQ Press, 1995).

5. Republicans seem to place more stock in party service than do Democrats but this has little formal effect on the candidate selection process.

6. Hugh Heclo, "Presidential and Prime Ministerial Selection," in Donald Matthews, *Perspectives on Presidential Selection* (Washington, DC: Brookings Institution, 1973); more recently, for congressional candidate recruitment, see Alan Ehrenhalt, *The United States of Ambition: Politicians, Power, and the Pursuit of Office* (New York: Times Books, 1991).

7. As per Andrew Busch, *Outsiders and Openness in the Presidential Nominating System* (Pittsburgh, PA: University of Pittsburgh, 1997).

8. Wayne, *Road to the White House*, pp. 182–83.

9. Zeigler, *Political Parties in Industrial Democracies*, p. 125.

10. Elijah Ben-Zion Kaminsky, "The Selection of French Presidents," in Donald Matthews, *Perspectives on Presidential Selection* (Washington, DC: Brookings Institution, 1973).

11. Pierce, *Choosing the Chief*, pp. 218–19.

12. Kaminsky, "The Selection of French Presidents."

13. The announcement came on December 11, 1994; see Szarka, "The Winning of the 1995 French Presidential Election," p. 159.

14. Alistair Cole, "La France Pour Tous?— The French Presidential Elections of 23 April and 7 May 1995," *Government & Opposition* 30(3) (1995): 327–46; and Shields, "France's Presidential Election," p. 321.

15. Hill, "Financing the Presidential Campaign," p. 95; another sign of the importance of polling is the fact that opinion polling is banned for the two weeks prior to the election.

16. Orttung, "Voters Face a Red-and-White Choice," p. 8.

17. Polsby and Wildavsky, *Presidential Elections*, pp. 68–69.

18. "Lexington: Steve Forbes and His Victims" *Economist*, January 30, 1999, p. 31.

19. Evan Thomas, "The Sons also Rise," *Newsweek*, November 16, 1998, pp. 44–48.

20. Polsby and Wildavsky, *Presidential Elections*, pp. 170–71.

21. Buell, "The Invisible Primary," pp. 20–24.

22. Kaminsky, "The Selection of French Presidents," p. 115.

23. Cole, "La France Pour Tous?" p. 331; Szarka, "The Winning of the 1995 French Presidential Election."

24. This was part of Chirac's strategy in giving Balladur the job of prime minister.

25. See Beck, *Party Politics in America*, pp. 200–204, for a good discussion of the distinction between the types of direct primaries; for our purposes the differences are minimal at best. William Mayer, "Caucuses: How They Work, What Difference They Make," in *In Pursuit of the White House: How We Choose Our Presidential Nominees* (Chatham, NJ: Chatham House, 1996), does a good job of explaining party caucuses, which are essentially party conferences where delegates from a lower level (e.g., local) are chosen to go to a party conference at the next level (e.g., county), which then chooses delegates to go to on (e.g., to regional caucuses) and so on, until they meet at the state level to choose delegates to the national convention.

26. Beck, *Party Politics in America*, pp. 218–21.

27. The reforms were enacted first by the Democrats, then the Republicans by virtue of the fact that they, by and large, became state law.

28. John Aldrich, "Presidential Selection," in George Edwards III, et al., *Researching the Presidency: Vital Questions, New Approaches* (Pittsburgh, PA: University of Pittsburgh, 1993). The new nomination system includes many of the factors which this book addresses (technology, political consultants, increased electoral prominence of independent groups, new campaign finance laws), as well as a decline in partisan identification.

29. See Ryan Barilleaux and Randall Adkins, "The Nominations: Process and Patterns," in Michael Nelson, *The 1992 Elections* (Washington, DC: CQ Press, 1993), for a discussion of this.

30. Walsh, "The Man to Beat."

31. Patterson, *Out of Order*, pp. 119–32.

32. Dodenhoff and Goldstein, "Resources, Racehorses, and Rules."

33. Both Iowa and New Hampshire have state laws that require their respective contests to be first. This has caused some problems within the Democratic Party, because although the party defers to these two states, other states (South Dakota, Wyoming, Delaware) have enacted legislation which schedules their contests before the official time period set by the party begins. This, in turn, forces both Iowa and New Hampshire to move their dates even further ahead (to before the official party window for delegate selection), which technically violates party rules; see Wayne, *Road to the White House*, p. 155.

34. Ibid., pp. 124–25.

35. From *CBS News Campaign Directory*, in Dodenhoff and Goldstein, "Resources, Racehorses, and Rules," p. 181. See Sabato, "Presidential Nominations: The Front-loaded Frenzy of '96," p. 81, for a detailed listing of candidate visits to all states during the 1996 primary season.

36. Dodenhoff and Goldstein, "Resources, Racehorses, and Rules," p. 174, Table 8.3.

37. Byron Shafer, *Bifurcated Politics: Evolution and Reform in the National Party Convention* (Cambridge, MA: Harvard, 1988).

38. Wayne, *Road to the White House*, p. 162.

39. Beck, *Party Politics in America*, pp. 236–40.

40. Ibid. Unlike efforts at organization-building, the Democrats have initiated most of the party reforms since 1968, with Republicans following.

41. Ibid., p. 233.

42. As per Shafer, *Bifurcated Politics*.

43. Larry David Smith, "The Party Platforms as Institutional Discourse: The Democrats and Republicans of 1988," *Presidential Studies Quarterly* 22(3) (1992): 531–43.

44. Judith H. Parris, *The Convention Problem: Issues in Reform of Presidential Nominating Procedures* (Washington, DC: Brookings Institution, 1972).

45. Terri Susan Fine, "Lobbying from Within: Government Elites and the Framing of the 1988 Democratic and Republican Party Platforms," *Presidential Studies Quarterly* 24(4) (1994): 855–63; see also L. Sandy Maisel, "The Platform-Writing Process: Candidate-Centered Platforms in 1992," in Robert Shapiro, *Understanding Presidential Elections: Trends and New Developments* (New York: Academy of Political Science, 1996).

46. Ronald Elving, "Party Platforms Helped Shape Fall Campaigns," *Congressional Quarterly Weekly Report*, October 22, 1988, p. 3041; Beth Donovan, "Abortion: Will the Big Tent Hold All?" *Congressional Quarterly Weekly Report*, Supplement: The Republican Convention, August 8, 1992, p. 19; Deborah Kalb, "Building with Broad Planks," *Congressional Quarterly Weekly Report*, Supplement: The Democratic Convention. August 17, 1996, p. 34; Alan Greenblatt, "The Platform Dance," *Congressional Quarterly Weekly Report*, Supplement: The Republican Convention. August 3, 1996, p. 14.

47. "Republicans: Convention Notes," *Time*, August 26, 1996, p. 21.

48. With the recent rise in the number of uncommitted superdelegates (and the Democrats' move to delegate selection based on proportional representation), the potential, albeit a small one, exists for a "brokered" convention in the future.

49. Wayne, *Road to the White House*, p. 184.

50. Safran, *The French Polity*, p. 117. Although the Rally for the Republic toyed with the idea of holding a direct primary in 1995 to determine the party nomination, they did not. In fact, the constitutionality of a direct primary nomination in France is in question, since it would, in the eyes of many French, constitute a third round of balloting; see Peter Fysh, "Candidates and Parties of the Right," in Robert Elgie, *Electing the French President: The 1995 Presidential Election* (New York: St. Martin, 1996), p. 82.

51. Of late the Supreme Court seems to be drifting toward giving some of the power to determine delegate selection criteria back to parties, allowing them "the right to regulate standards for admission to it, even overriding enactments of state legislatures on the subject of primary elections." See Polsby and Wildavsky, *Presidential Elections*, p. 64, note 40.

52. Kay Lawson, "Constitutional Change and Party Development in France, Nigeria, and the United States," in Louis Maisel and Joseph Cooper, *Political Parties: Development and Decay* (London, UK: Sage, 1978), p. 152.

53. Jean and Monica Charlot, "France," p. 138.

54. Marie-France Toinet, "The Elections of 1981," p. 15.

55. Cole, "La France Pour Tous?" p. 333.

56. Zeigler, *Political Parties in Industrial Democracies*, p. 120.

57. Roy C. Macridis, *French Politics in Transition* (Cambridge, MA: Winthrop, 1975).

58. Jean and Monica Charlot, "France," pp. 138–39.

59. Safran, *The French Polity*, p. 111.

60. Maarek, "New Trends in French Political Communication," p. 357.

61. Laura Belin, "Zyuganov Tries to Broaden an Already Powerful Left-Wing Coalition," *Transition*, 2(11) (1996): 12–17.

62. Ibid., p. 12; McFaul, *Russia's 1996 Presidential Election*, p. 37.

63. Orttung, "Voters Face a Red-and-White Choice," p. 6.

64. Treisman, "Why Yeltsin Won," p. 75.

65. McFaul, *Russia's 1996 Presidential Election*, pp. 44–45.

66. Polsby and Wildavsky, *Presidential Elections*, p. 191.

67. Report by the Center for Public Integrity, quoted in the *Orange County Register*, December 14, 1996.

68. "Bush, Perot Outspend Clinton: Democrat Finds It Difficult to Keep up with Incumbent's Perks," *Houston Chronicle*, October 31, 1992, p. A19.

69. Wayne, *Road to the White House*, pp. 221, 224.

70. Technically Maine and Nebraska laws do not require that their electors be awarded by the winner-take-all system; in practice, however, they are.

71. Wayne, *Road to the White House*, p. 225.

72. Polsby and Wildavsky, *Presidential Elections*, p. 66.

73. Wayne, *Road to the White House*, pp. 225–26.

74. Trent and Friedenberg, *Political Campaign Communication*, pp. 182–83.

75. Ibid., p. 220; also, Dinkin, *Campaigning in America*, p. 171.

76. Polsby and Wildavsky, *Presidential Elections*, pp. 183–84; Wayne, *Road to the White House*, pp. 229–30.

77. Wayne, *Road to the White House*, pp. 288–89.

78. Polsby and Wildavsky, *Presidential Elections*, p. 205.

79. Sabato, *The Rise of Political Consultants*, p. 73.

80. Wayne, *Road to the White House*, pp. 128–31.

81. Ibid., p. 92.

82. Polsby and Wildavsky, *Presidential Elections*, p. 212.

83. Democratic pollster Mark Mellman, quoted in ibid., p. 209.

84. Ibid., p. 210.

85. Wayne, *Road to the White House*, p. 129; see also Sabato, "Presidential Nominations: The Front-loaded Frenzy of '96," pp. 74–76.

86. Polsby and Wildavsky, *Presidential Elections*, pp. 186–88, and Wayne, *Road to the White House*, pp. 233–34.

87. Wayne, *Road to the White House*, p. 234.

88. Dinkin, *Campaigning in America*, p. 161.

89. Friedenberg, *Communication Consultants in Political Campaigns*.

90. Ibid., pp. 82–89.

91. Ibid., pp. 177–83.

92. Polsby and Wildavsky, *Presidential Elections*, pp. 193–200.

93. Wayne, *Road to the White House*, pp. 217–20.

94. Ibid., p. 219.

95. Ibid., pp. 218–19.

96. Friedenberg, *Communication Consultants in Political Campaigns*, p. 118.

97. Videocassettes are also a way to supply "feeds" to local news channels. About 10 percent of local stations used these campaign-produced "news releases" in 1992, often without knowing who their source was (Wayne, *Road to the White House*, p. 132).

98. Sabato, *The Rise of Political Consultants*, p. 201.

99. Friedenberg, *Communication Consultants in Political Campaigns*, p. 184.

100. Ibid., pp. 183–91.

101. Varoga, "Campaign Doctor."

102. Dinkin, *Campaigning in America*, p. 173, from Witcover, *Marathon*.

103. Graber, *Mass Media and American Politics*, p. 237.

104. Hill, "Financing the Presidential Campaign," p. 87.

105. Maarek, "New Trends in French Political Communication," p. 364.

106. Lawson and Ysmal, "France: The 1988 Presidential Campaign," p. 115.

107. See, for example, Singer, "Letters from Europe," or Maarek, "New Trends in French Political Communication.

108. Catherine Fieschi, "The Other Candidates: Voynet, Le Pen, de Villiers and

Cheminade," in John Gaffney and Lorna Milne, *French Presidentialism and the Election of 1995* (Aldershot, UK: Ashgate, 1997), pp. 143–44. In addition, election laws gave candidate Le Pen government-sponsored television time during the presidential campaign itself.

109. White et al., *How Russia Votes*, p. 253.

110. Anna Paretskaya, *OMRI Russian Presidential Election Survey*, Number 11. June 27, 1996.

111. McFaul, *Russia's 1996 Presidential Election*, pp. 46–47.

112. Irina Niyudovaya, deputy leader of Komsomol, quoted in Donne, "Yeltsin Strikes Chord with the Young at Red Square Concert."

CHAPTER SEVEN

1. Martin Wattenberg, *The Rise of Candidate-centered Politics: Presidential Elections of the 1980s* (Cambridge, MA: Harvard, 1991).

2. An edited collection by David Butler and Austin Ranney "explores the extent of . . . Americanization [in political campaigns] and its limits" (*Electioneering: A Comparative Study of Continuity and Change* [Oxford, UK: Clarendon, 1992], p. 8). For Shaun Bowler and David Farrell (*Electoral Strategies and Political Marketing* [New York: St. Martin, 1992]) and Lawrence LeDuc et al. (*Comparing Democracies: Elections and Voting in Global Perspectives* [Thousand Oaks, CA: Sage, 1996]) the focus is similar, as well as for Dennis Kavanagh (*Election Campaigning: The New Marketing of Politics* [Oxford, UK: Basil Blackwell, 1995]), looking at (for) an "American" model of campaigning in Great Britain. There is, as might be expected, some dissent over the extent of the spread of "American" style campaigning; see, for example, Margaret Scammel, "The Wisdom of the War Room: U.S. Campaigning and Americanization," Research Paper, The Joan Shorenstein Center for Press, Politics, and Public Policy, Cambridge, MA: Harvard, 1997.

3. David Swanson and Paolo Mancini, *Politics, Media, and Modern Democracy: An International Study of Innovations in Electoral Campaigning and Their Consequences* (Westport, CT: Praeger, 1996).

4. Andrew M. Appleton and Daniel S. Ward insightfully note that in the "party's over" debate, the difference between the "declinists" and the "revivalists" arguments pivots on the distinction being made in this research, namely, that the "declinists" look at the party-in-the-electorate, while "revivalists" look at party organizations ("Measuring Party Organization in the United States," *Party Politics* 1[1] [1994]: 113–31).

5. Swanson and Mancini, *Politics, Media, and Modern Democracy*.

6. Friedenberg, *Communication Consultants in Political Campaigns*, pp. 1–30, does an outstanding job of discussing the history of political consultancy as well as its emergence as an industry.

7. Excellent review essays can be found in Gabriel Almond, *Political Development: Essays in Heuristic Theory* (Boston: Little, Brown, and Co., 1970), or Samuel Huntington, "The Change to Change," *Comparative Politics* 3(1971):283–322.

8. See Dalton, *Citizen Politics*, for a thorough and readable overview of "new politics."

9. Herrnson, "National Party Organizations at Century's End," p. 62.

10. Those interested in following developments in Russia can do so online, with daily reports from Radio Free Europe/Radio Liberty, <http://www.rferl.org/>.

11. Parties still play a large role in the candidate selection process for parliamentary and congressional elections.

12. O'Shaughnessy, *The Phenomenon of Political Marketing*, p. 231.

13. Bert Rockman, "Presidential Studies: The One, the Few, and the Many," in Herbert Weisberg, *Political Science: The Science of Politics* (New York: Agathon, 1986), p. 117.

14. William Mayer, "The Presidential Nominations," in Gerald Pomper, *The Election of 1996: Reports and Interpretations* (Chatham, NJ: Chatham House, 1997), p. 28; see also Randall E. Adkins, "Strategic Politicians and the Presidency: An Examination of the Dynamic Nature of Presidential Ambition in a Post-modern Nominating Environment," (Ph.D. dissertation, Miami University, Oxford, OH, 1995.

15. James W. Ceaser, *Presidential Selection: Theory and Development* (Princeton, NJ: Princeton, 1979).

16. This also suggests that examinations of the political, social, economic, and cultural aspects of extreme politics (undoubtedly important) may to some extent miss the mark in trying to explain them.

17. John Aldrich makes this latter point in "Methods and Actors: The Relationship of Processes to Candidates," in Alexander Heard and Michael Nelson, *Presidential Selection*, (Durham, NC: Duke, 1987).

18. Nelson Polsby, *Consequences of Party Reform* (Oxford, UK: Oxford University, 1983), p. 89.

19. Richard Neustadt, the dean of presidential scholars, cautioned presidents about too much reliance on this aspect of presidential power (*Presidential Power and the Modern Presidents: The Politics of Leadership from Roosevelt to Reagan* [New York: The Free Press, 1990]).

20. See Richard Rose, "Learning to Govern or Learning to Campaign?" in Heard and Nelson, *Presidential Selection*, p. 55, who, it must be noted, was examining only presidential selection in the United States.

21. See, for example, G. Bingham Powell, *Contemporary Democracies: Participation, Stability and Violence* (Cambridge, MA: Harvard, 1982).

22. Larry Diamond, "Introduction: In Search of Consolidation," in *Consolidating the Third Wave Democracies* (Baltimore: Johns Hopkins, 1997), p. xxv.

23. Juan Linz, "The Perils of Presidentialism,"*Journal of Democracy* 1(1990):51–69; or, extended, with Arturo Valenzuela, *The Failure of Presidential Democracy* (Baltimore: Johns Hopkins, 1994).

24. James Davis, *The President as Party Leader* (Westport CT: Greenwood, 1992).

25. Ibid.

26. Aldrich's discussion of this topic is excellent ("Presidential Selection," 1993).

27. Charles Jones, "The Clinton Administration in the Separated System: A Presidency at Risk," *extensions: A Journal of the Carl Albert Congressional Research and Studies Center* (1996): 4.

28. Charles Jones, *The Presidency in a Separated System* (Washington, DC: Brookings Institution, 1994), p. 294.

29. Lester G. Seligman and Cary R. Covington, *The Coalitional Presidency* (Chicago, IL: Dorsey, 1989); Milkis, *The Presidency and Political Parties.*

30. Lowi, *The Personal President.*

31. Ceaser, *Presidential Selection.*

32. Alexander Heard and Michael Nelson, "Change and Stability in Choosing Presidents," in their *Presidential Selection.*

33. Polsby, *Consequences of Party Reform*, p. 75.

34. Gerald Pomper and Susan Lederman, *Elections in America: Control and Influence in Democratic Politics* (New York: Longman's, 1980); Hans-Dieter Klingemann, Richard Hofferbert, and Ian Budge, *Parties, Policies, and Democracy* (Boulder, CO: Westview, 1994).

35. Samuel Huntington, *The Third Wave: Democratization in the Late Twentieth Century* (Norman: University of Oklahoma, 1991); Gerald Easter, "Preference for Presidentialism: Postcommunist Regime Change in Russia and the NIS," *World Politics* 49(1997):184–211.

Bibliography

Abramson, Paul R., John H. Aldrich, and David W. Rhode. 1998. *Change and Continuity in the 1996 Elections.* Washington, DC: CQ Press.

Adkins, Randall E. 1995. "Strategic Politicians and the Presidency: An Examination of the Dynamic Nature of Presidential Ambition in a Post-modern Nominating Environment." Ph.D. dissertation, Department of Political Science, Miami University, Oxford, OH.

Agranoff, Robert. 1976. *The New Style in Election Campaigns.* Second Edition. Boston: Holbrook.

Aldrich, John H. 1987. "Methods and Actors: The Relationship of Processes to Candidates." In Alexander Heard and Michael Nelson, eds., *Presidential Selection.* Durham, NC: Duke.

———. 1993. "Presidential Selection." In George C. Edwards III, John H. Kessel, and Bert A. Rockman, eds., *Researching the Presidency: Vital Questions, New Approaches.* Pittsburgh, PA: University of Pittsburgh.

———. 1995. *Why Parties? The Origin and Transformation of Political Parties in America.* Chicago: University of Chicago.

Alexander, Herbert E. 1992. *Financing Politics: Money, Elections, and Political Reform.* Fourth Edition. Washington, DC: CQ Press.

Almond, Gabriel A. 1970. *Political Development: Essays in Heuristic Theory.* Boston: Little, Brown, and Co.

Ansolabehere, Stephen, Roy Behr, and Shanto Iyengar. 1993. *The Media Game: American Politics in the Television Age.* New York: Macmillan.

Appleton, Andrew M., and Daniel S. Ward. 1994. "Measuring Party Organization in the United States." *Party Politics* 1(1): 113–31.

———. 1997. "Party Response to Environmental Change: A Model of Organizational Innovation." *Party Politics* 3(3): 341–62.

Avril, Pierre. 1994. "Regulation of Political Finance in France." In Herbert E.

Alexander and Rei Shiratori, eds., *Comparative Political Finance Among the Democracies*. Boulder, CO: Westview.

Baer, Denise, and David A. Bositis. 1993. *Politics and Linkage in a Democratic Society*. Englewood Cliffs, NJ: Prentice Hall.

Barilleaux, Ryan J. 1996. *American Government in Action: Principle, Process, and Politics*. Upper Saddle River, NJ: Prentice Hall.

Barilleaux, Ryan J., and Randall E. Adkins. 1993. "The Nominations: Process and Patterns." In Michael Nelson, ed., *The 1992 Elections*. Washington, DC: CQ Press.

Baumgartner, Jody C. 1998. "Electing Presidents and Other Potentates." In Ryan J. Barilleaux, ed., *Presidential Frontiers: Underexplored Issues in White House Politics*. Westport, CT: Praeger.

———. 1998a. "Comparative Presidential Selection: An Organizational Approach." Ph.D. dissertation, Department of Political Science, Miami University, Oxford, OH.

———. 1999. "Hunker Democrats (1848)." In Ronald Hayduk, Immanuel Ness, and James Ciment, eds., *Encyclopedia of American Third Parties*. M. E. Sharpe.

Beck, Paul Allen. 1997. *Party Politics in America*. Eighth Edition. New York: Longman.

Belin, Laura. 1996. "Zyuganov Tries to Broaden an Already Powerful Left-Wing Coalition." *Transition* 2(11): 12–17.

———. 1996a. *OMRI Daily Digest*. Number 112, Part 1. June 10, 1996.

———. 1996b. *OMRI Daily Digest*. Number 116, Part 1. June 14, 1996.

———. 1996c. *OMRI Russian Presidential Election Survey*. Number 10: June 21, 1996.

———. 1996d. *OMRI Daily Digest*. Number 122, Part 1. June 24, 1996.

Bell, David S., ed. 1982. *Contemporary French Political Parties*. London, UK: Croom Helm.

Bernstein, Carl, and Bob Woodward. 1974. *All the President's Men*. New York: Simon and Schuster.

Bibby, John F. 1998. "State Party Organizations: Coping and Adapting to Candidate-Centered Politics and Nationalization." In L. Sandy Maisel, ed., *The Parties Respond*. Second Edition. Boulder, CO: Westview.

Bibby, John F., and L. Sandy Maisel. 1998. *Two Parties—Or More? The American Party System*. Boulder, CO: Westview.

"Big DNC Donations Linked to Coffees." 1997. *Washington Post*, January 28, 1997, p. A2.

Binkley, Wilfred E. 1962. *American Political Parties: Their Natural History*. Fourth Edition, Enlarged. New York: Alfred E. Knopf.

Boilard, Steve D. 1998. *Russia at the Twenty-First Century: Political and Social Change in the Post-Soviet Era*. Fort Worth, TX: Harcourt Brace College.

Bowler, Shaun, and David M. Farrell, eds. 1992. *Electoral Strategies And Political Marketing*. New York: St. Martin.

———. 1992a. "Conclusion: The Contemporary Election Campaign." In Shaun Bowler and David M. Farrell, eds., *Electoral Strategies And Political Marketing*. New York: St. Martin.

Bryce, James. 1995. *The American Commonwealth*. Vol. 2. Indianapolis: Liberty Fund.

Buchanan, Bruce. 1995. "The Presidency and the Nominating Process." In Michael Nelson, ed., *The Presidency and the Political System*. Washington, DC: CQ Press.

Buell, Emmett H. 1996. "The Invisible Primary." In William G. Mayer, ed., *In Pursuit of the White House: How We Choose Our Presidential Nominees*. Chatham, NJ: Chatham House.

Burnham, Walter Dean. 1970. *Critical Elections and the Mainsprings of American Politics*. New York: Norton.

Busch, Andrew E. 1997. *Outsiders and Openness in the Presidential Nominating System*. Pittsburgh, PA: University of Pittsburgh.

"Bush, Perot Outspend Clinton: Democrat Finds It Difficult to Keep up with Incumbent's Perks." 1992. *Houston Chronicle*, October 31, p. A19.

Butler, David, and Austin Ranney, eds. 1992. *Electioneering: A Comparative Study of Continuity and Change*. Oxford, UK: Clarendon.

Campaigns and Elections. 1997. "Scorecard." 17(12): 20–51.

———. 1997a. 17(12): 55.

———. 1998. (Front Cover). 19(3).

Carey, John M. 1997. "Institutional Design and Party Systems." In Larry Diamond et al., eds., *Consolidating the Third Wave Democracies*. Baltimore: Johns Hopkins.

Ceaser, James W. 1979. *Presidential Selection: Theory and Development*. Princeton, NJ: Princeton.

Charlot, Jean, and Monica Charlot. 1992. "France." In David Butler and Austin Ranney, eds., *Electioneering: A Comparative Study of Continuity and Change*. Oxford, UK: Clarendon.

Chinoy, Ira. 1996. "In Quest for Presidency, Candidates Learned They Could Bank on Finance Laws." *Washington Post*, November 5, p. A17.

———. 1997. "In Presidential Race, TV Ads Were Biggest '96 Cost By Far." *Washington Post*, March 31, p. A19.

Clark, Charles S. 1996. "Political Consultants: The Issues." *The CQ Researcher* 6(37): 867–73.

Cole, Alistair M. 1989. "Factionalism, the French Socialist Party and the Fifth Republic: An Explanation of Intra-party Divisions." *European Journal of Political Research*. 17:77–94.

———, ed. 1990. *French Political Parties in Transition*. Aldershot, UK: Dartmouth.

———. 1993. "The Presidential Party and the Fifth Republic." *West European Politics* 16(2): 49–66.

———. 1995. "La France Pour Tous?—The French Presidential Elections of 23 April and 7 May 1995." *Government & Opposition* 30(3): 327–346.

Colorado Republican Federal Campaign Committee v. FEC, U.S., 64 U.S.L.2 4663. 1996.

Congressional Quarterly. 1997. "Selecting the President: From 1789 to 1996." Washington, DC: CQ Press.

Cook, Rhodes. 1989. "The Nominating Process." In Michael Nelson, ed., *The Elections of 1988*. Washington, DC: CQ Press.

Corrado, Anthony. 1996. "The Changing Environment of Presidential Campaign

Finance." In William G. Mayer, ed., *In Pursuit of the White House: How We Choose Our Presidential Nominees*. Chatham, NJ: Chatham House.

———. 1997. "Financing the 1996 Elections." In Gerald M. Pomper, ed., *The Election of 1996: Reports and Interpretations*. Chatham, NJ: Chatham House.

Cronin, Thomas E., ed. 1989. *Inventing the American Presidency*. Lawrence University Press of Kansas.

Crouse, Timothy. 1973. *The Boys on the Bus*. New York: Random House.

Dalton, Russell J. 1996. *Citizen Politics: Public Opinion and Political Parties in Advanced Industrial Democracies*. Second Edition. Chatham, NJ: Chatham House.

Davis, James W. 1980. *Presidential Primaries: Road to the White House*. Westport, CT: Greenwood.

———. 1992. *The President as Party Leader*. Westport, CT: Greenwood.

———. 1997. *U.S. Presidential Primaries and the Caucus-convention System: A Sourcebook*. Westport, CT: Greenwood.

DeBardeleben, Joan. 1997. *Russian Politics in Transition*. Second Edition. Boston: Houghton Mifflin.

De Gaulle, Charles. 1992. "The Bayeux Manifesto." In Arend Lijphart, ed., *Parliamentary Versus Presidential Government*. Oxford, UK: Oxford University.

Diamond, Edwin, and Robert A. Silverson. 1995. *White House to Your House: Media and Politics in Virtual America*. Cambridge, MA: MIT.

Diamond, Larry. 1997. "Introduction: In Search of Consolidation." In Larry Diamond et al., eds., *Consolidating the Third Wave Democracies*. Baltimore: Johns Hopkins.

Dinkin, Robert J. 1989. *Campaigning in America: A History of Election Practices*. Westport, CT: Greenwood.

Dinnerstein, Leonard. 1971. "Election of 1880." In Arthur M. Schlesinger, Jr., and Fred L. Israel, eds., *History of American Presidential Elections, 1789–1968*. New York: Chelsea House.

Dodenhoff, David, and Kenneth Goldstein. 1998. "Resources, Racehorses, and Rules: Nominations in the 1990s." In L. Sandy Maisel, ed., *The Parties Respond*. Second Edition. Boulder, CO: Westview.

Donne, Bronwyn. 1996. "Yeltsin Strikes Chord with the Young at Red Square Concert." *The Times*, June 11.

Donovan, Beth. 1992. "Abortion: Will the Big Tent Hold All?" *Congressional Quarterly Weekly Report*. Supplement: The Republican Convention, August 8, pp. 17–19.

Dore, Isaak I. 1995. "The Distribution of Governmental Power under the Constitution in Russia." *Parker School Journal of East European Law* 2(6): 673–705.

Drysch, Thomas. 1993. "The New French System of Political Finance." In Arthur B. Gunlicks, ed., *Campaign and Party Finance in North America and Western Europe*. Boulder, CO: Westview.

Dulio, David A. 1999. "Just Win Baby! Campaign Consultants, Ethical Standards, and Campaign Reform." Paper presented at the Annual Meeting of the Midwest Political Science Association, Chicago, IL, April 15–17.

Dulio, David A., Donald L. Goff, and James A. Thurber. 1999. "Untangled Web: Internet Use During the 1998 Election." *PS: Political Science and Politics*. 32(1): 53–59.

Dulio, David A., Candice J. Nelson, and James A. Thurber. 1999. "Campaign Elites: The Attitudes and Roles of Professional Political Consultants." Paper presented at the Annual Meeting of the Western Political Science Association, Seattle, WA, March 25–27.

Duverger, Maurice. 1965. *Political Parties: Their Organization and Activity in the Modern State.* Translated by Barbara and Robert North. Second Edition. New York: Wiley.

——. 1992. "A New Political System Model." In Arend Lijphart, ed., *Parliamentary Versus Presidential Government.* Oxford, UK: Oxford University.

Easter, Gerald. 1997. "Preference for Presidentialism: Postcommunist Regime Change in Russia and the NIS." *World Politics* 49: 184–211.

Ehrenhalt, Alan. 1991. *The United States of Ambition: Politicians, Power, and the Pursuit of Office.* New York: Times Books.

Elving, Ronald D. 1988. "Party Platforms Helped Shape Fall Campaigns." *Congressional Quarterly Weekly Report,* October 22, pp. 3041–44.

Epstein, Leon D. 1986. *Political Parties in the American Mold.* Madison: University of Wisconsin.

Farrell, David M. 1996. "Campaign Strategies and Tactics." In Lawrence LeDuc, Richard G. Niemi, and Pippa Norris, eds., *Comparing Democracies: Elections And Voting In Global Perspectives.* Thousand Oaks, CA: Sage.

——. 1998. "Political Consultancy Overseas: The Internationalization of Campaign Consultancy." *PS: Political Science and Politics* 31(2): 171–76.

Faucheux, Ron, ed. 1995. *The Best of the Best from Campaigns & Elections: The Road to Victory: The Complete Guide to Winning in Politics.* Dubuque, IA: Kendall/Hunt.

Fieschi, Catherine. 1997. "The Other Candidates: Voynet, Le Pen, de Villiers and Cheminade." In John Gaffney and Lorna Milne, eds., *French Presidentialism and the Election of 1995.* Aldershot, UK: Ashgate.

Fine, Terri Susan. 1994. "Lobbying from Within: Government Elites and the Framing of the 1988 Democratic and Republican Party Platforms." *Presidential Studies Quarterly* 24(4): 855–863.

Finer, S. E., Vernon Bogdanor, and Bernard Rudden. 1995. *Comparing Constitutions.* Oxford, UK: Clarendon.

Fish, M. Steven. 1995. "The Advent of Multipartism in Russia, 1993–95." *Post-Soviet Affairs.* 11(4): 340–83.

——. 1997. "The Pitfalls of Russian Superpresidentialism." *Current History* 96(612): 326–31.

"France's Right: New Name, Old Confusion." 1998. *Economist,* May 23, pp. 46–47.

Frantzich, Stephen E. 1989. *Political Parties in the Technological Age.* New York: Longman.

Frears, J. R. 1977. *Political Parties and Elections in the French Fifth Republic.* London, UK: C. Hurst.

Friedenberg, Robert V. 1997. *Communication Consultants in Political Campaigns: The Ballot Box Warriors.* Westport, CT: Praeger.

Fysh, Peter. 1996. "Candidates and Parties of the Right." In Robert Elgie, ed., *Electing the French President: The 1995 Presidential Election.* New York: St. Martin.

Germond, Jack, and Jules Witcover. 1993. *Mad as Hell: Revolt at the Ballot Box.* New York: Warner Books.

Gerstlé, Jacques. 1991. "Election Communication in France." In Frederick J. Fletcher, ed., *Media, Elections, and Democracy.* Toronto: Dundurn.

Gibson, James L., and Susan E. Scarrow. 1993. "State and Local Party Organizations in American Politics." In Eric M. Uslaner, ed., *American Political Parties: A Reader.* Itasca, IL: F. E. Peacock.

Goldman, Peter, et al. 1994. *Quest for the Presidency, 1992.* College Station: Texas A&M.

Graber, Doris A. 1993. "Political Communication: Scope, Progress, Promise." In Ada W. Finifter, ed., *Political Science: The State of the Discipline II.* Washington, DC: APSA.

———. 1997. *Mass Media and American Politics.* Fifth Edition. Washington, DC: CQ Press.

Greenblatt, Alan. 1996. "The Platform Dance." *Congressional Quarterly Weekly Report.* Supplement: The Republican Convention, August 3, pp. 13–16.

Griggs, Steven. 1996. "Candidates and Parties of the Left." In Robert Elgie, ed, *Electing the French President: The 1995 Presidential Election.* New York: St. Martin.

Hadley, Arthur T. 1976. *The Invisible Primary.* Englewood Cliffs, NJ: Prentice Hall.

Hamilton, Alexander, James Madison, and John Jay. 1961. *The Federalist.* New York: Barnes and Noble.

Harris, John F. 1998. "Clinton's Campaign Consultants Reaped Millions from TV Ads." *Washington Post*, January 4, p. A4.

Hayes, Nick. 1996. "Yeltsin Then and Now." *Star Tribune*, June 20, p. 24A.

Heard, Alexander, and Michael Nelson. 1987. "Change and Stability in Choosing Presidents." In Alexander Heard and Michael Nelson, eds., *Presidential Selection.* Durham, NC: Duke.

Heclo, Hugh. 1973. "Presidential and Prime Ministerial Selection." In Donald R. Matthews, ed., *Perspectives on Presidential Selection.* Washington, DC: Brookings Institution.

Hendrie, Paul. 1999. "Giving Double to Keep Gore out of Trouble." *Capital Eye* 6(3): 5.

———. 1999a. "FEC May Revise Cyberspace Campaign Rules." *Capital Eye* 6(3): 7.

Herrnson, Paul S. 1988. *Party Campaigning in the 1980s.* Cambridge, MA: Harvard.

———. 1998. *Congressional Elections: Campaigning at Home and in Washington.* Second Edition. Washington, DC: CQ Press.

———. 1998a. "National Party Organizations at Century's End." In L. Sandy Maisel, ed., *The Parties Respond.* Third Edition. Boulder, CO: Westview.

Hill, Irène. 1997. "Financing the Presidential Campaign." In John Gaffney and Lorna Milne, eds., *French Presidentialism and the Election of 1995.* Aldershot, UK: Ashgate.

Humphreys, Peter J. 1996. *Mass Media and Media Policy in Western Europe.* Manchester, UK: Manchester University.

Huntington, Samuel P. 1968. *Political Order in Changing Societies.* New Haven: Yale.

———. 1971. "The Change to Change." *Comparative Politics* 3: 283–322.

———. 1991. *The Third Wave: Democratization in the Late Twentieth Century*. Norman: University of Oklahoma.

Jackson, Brooks. 1997. "Financing the 1996 Campaign: The Law of the Jungle." In Larry J. Sabato, ed., *Toward the Millennium: The Elections of 1996*. Boston: Allyn and Bacon.

Jalonick, Mary Clare. 1999. "Rating 2000 Presidential Campaign Web Sites." *Campaigns & Elections*, July, p. 36.

Jamieson, Kathleen Hall. 1992. *Packaging the Presidency: A History and Criticism of Presidential Campaign Advertising*. Second Edition. New York: Oxford University.

Janda, Kenneth. 1993. "Comparative Political Parties: Research and Theory." In Ada W. Finifter, *Political Science: The State of the Discipline II*. Washington, DC: APSA.

Johnston, Anne, and Jacques Gerstlé. 1995. "The Role of Television Broadcasts in Promoting French Presidential Candidates." In Lynda Lee Kaid, ed., *Political Advertising in Western Democracies: Parties & Candidates on Television*. Thousand Oaks, CA: Sage.

Jones, Charles O. 1994. *The Presidency in a Separated System*. Washington, DC: Brookings Institution.

———. 1996. "The Clinton Administration in the Separated System: A Presidency at Risk." *extensions: A Journal of the Carl Albert Congressional Research and Studies Center*. Spring, pp. 3–9.

Just, Marion R. 1996. *Crosstalk: Citizens, Candidates, and the Media in a Presidential Campaign*. Chicago: University of Chicago.

Kalb, Deborah. 1996. "Building with Broad Planks." *Congressional Quarterly Weekly Report*. Supplement: The Democratic Convention, August 17, pp. 33–35.

Kaminsky, Elijah Ben-Zion. 1973. "The Selection of French Presidents." In Donald R. Matthews, ed., *Perspectives on Presidential Selection*. Washington, DC: Brookings Institution.

Kaplan, Sheila. 1999. "Campaign 2000, by the Numbers." *U.S. News & World Report*, January 18, pp. 20–21.

Kavanagh, Dennis. 1995. *Election Campaigning: The New Marketing of Politics*. Oxford, UK: Basil Blackwell.

Kessel, John H. 1992. *Presidential Campaign Politics*. Fourth Edition. Pacific Grove, CA: Brooks/Cole.

Key, V. O., Jr. 1964. *Politics, Parties, & Pressure Groups*. Fifth Edition. New York: Crowell.

King, Anthony. 1993. "Foundations of Power." In George C. Edwards III, John H. Kessel, and Bert A. Rockman, eds., *Researching the Presidency: Vital Questions, New Approaches*. Pittsburgh, PA: University of Pittsburgh.

Klingemann, Hans-Dieter, Richard I. Hofferbert, and Ian Budge. 1994. *Parties, Policies, and Democracy*. Boulder, CO: Westview.

Knapp, Andrew. 1994. *Gaullism since de Gaulle*. Aldershot, UK: Darthmouth.

Kolodny, Robin, and Angela Logan. 1998. "Political Consultants and the Extension of Party Goals." *PS: Political Science and Politics* 31(2): 155–59.

Kramer, Michael. 1996. "Rescuing Boris." *Time*, July 15, pp. 28–37.

Lawson, Kay. 1978. "Constitutional Change and Party Development in France,

Nigeria, and the United States." In Louis Maisel and Joseph Cooper, eds., *Political Parties: Development and Decay*. London, UK: Sage.

Lawson, Kay, and Colette Ysmal. 1992. "France: The 1988 Presidential Campaign." In Shaun Bowler and David M. Farrell, eds., *Electoral Strategies and Political Marketing*. New York: St. Martin.

LeDuc, Lawrence, Richard G. Niemi, and Pippa Norris, eds. 1996. *Comparing Democracies: Elections and Voting in Global Perspectives*. Thousand Oaks, CA: Sage.

"Lexington: Steve Forbes and His Victims." 1999. *Economist*, January 30, p. 31.

Lijphart, Arend. 1992. "Introduction." In Arend Lijphart, ed., *Parliamentary Versus Presidential Government*. Oxford, UK: Oxford University.

Linz, Juan J. 1990. "The Perils of Presidentialism." *Journal of Democracy* 1: 51–69.

Linz, Juan J., and Arturo Valenzuela. 1994. *The Failure of Presidential Democracy*. Vols. 1 & 2. Baltimore: Johns Hopkins.

Lowi, Theodore J. 1985. *The Personal President: Power Invested, Promise Unfulfilled*. Ithaca, NY and London, UK: Cornell.

Luntz, Frank I. 1988. *Candidates, Consultants, and Campaigns*. Oxford, UK: Basil Blackwell.

Maarek, Philippe J. 1997. "New Trends in French Political Communication: The 1995 Presidential Elections." *Media, Culture, and Society* 19: 357–68.

Machin, Howard. 1989. "Stages and Dynamics in the Evolution of the French Party System." *West European Politics* 12(4): 59–81.

———. 1993. "The President, the Parties and Parliament." In Jack Hayward, ed., *De Gaulle to Mitterand: Presidential Power in France*. New York: New York University.

———. 1996. "The 1995 Presidential Election Campaign." In Robert Elgie, ed., *Electing the French President: The 1995 Presidential Election*. New York: St. Martin.

Machin, Howard, and Vincent Wright. 1982. "Why Mitterand Won: The French Presidential Elections of April-May 1981." *West European Politics* 5(1): 5–35.

Macridis, Roy C. 1975. *French Politics in Transition*. Cambridge, MA: Winthrop.

Mainwaring, Scott, and Matthew S. Shugart. 1997. "Juan Linz, Presidentialism, and Democracy: A Critical Appraisal." *Comparative Politics* 29(4): 449–72.

Maisel, L. Sandy. 1996. "The Platform-Writing Process: Candidate-Centered Platforms in 1992." In Robert Y. Shapiro, ed., *Understanding Presidential Elections: Trends and New Developments*. New York: Academy of Political Science.

Marcus, Ruth, and Ira Chinoy. 1996. "Lack of Primary Season Foe Leaves Clinton in the Money; President Saved for August Spending Spree." *Washington Post*, August 24, p. A1.

Marshall, Thomas R. 1981. *Presidential Nominations in a Reform Age*. Westport, CT: Praeger.

Mayer, William G. 1996. "Caucuses: How They Work, What Difference They Make." In William G. Mayer, ed., *In Pursuit of the White House: How We Choose Our Presidential Nominees*. Chatham, NJ: Chatham House.

———. 1997. "The Presidential Nominations." In Gerald M. Pomper, ed., *The Election of 1996: Reports and Interpretations*. Chatham, NJ: Chatham House.

McAllister, Ian, and Stephen White. 1995. "Democracy, Political Parties and Party Formation in Postcommunist Russia." *Party Politics* 1: 49–72.

McCubbins, Matthew D., ed. 1992. *Under the Watchful Eye: Managing Presidential Campaigns in the Television Era.* Washington, DC: CQ Press.

McDonald, Forrest. 1994. *The American Presidency: An Intellectual History.* Lawrence: University Press of Kansas.

McFaul, Michael. 1996. "Russia's 1996 Presidential Elections." *Post-Soviet Affairs* 12(4): 318–50.

———. 1997. *Russia's 1996 Presidential Election: The End of Polarized Politics.* Stanford, CA: Stanford.

———. 1997a. "Russia's Rough Ride." In Larry Diamond et al., eds., *Consolidating the Third Wave Democracies.* Baltimore: Johns Hopkins.

McGinniss, Joe. 1969. *The Selling of the President, 1968.* New York: Trident Press.

Melder, Keith E. 1992. *Hail to the Candidate: Presidential Campaigns from Banners to Broadcasts.* Washington, DC: Smithsonian Institution.

Milkis, Sidney M. 1993. *The Presidency and Political Parties: The Transformation of the American Party System Since the New Deal.* Oxford, UK: Oxford University.

"Money Behind the Clinton Campaign." 1996. *Washington Post*, August 24, p. A11.

"Money Behind the Dole Campaign." 1996. *Washington Post*, April 18, p. A3.

Morvant, Penny. 1996. *OMRI Daily Digest.* Number 73, Part 1. April 12.

———. 1996a. *OMRI Daily Digest.* Number 91, Part 1. May 10.

Napolitan, Joseph. 1972. *The Election Game and How to Win It.* Garden City, NY: Doubleday.

Nelson, Michael. 1982. "Sentimental Science: Recent Essays on the Politics of Presidential Selection." *Congress and the Presidency* 9: 99–106.

———, ed. 1997. *The Elections of 1996.* Washington, DC: CQ Press.

Neustadt, Richard E. 1990. *Presidential Power and the Modern Presidents: The Politics of Leadership from Roosevelt to Reagan.* New York: The Free Press.

Niemi, Richard G., and Harold W. Stanley. 1994. *Vital Statistics on American Politics.* Fourth Edition. Washington, DC: CQ Press.

Niemi, Richard G., and Herbert F. Weisberg. 1984. "Introduction: The Study of Voting and Elections." In Richard G. Niemi and Herbert F. Weisberg, eds., *Controversies in Voting Behavior.* Second Edition. Washington, DC: CQ Press.

Nimmo, Dan D. 1996. "Politics, Media, and Modern Democracy: The United States." In David L. Swanson and Paolo Mancini, eds., *Politics, Media, and Modern Democracy: An International Study of Innovations In Electoral Campaigning and Their Consequences.* Westport, CT: Praeger.

Orange County Register. 1996. Lexis/Nexis Database. December 14.

Ornstein, Norman J., Thomas E. Mann, and Michael J. Malbin. 1998. *Vital Statistics on Congress, 1997–1998.* Washington, DC: CQ Press.

Orttung, Robert W. 1996. "Voters Face a Red-and-White Choice." *Transition* 2(11): 6–17.

———. 1996a. *OMRI Daily Digest.* Number 71, Part 1, April 10.

———. 1996b. *OMRI Russian Presidential Election Survey.* Number 2, May 10.

———. 1996c. *OMRI Russian Presidential Election Survey.* Number 3, May 16.

———. 1996d. *OMRI Daily Digest.* Number 105, Part 1, May 30.

————. 1996e. *OMRI Russian Presidential Election Survey*. Number 7, June 7.

————. 1996f. *OMRI Russian Presidential Election Survey*. Number 9, June 14.

————. 1996g. *OMRI Russian Presidential Election Survey*. Number 11, June 27.

O'Shaughnessy, Nicholas. 1990. *The Phenomenon of Political Marketing*. New York: St. Martin.

Paretskaya, Anna. 1996. *OMRI Russian Presidential Election Survey*. Number 11, June 27.

Parris, Judith H. 1972. *The Convention Problem: Issues in Reform of Presidential Nominating Procedures*. Washington, DC: Brookings Institution.

Patterson, Thomas E. 1994. *Out of Order*. New York: Vintage Books.

Paul, James C. N. 1951. *Rift in the Democracy*. Philadelphia: University of Pennsylvania.

Peskin, Allan. 1978. *Garfield*. Kent, OH: Kent State.

Pew Research Center. 1998. "The Views of Political Consultants: Don't Blame Us." <http://www.people-press.org/com98rpt.htm>.

Pierce, Roy. 1995. *Choosing the Chief: Presidential Elections in France and the United States*. Ann Arbor: University of Michigan.

Pika, Joseph A., and Richard A. Watson. 1996. *The Presidential Contest, with a Guide to the 1996 Presidential Race*. Fifth Edition. Washington, DC: CQ Press.

Polsby, Nelson W. 1983. *Consequences of Party Reform*. Oxford, UK: Oxford University.

Polsby, Nelson W., and Aaron Wildavsky. 1996. *Presidential Elections: Strategies and Structures in American Politics*. Ninth Edition. Chatham, NJ: Chatham House.

Pomper, Gerald M. 1970. "Campaigning: The Art & Science of Politics." *Polity* 2(4): 533–39.

————, ed. 1997. *The Elections of 1996: Reports and Interpretations*. Chatham, NJ: Chatham House.

Pomper, Gerald M., and Susan S. Lederman. 1980. *Elections in America: Control and Influence in Democratic Politics*. Second Edition. New York: Longman's.

Powell, G. Bingham. 1982. *Contemporary Democracies: Participation, Stability and Violence*. Cambridge, MA: Harvard.

Raymond, Gino. 1994. "The Decline of the Established Parties." In Gino Raymond, ed., *France During the Socialist Years*. Brookefield, VT: Dartmouth.

Reichley, James A. 1985. "The Rise of National Parties." In John E. Chubb and Paul E. Peterson, eds., *The New Direction in American Politics*. Washington, DC: Brookings Institution.

————. 1992. *The Life of the Parties: A History of American Political Parties*. New York: Free Press.

Remnick, David. 1996. "Letter from Russia: Gorbachev's Last Hurrah." *New Yorker*, March 11, 68–83.

————. 1996a. "Letter from Russia: War for the Kremlin." *New Yorker*, July 22, 40–57.

"Republicans: Convention Notes." 1996. *Time*, August 26, pp. 20–21.

Riordon, William. 1991. *Plunkitt of Tammany Hall*. New York: Meridian.

Rockman, Bert A. 1986. "Presidential Studies: The One, the Few, and the Many."

In Herbert F. Weisberg, ed., *Political Science: The Science of Politics*. New York: Agathon.

Rose, Richard. 1987. "Learning to Govern or Learning to Campaign?" In Alexander Heard and Michael Nelson, eds., *Presidential Selection*. Durham, NC: Duke.

Rosenbloom, David Lee. 1973. *The Election Men: Professional Campaign Managers and American Democracy*. New York: Quadrangle Books.

Rosenstiel, Tom. 1993. *Strange Bedfellows: How Television and the Presidential Candidates Changed American Politics, 1992*. New York: Hyperion.

Royer, Charles T., ed. 1997. *Campaign for President: The Managers Look at '96*. Hollis, NH: Puritan.

Russell, Francis. 1976. *The President Makers: From Mark Hanna to Joseph P. Kennedy*. Boston: Little, Brown, and Company.

Sabato, Larry J. 1981. *The Rise of Political Consultants: New Ways of Winning Elections*. New York: Basic Books.

———. 1988. *The Parties Just Begun: Shaping Political Parties for America's Future*. Boston: Little, Brown.

———. 1994. "Open Season: How the News Media Covers Presidential Campaigns in the Age of Attack Journalism." In Doris A. Graber, ed., *Media Power in Politics*. Third Edition. Washington, DC: CQ Press.

———. 1997. "Presidential Nominations: The Front-loaded Frenzy of '96." In Larry J. Sabato, ed., *Toward the Millennium: The Elections of 1996*. Boston: Allyn and Bacon.

———. 1997a. "The Conventions: One Festival of Hope, One Celebration of Impending Victory." In Larry J. Sabato, ed., *Toward the Millennium: The Elections of 1996*. Boston: Allyn and Bacon.

Safran, William. 1995. *The French Polity*. Fourth Edition. New York: Longman.

Sakwa, Richard. 1993. "Parties and the Multiparty System in Russia." *RFE/RL Research Report* 2(31): 7–15.

Salmore, Barbara G., and Stephen A. 1989. *Candidates, Parties, and Campaigns: Electoral Politics in America*. Second Edition. Washington, DC: CQ Press.

Scammel, Margaret. 1997. "The Wisdom of the War Room: U.S. Campaigning and Americanization." Research Paper R-17, The Joan Shorenstein Center for Press, Politics, and Public Policy. Cambridge, MA: Harvard.

Schattschneider, E. E. 1942. *Party Government*. New York: Farrar and Rinehart.

Schlesinger, Arthur M., Jr., and Fred L. Israel, eds. 1971. *History of American Presidential Elections, 1789–1968*. New York: Chelsea House.

Searls, Ella. 1982. "The Giscardians and Party Politics." In David S. Bell, ed., *Contemporary French Political Parties*. London, UK: Croom Helm.

Seligman, Lester G., and Cary R. Covington. 1989. *The Coalitional Presidency*. Chicago: Dorsey.

Selnow, Gary W. 1994. *High-tech Campaigns: Computer Technology in Political Communication*. Westport, CT: Praeger.

Shafer, Byron E. 1988. *Bifurcated Politics: Evolution and Reform in the National Party Convention*. Cambridge, MA: Harvard.

Shea, Daniel M. 1996. *Campaign Craft: The Strategies, Tactics, and Art of Political Campaign Management*. Westport, CT: Praeger.

Shields, James G. 1989. "Barre, Chirac, Le Pen et al.: France's Fragmented Right." *Contemporary Review* 254(1476): 1–6.

———. 1995. "France's Presidential Election: The Gaullist Restoration." *Political Quarterly* 66(4): 320–27.

Sibley, Joel H. 1998. "From 'Essential to the Existence of Our Institutions' to 'Rapacious Enemies of Honest and Responsible Government': The Rise and Fall of American Parties, 1790–2000." In L. Sandy Maisel, ed., *The Parties Respond*. Third Edition. Boulder, CO: Westview.

Simon, Roger. 1999. "Backstage at the Opening." *U.S. News & World Report*, June 28, pp. 20–22.

Singer, Daniel. 1988. "Letters from Europe: The Mitterand-Chirac-Barre Show." *The Nation*, April 16, pp. 524–26.

Slonim, Shlomo. 1989. "Designing the Electoral College." In Thomas E. Cronin, ed., *Inventing the American Presidency*. Lawrence: University Press of Kansas.

Smith, Larry David. 1992. "The Party Platforms as Institutional Discourse: The Democrats and Republicans of 1988." *Presidential Studies Quarterly* 22(3): 531–43.

Spencer, Ivor D. 1959. *The Victor and the Spoils: A Life of William L. Marcy*. Providence, RI: Brown University.

Stanley, Harold W. 1997. "The Nominations: Republican Doldrums, Democratic Revival." In Michael Nelson, ed., *The Elections of 1996*. Washington, DC: CQ Press.

Stanley, Harold W., and Richard G. Niemi. 1998. *Vital Statistics on American Politics, 1997–1998*. Sixth Edition. Washington, DC: CQ Press.

Stephanopoulos, George. 1999. "The New Rules of the Road." *Newsweek*, February 8, pp. 34–35.

Stevens, Anne. 1996. *The Government and Politics of France*. Second Edition. New York: St. Martin.

Susser, Bernard. 1992. "From Burgess to Behavioralism and Beyond." In Bernard Susser, ed., *Approaches to the Study of Politics*. New York: Macmillan.

Swanson, David L., and Paolo Mancini, eds. 1996. *Politics, Media, and Modern Democracy: An International Study of Innovations in Electoral Campaigning and Their Consequences*. Westport, CT: Praeger.

Szarka, Joseph. 1996. "The Winning of the 1995 French Presidential Election." *West European Politics* 19(1): 151–67.

Texier, Cristophe. 1996. "Chronology of the Campaign." In Robert Elgie, ed., *Electing the French President: The 1995 Presidential Election*. New York: St. Martin.

Thomas, Evan. 1998. "The Sons Also Rise." *Newsweek*, November 16, pp. 44–48.

Thompson, Hunter S. 1973. *Fear and Loathing: On the Campaign Trail '72*. New York: Warner Books.

Thornson, Carla. 1993. "Russia's Draft Constitution." *RFE/RL Research Report* 2(48): 9–15.

Thurber, James A. 1998. "The Study of Campaign Consultants: A Subfield in Search of a Theory." *PS: Political Science and Politics* 31(2): 145–49.

Thurber, James A., and David A. Dulio. 1999. "Industry Portrait: Political Consultants." *Campaigns & Elections*, July, pp. 27–28, 71.

Tindall, George Brown, and David E. Shi. 1996. *America: A Narrative History.* Fourth Edition. New York: W. W. Norton.

Toinet, Marie-France. 1988. "The Elections of 1981: Background and Legal Setting." In Howard R. Penniman, ed., *France at the Polls, 1981 and 1986: Three National Elections.* Durham, NC: Duke.

Treisman, Daniel. 1996. "Why Yeltsin Won." *Foreign Affairs* 75(5): 64–77.

Trent, Judith S., and Robert V. Friedenberg. 1995. *Political Campaign Communication: Principles and Practices.* Third Edition. Westport, CT: Praeger.

Troy, Gil. 1996. *See How They Ran: The Changing Role of the Presidential Candidate.* Revised and Expanded Edition. Cambridge, MA: Harvard.

Varoga, Craig. 1999. "Campaign Doctor." *Campaigns & Elections,* July, p. 77.

Wahl, Nicholas. 1959. "The French Constitution of 1958: The Initial Draft and Its Origins." *American Political Science Review* 53 (June).

Walsh, Kenneth T. 1999. "The Man to Beat." *U.S. News & World Report,* March 15, pp. 18–21.

Ware, Alan. 1996. *Political Parties and Party Systems.* Oxford, UK: Oxford University.

"Washington Whispers: Family Ties." 1999. *U.S. News & World Report,* June 21, p. 9.

"Washington Whispers: Opponents Invited." 1999. *U.S. News & World Report,* June 28, p. 8.

"Washington Whispers: Sucker Punch." 1999. *U.S. News & World Report,* July 26, p. 8.

"Washington Whispers: Betting on Victory." 1999. *U.S. News & World Report,* August, 9, p. 8.

Wattenberg, Martin. 1991. *The Rise of Candidate-centered Politics: Presidential Elections of the 1980s.* Cambridge, MA: Harvard.

Watzman, Nancy. 1999. "Virtual Fund-raising: Force for Democracy or a New Edge for Incumbents?" *Capital Eye* 6(3): 6.

Wayne, Stephen J. 1997. *The Road to the White House: The Politics of Presidential Elections.* Post-election Edition. New York: St. Martin.

White, Stephen, and Ian McAllister. 1996. "The CPSU and Its Members: Between Communism and Postcommunism." *British Journal of Political Science* 26: 105–22.

White, Stephen, Richard Rose, and Ian McAllister. 1997. *How Russia Votes.* Chatham, NJ: Chatham House.

White, Theodore H. 1961. *The Making of the President, 1960.* New York: Atheneum.

———. 1961a. *La Victoire de Kennedy ou Comment on Fait un Président.* Paris: Robert Laffont.

———. 1973. *The Making of the President, 1972.* New York: Atheneum.

Whitney, Craig R. 1997. "Common Currency: Do Francs and Yen Corrupt? Absolutely." *New York Times,* March 16, sec. 4, pp. 1, 4.

Wilson, James Q. 1962. *The Amateur Democrat: Club Politics in Three Cities.* Chicago: University of Chicago.

Witcover, Jules. 1977. *Marathon: The Pursuit of the Presidency, 1972–1976.* New York: Viking.

Woodward, Bob. 1996. *The Choice.* New York: Simon & Schuster.

Wright, Vincent. 1989. *The Government and Politics of France*. New York: Holmes
    and Meier.
Zeigler, Harmon. 1993. *Political Parties in Industrial Democracies*. Itasca, IL: F. E.
    Peacock.
Zlobin, Nikolai V. 1993. "The Political Spectrum." In Alexander Dallin, ed., *Po-
    litical Parties in Russia*. Berkeley: University of California.

Index

About the Author

JODY C BAUMGARTNER is Professor of Political Science at the International College at Beijing. He has published articles on American politics and the presidency.

ISBN 0-275-96760-3

90000>

EAN

9 780275 967604

HARDCOVER BAR CODE

DATE